BLACK AMERICA SERIES

AFRICAN AMERICANS OF WESTERN LONG ISLAND

BLACK AMERICA SERIES

AFRICAN AMERICANS OF WESTERN LONG ISLAND

Jerry Komia Domatob, Ph.D

ARCADIA PUBLISHING

ISBN 978-0-7385-1067-5

Published by Arcadia Publishing
Charleston SC, Chicago IL, Portsmouth NH, San Francisco CA

Printed in the United States of America

Library of Congress Catalog Card Number: 2002106584

For all general information contact Arcadia Publishing at:
Telephone 843-853-2070
Fax 843-853-0044
E-mail sales@arcadiapublishing.com
For customer service and orders:
Toll-Free 1-888-313-2665

Visit us on the Internet at www.arcadiapublishing.com

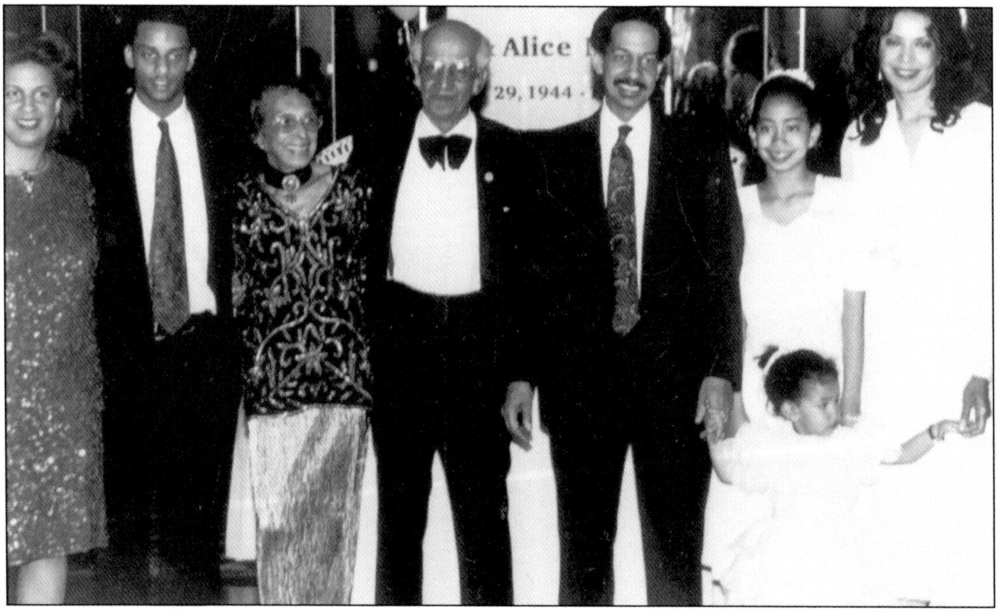

This book is dedicated to the late William Brazier, who motivated the author to research and write this book. Brazier, the great-grandson of Bishop Daniel A. Payne, founder of Wilberforce University in Ohio, pioneered the first black newspaper on Long Island, the *Weekly Voice*. He served as a school administrator in Harlem and his wife, Alice Marie Brazier, was a social worker. The couple (third and fourth from the left) celebrated their 50th wedding anniversary in 1994. Shown with them at the Plainview Holiday Inn, from left to right, are daughter Michele Mohammed, a guidance counselor in Harlem; grandson Barry Mohammed, a social studies teacher in Brentwood; son Tony Brazier, a vice president at J.P. Morgan/Chase; granddaughters Jennifer and Kimberly Brazier; and daughter-in-law Bernice Brazier.

CONTENTS

ACKNOWLEDGMENTS

The success of any historical project depends on the contributions and goodwill of people who provide assistance. This book reaped the rewards of noble and humane gestures from many kind, generous friends who took the time and effort to explain and clarify issues.

Going back earlier, however, my late father, Vincent Phillip Domatob, and my mother, Pauline Kahkiti Domatob, deserve honor for their diligence and dedication in placing me on the achievement track. I am immensely grateful to both of them.

To the many friends who helped me in this endeavor, I offer my sincere thanks: Mimmie Gladden, Larry Toler, Shirley Bailey, Claire Conquest, Cynthia Richardson, Scharron Gripper, Sue Taylor, Jim Banks, Bishop Nichols, Diane Robinson, Marcia White, Rev. Reggie Tuggle, Diane Robinson, Kimberly Grant, LaVada Felder, Rev. Alfred Coverdale, Bishop Frank White, Honorable Joan Johnson, Honorable Patrick Williams, Honorable Hezekiah Brown, Honorable Barbara Paton, Mr. and Mrs. Ed Monroe, the late Pastor Bullock, Little Zion Church of Center Moriches, Rhia Warren, the Majority Press Office of Nassau County and the Minority Press Office, Jack Profit, Andreaus Guilty, John Kearse, JoAnn Braxton, Rachel Davis, Bridget Wilson, Pastor Pearson, Rev. and Mrs. Washington, Pastor Phillip Elliot, Delores Smith, Rev. and Mrs. Johns, David Briggs, Jerry Jackson, Dr. Marc Fasanella, Dr. Bob Pattison, Prof. Phyllis K. Sullivan, and many others.

A number of people went even further and welcomed the project with unabated zeal. I am most grateful to all of them: Joe Turner. who provided motivation, photographs, research, and information; Adrian Fassett, Brenda Simmons, and the entire team at the Suffolk County Equal Opportunity Commission in Patchogue, who offered positive contributions, suggestions, and strategies; Gary Coley, who put much time, effort, and expertise into the project; LaVada Felder, who offered wisdom and a fresh perspective; Emily Moore, who dug deep into her archives; J Stewart Moore and Victoria Moore, who contributed pictures and information; Jean Dember, who offered needed support; Delano Stewart, who provided prodigious assistance; Willie Houston, Mildred Clayton, Rev. Alston, and Julius and Joysetta Pearse, who together introduced me to the genealogical society in grand style; and Honorable Janice Tinsley-Colbert, Robert Wilson, Elsie Owens, Pastor Dozier, Mildred Clayton, and Willie Houston, who each spurred me along.

Finally, my editor, Pam O'Neil, whose professionalism and diligence is remarkable, deserves praise for excellence and meticulousness. If I have left out names of some who generously helped with this project, it is not by design but rather is an honest mistake. Please accept my heartfelt appreciation. Enjoy this book to which so many people added so much.

—Jerry Komia Domatob, Ph.D.

Preface

African American Legacy

The renowned African American scholar W.E.B. Du Bois wrote in chapter 1 of *The Souls of Black Folks* (1903) that "Throughout history, the powers of single blacks flash here and there like falling stars, and die sometimes before the world has rightly gauged their brightness." His comment applies to Long Island, especially for most Americans and even international observers who think of it as a locality that is suburban, affluent, and most of all, white. However, this is not, nor has it ever been the true face of our community. From the very first settlement in the 1640s, people of African descent have been major contributors to the history, culture, and social and economic life on Long Island.

Historical documents provide ample evidence of African American accomplishments in Long Island towns, villages, churches, and individual residences. Whether operating as slaves or citizens, colonized or liberated folks, African Americans have excelled as poets, musicians, athletes, entrepreneurs, military men, and revered community leaders. Notwithstanding, most of these contributions have often gone unnoted, unremarked, and most commonly, uncelebrated.

In *African Americans of Western Long Island*, Dr. Jerry Komia Domatob seeks to remedy this oversight, giving voice and recognition to those who quietly but significantly helped forge and shape the community. His quest to focus on prominent personalities and their achievements honors a people, who have been overlooked and restores an absent but integral piece of Long Island's historical and cultural narrative. Through this restoration, Dr. Domatob gives the world a second opportunity to gauge and reflect on the brightness and richness of our stars.

—Adrian Fassett
Suffolk County Economic Opportunity Council

A Rich Pictorial History

Dr. Jerry Komia Domatob's pictorial book *African Americans of Western Long Island* focuses on prominent African American educators, lawyers, business entrepreneurs, politicians, entertainers, and pastors. It also highlights various organizations and fraternities in western Long Island. Many of the pictures spotlight the achievements of deceased African American leaders, whose legacies need to be recorded.

Dr. Domatob, an African from the Cameroon, offers a rich history that African Americans should emulate and endeavor to surpass. In writing this history, he sends a message that we should capture and value, as it documents the accomplishments of individuals and groups who have contributed to the development of western Long Island and, indeed, the world.

Read this little yet giant book and absorb the lesson. If it inspires you to know more about the individuals or organizations highlighted, embark upon that mission. It will be a stride in the right direction. We commend Dr. Domatob's initiative, tenacity, and dedication.

—Rev. Charles A. Coverdale
Pastor of the First Baptist Church of Riverhead

INTRODUCTION

African Americans of Western Long Island provides a new perspective on Long Island's rich historical heritage. Focusing on the African American community living in the western half of the island, the book offers a positive glimpse of the evolution of this group and of its individual contributions and achievements throughout the 20th century.

Through photographs, portraits, posters, and narrative, the book highlights major accomplishments in the social, political, economic, and cultural arenas. It presents pioneer jurists, pastors, educators, and others from the communities centered around Hempstead, Roosevelt, Freeport, Huntington, Babylon, Islip, Stony Brook, and Gordon Heights.

Currently teaching at Fordham University at Lincoln Center, the author has also taught at Long Island University's Southampton College, the University of Northern Iowa, and the University of Maiduguri, Nigeria, West Africa. He has a doctoral degree from Ohio University and two master's degrees from Carleton University. He is the author of several books, including *African Americans of Eastern Long Island,* published by Arcadia in 2001.

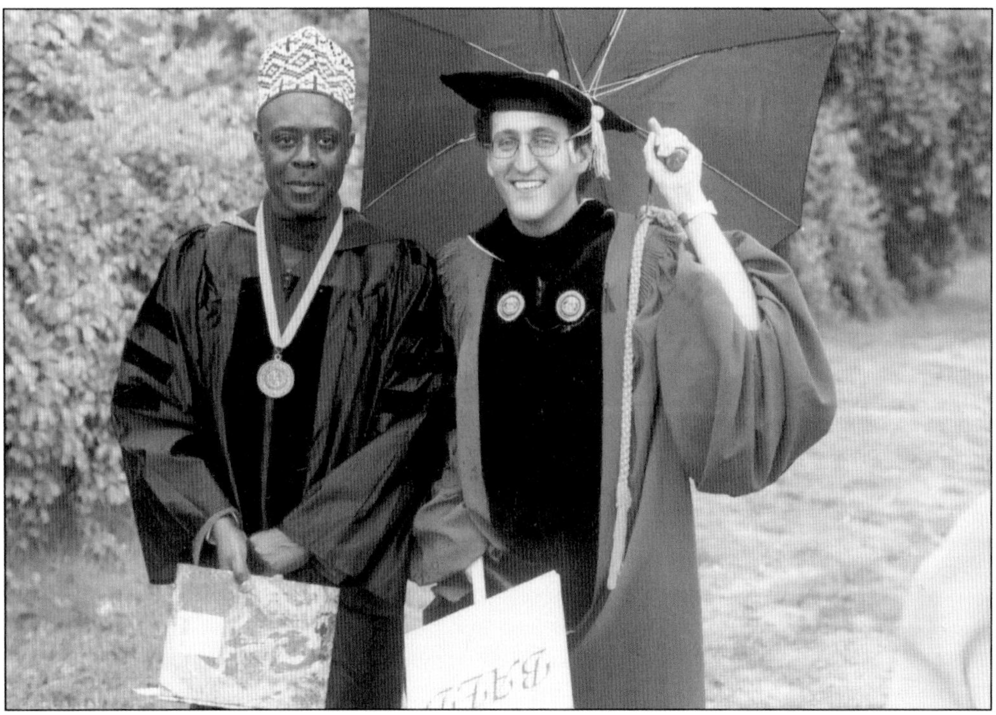

As the rain lets up, author Jerry Komia Domatob (left) stops outside for a moment with Dr. Scott Carlin of Southampton College, Long Island University.

One

Hempstead
Challenge and Change

Although many African Americans were imported into Hempstead by slave masters, those who migrated here from the South in the post–Civil War era came in hopes of improving their poor economic circumstances. Battered by the perceptions and realities of harsh southern segregation, they arrived and took jobs as farmers, landscapers, domestic workers, and medical aids. A few of them made homes for themselves and established roots in the area from the early postwar years in the 1900s.

However, the recorded history of their adopted city goes back to 1643. In that year the local Native Americans conveyed 64,000 acres of land to the Dutch in exchange for goods, gunpowder, and cloth. The Dutch called the area Heemstede, or "town spot," and remained in control for two decades, from 1643 to 1663. Later, the English ruled for two decades, from 1663 to 1783. Hempstead was incorporated as a village in 1853. By the late 1800s, it had become a major trading and merchant center. After World War II, it experienced a big boom as population swelled and new businesses opened.

African Americans have made strides in this city—some modest and some major. There are professionals in all sectors of life: the church, government, commerce, law, and business. A few of them live the American dream of riches. In the 1990s, Hempstead elected the first African American mayor on Long Island, James Garner, a tall and charismatic leader. The city is also the home of activist Dorothy Goosby, who helped promote African Americans in the political arena, and many other prominent personalities. In addition, the city has one of the community's foremost institutions, the African American Museum, and an abundance of churches.

Hempstead, today, represents the paradox of challenge and change. It is fast developing into a sprawling city with its own churches, schools, malls, and houses. Although cynics and pessimists castigate Hempstead for congestion, crimes, confusion, and chaos, its positive and visible African American presence evokes images of hope and success.

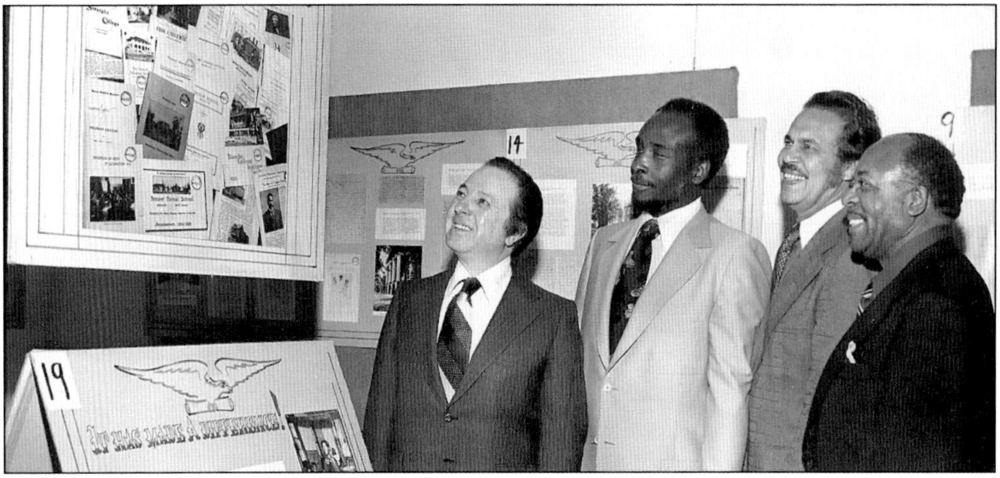

The African American Museum of Nassau County is unique. Established as a Black History Exhibit Center in 1970, the museum is the foremost cultural center for African Americans on Long Island. It organizes and holds exhibits, educational programs, conferences, films, workshops, concerts, and meetings throughout the year. Located in Hempstead and operated under the Nassau County Department of Recreation and Parks, the museum includes an exhibition center and an auditorium and is accredited by the American Association of Museums. Pictured with his colleagues in the 1970s is Leroy Ramsey, Ph.D., (second from left), the man often referred to as the museum's founder. Ramsey, with multiple degrees from Jackson State and Boston University, is a novelist, analyst, and professor who has also served as a minority affairs director and a military historian. (Courtesy of Dr. Leroy Ramsey.)

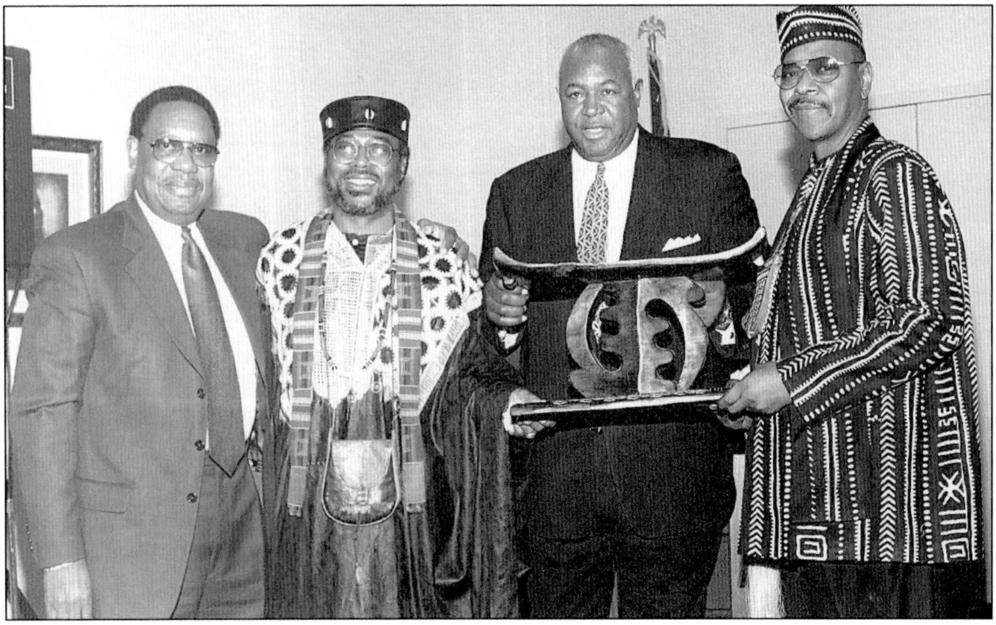

Hempstead Mayor James A. Garner (third from left) donates an African artifact, a stool, to the African American museum. With Garner, from left to right, are Hezekiah Brown, former village trustee and deputy county executive; William Houston, director of the African American Museum; and Rassan Hoskin, executive director-producer of the local television show *Shaka's Kraal.* (Courtesy of Willie Houston and the African American Museum.)

In 1989, James A. Garner became the first African American mayor on Long Island. Before his election as mayor, a position he still holds, Garner served Hempstead as a trustee, beginning in 1984. He comes from a family with an impressive history on Long Island. (Courtesy of Mayor James A. Garner.)

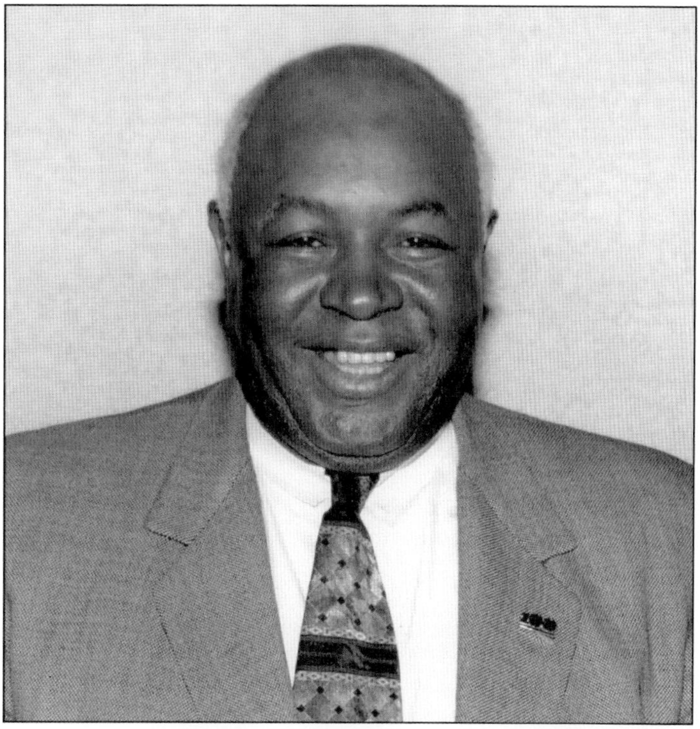

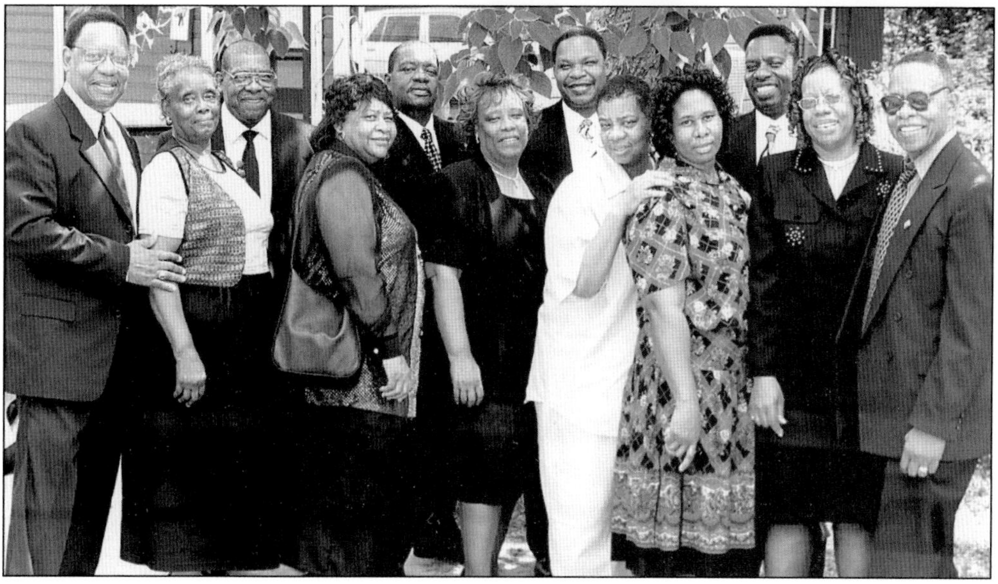

Hezekiah Brown (left) is the first African American Democrat to serve as deputy county executive in Nassau County. Born in Prichard, Alabama, he enlisted in the army in 1956. Over the years, he has served locally as a trustee of the village of Hempstead and a member of the Hempstead Village School Board. Additionally, he was an administrator at Cornell University, an arbitrator and chief mediator for the state of New York, and a federal mediator. He is pictured with family members, from left to right, Margaret Randolph, Jonnie Brown, Roberta Rouse, Cozy Brown, Doris Rogers, Tommie Brown, Theresa Angel, Patricia Bewwick, Nathaniel Brown, Sammie Clemons, and Willie Brown.

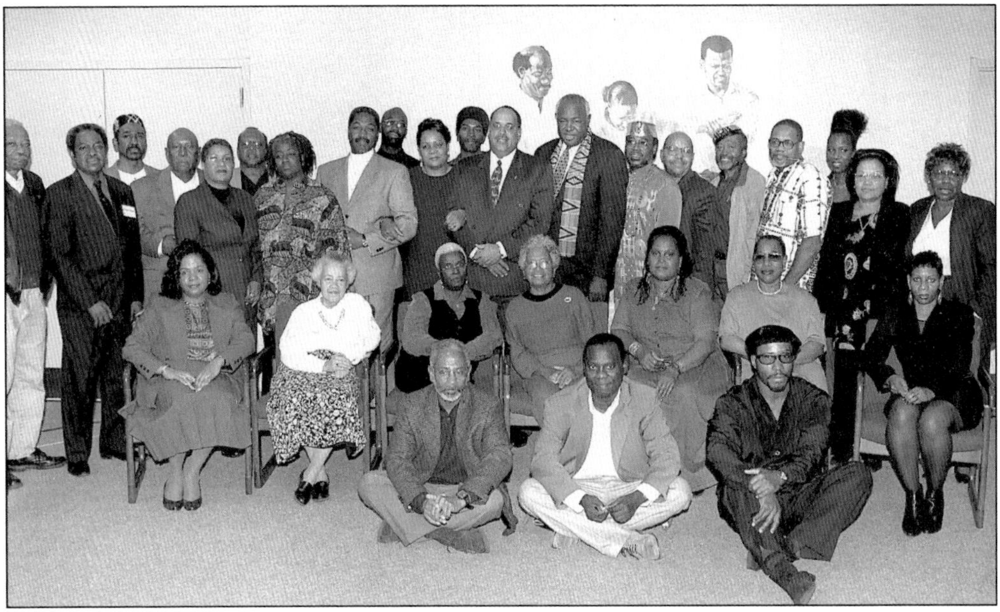

Shown are the founding and current members of the Long Island Black Artists Association, established in the 1970s. The association is one of the few Long Island organizations for African American artists. Along with exhibits and conferences, the group holds workshops and training sessions. (Courtesy of Willie Houston and the African American Museum.)

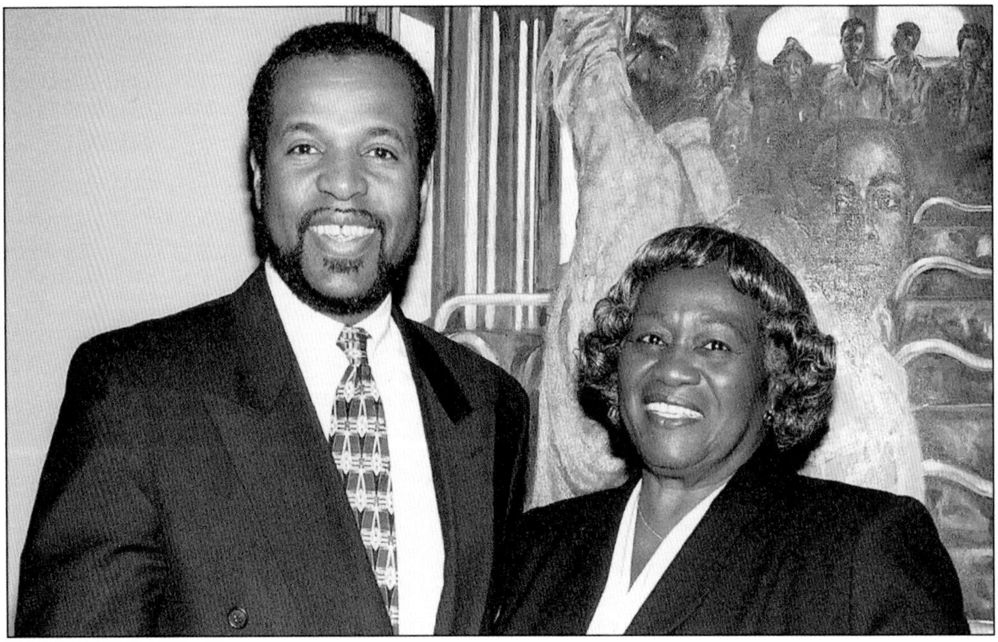

Dorothy Goosby and Frederick K. Brewington are prominent leaders and civil rights activists. Dorothy Goosby is the first black councilwoman in Hempstead's history. Fred Brewington is the civil rights lawyer who instituted the case *Goosby* v. *the Town of Hempstead,* which ultimately led to the election of African Americans to the city council. At the county level, his arguments that minorities were not represented in the legislature helped bring about African American representation in the Nassau County Legislature. (Courtesy of Dorothy Goosby.)

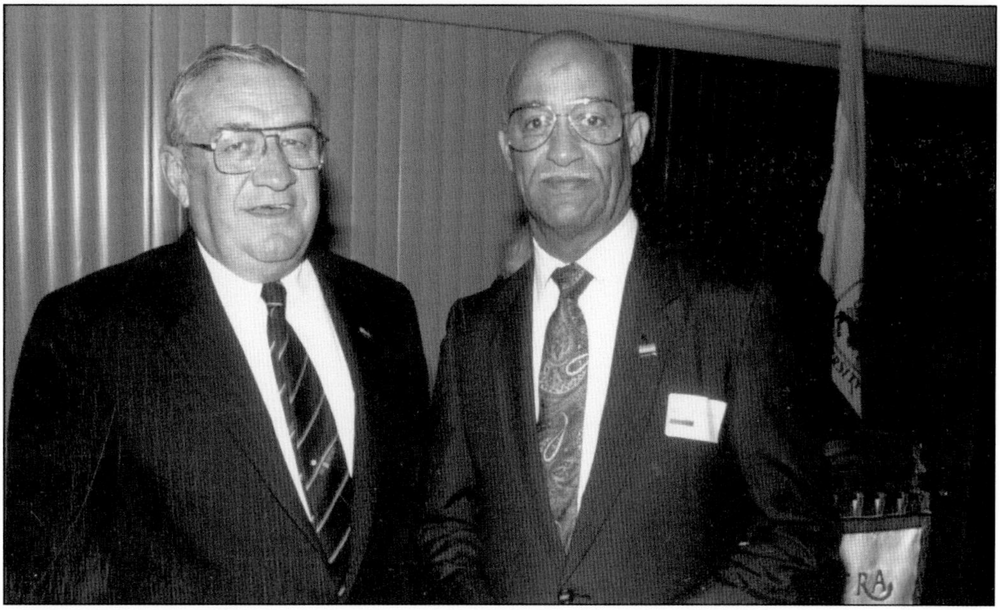

Roland H. Davis (right) receives an award from Dr. James M. Shuart, president of Hofstra University in Hempstead. A consultant to the president of Hofstra, Davis served in the U.S. Army from 1946 to 1966, earned a bachelor's degree from Long Island University in 1961, and received a master's degree in social work from Adelphi University in 1969. From 1979 to 1992, he served as coordinator of community development and an affirmative action officer. Along with serving on numerous clubs, committees, boards, and organizations, he cut the ribbon for the opening of headquarters at 9 Centre Street, Hempstead, of 100 Black Men, a group of distinguished African Americans who award scholarships and sponsor projects to encourage positive developments on Long Island. (Courtesy of Roland H. Davis.)

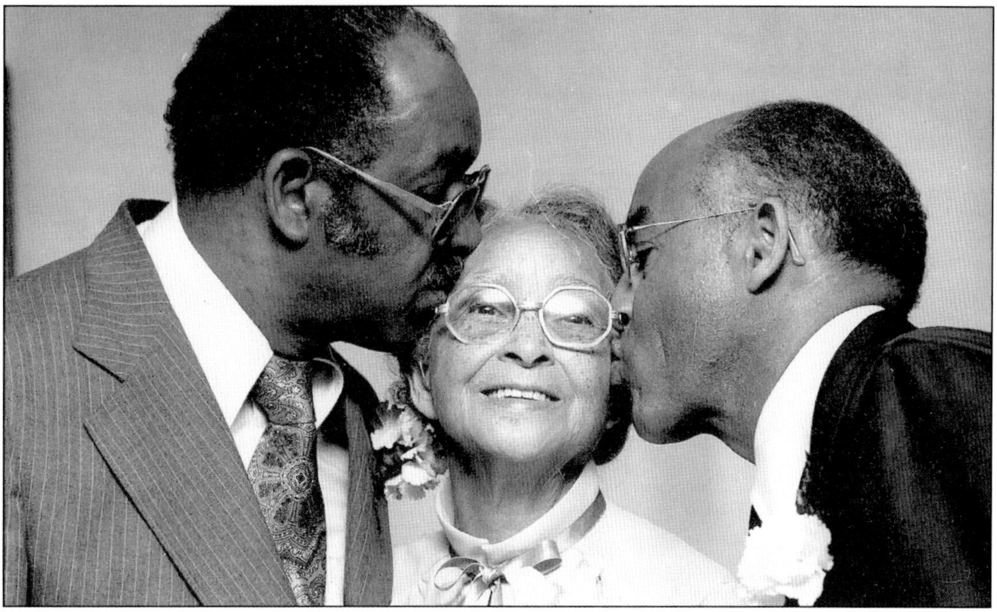

Dr. Sylvester S. Davis Jr. (left), a physician, and Roland H. Davis salute their mother, Amaza Davis, on her 80th birthday, May 5, 1978. (Courtesy of Roland H. Davis.)

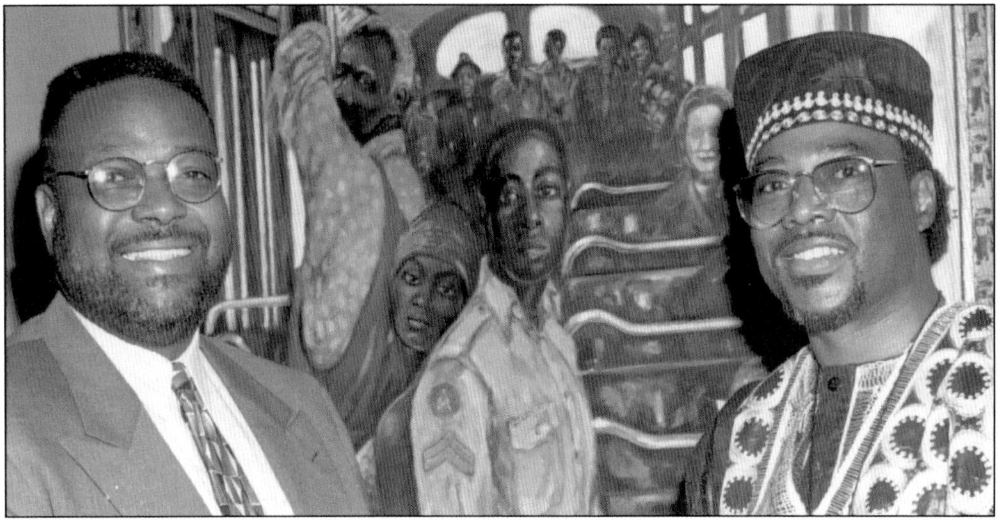

Curtis Fisher (left) was one of the first African American deputy county executives. He was appointed to that office by Thomas Gulotta, county executive. Fisher was also one of the first African Americans to serve on the town board. With him is William Houston of the African American Museum. (Courtesy of Willie Houston.)

Political and judicial leaders attend an Operation Get Ahead scholarship breakfast honoring high school seniors from Hempstead, Roosevelt, and Freeport. From left to right are Curtis Fisher, Alfred D. Cooper, district court judge; Dorothy Goosby, Hempstead town councilwoman; Patrick Williams, Nassau County legislator; Tina Hodge-Bowles, Operation Get Ahead executive director; Roger Corbin, Nassau County legislator; Hezekiah Brown, deputy county executive; and Cynthia Diaz Wilson, judge. (Courtesy of Gary Coley and the Community Journal.)

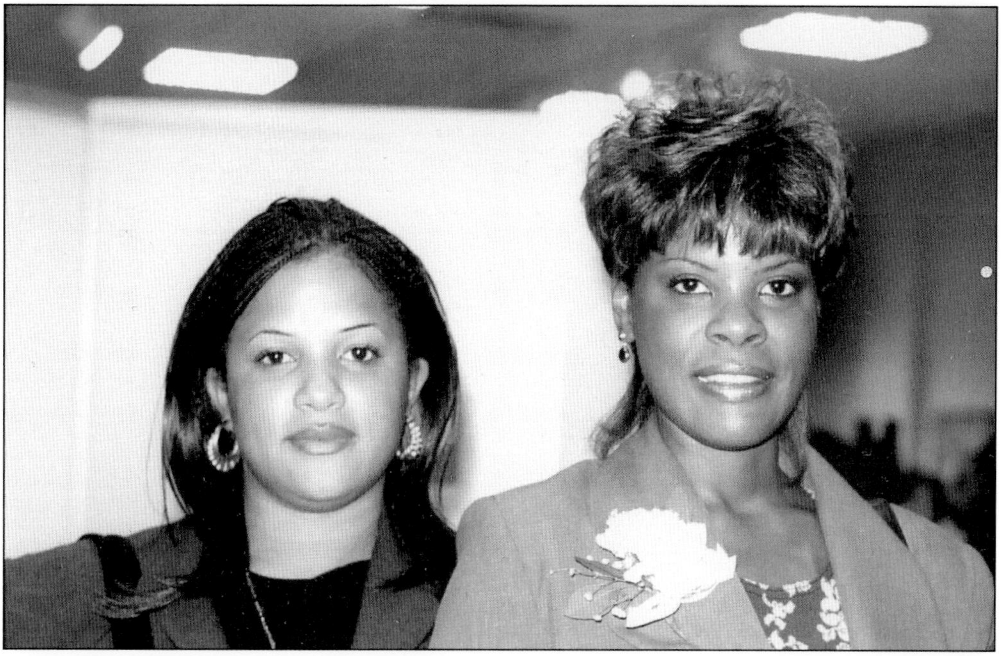

Visiting the African American Museum are Michelle Martin (left), who was born and raised in Hempstead, and her mother, Shirley Martin, secretary to the mayor of Hempstead. (Author's collection.)

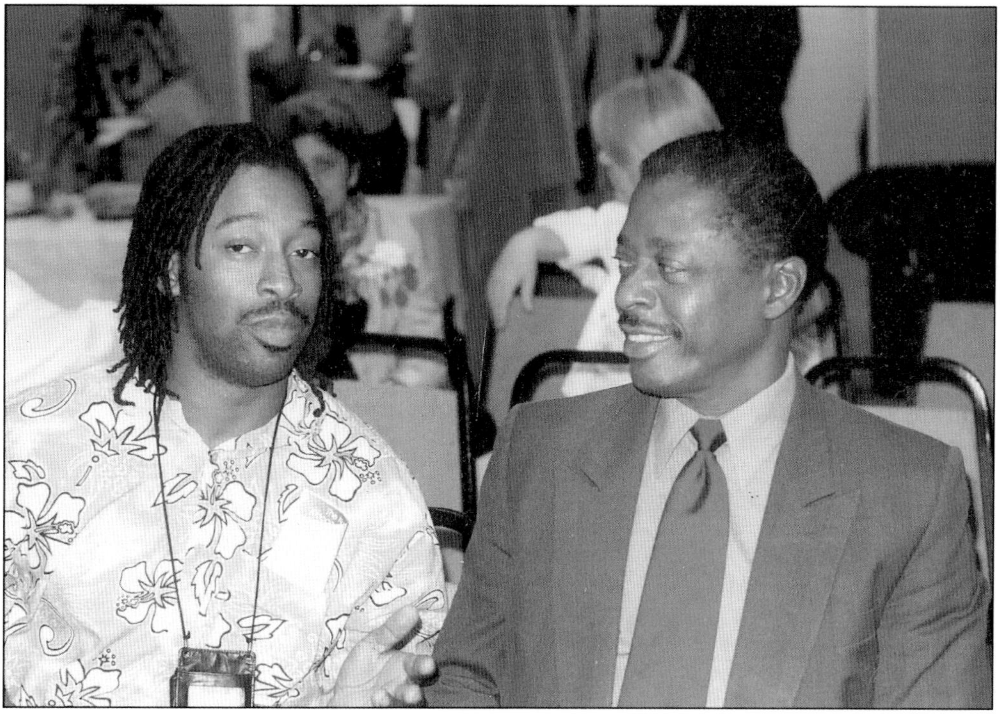

Andreaus Guilty (left), a founder of the Media Center in Roosevelt, and Delano Stewart, journalist and publisher of *Point of View*, reflect on community issues at the African American Museum in Hempstead. (Author's collection.)

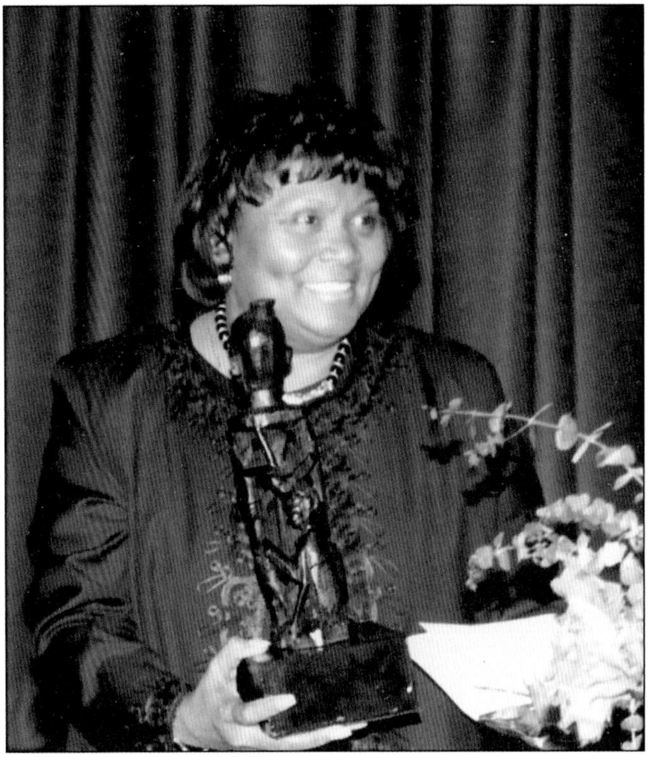

Phyllis Gates-Young, the founding pastor of Miracle Christian Center in Hempstead, speaks at a Kwanza ceremony in Freeport. She holds associate's and bachelor's degrees from Long Island University. Her two children are also preachers and church leaders. (Courtesy of Emily Moore.)

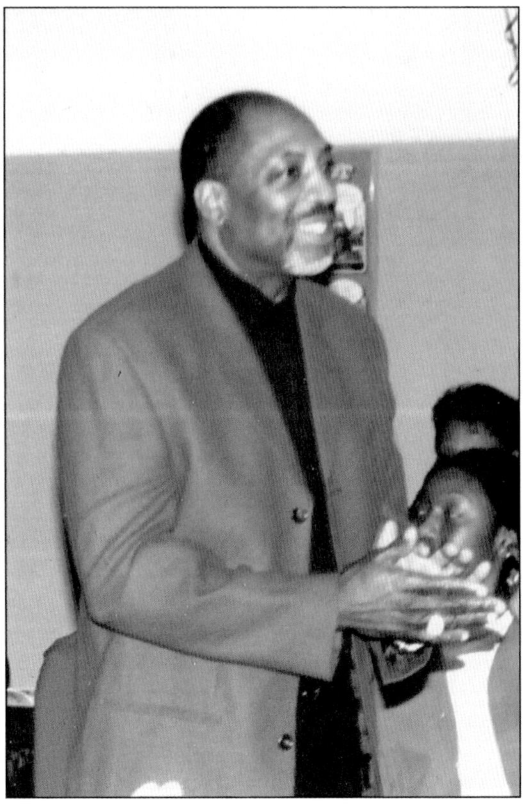

Ted Adams, director of the Salvation Army Community Center, is popular basketball coach. He has served in Hempstead for over two decades, dedicating his life to children in the community. (Courtesy of Emily Moore.)

Hazel Dukes is a political leader, activist, and community mobilizer. A prominent member of the National Association for the Advancement of Colored People (NAACP), she has led the organization in several capacities. (Courtesy of Emily Moore.)

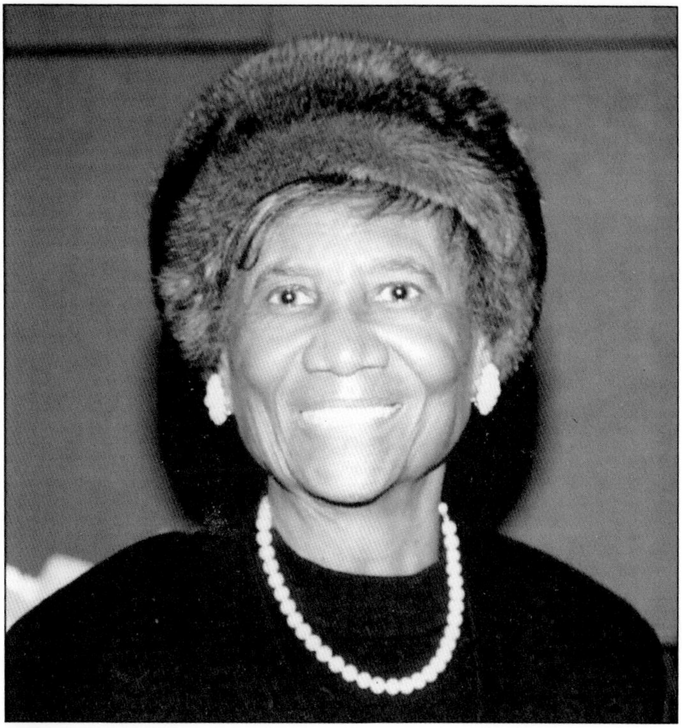

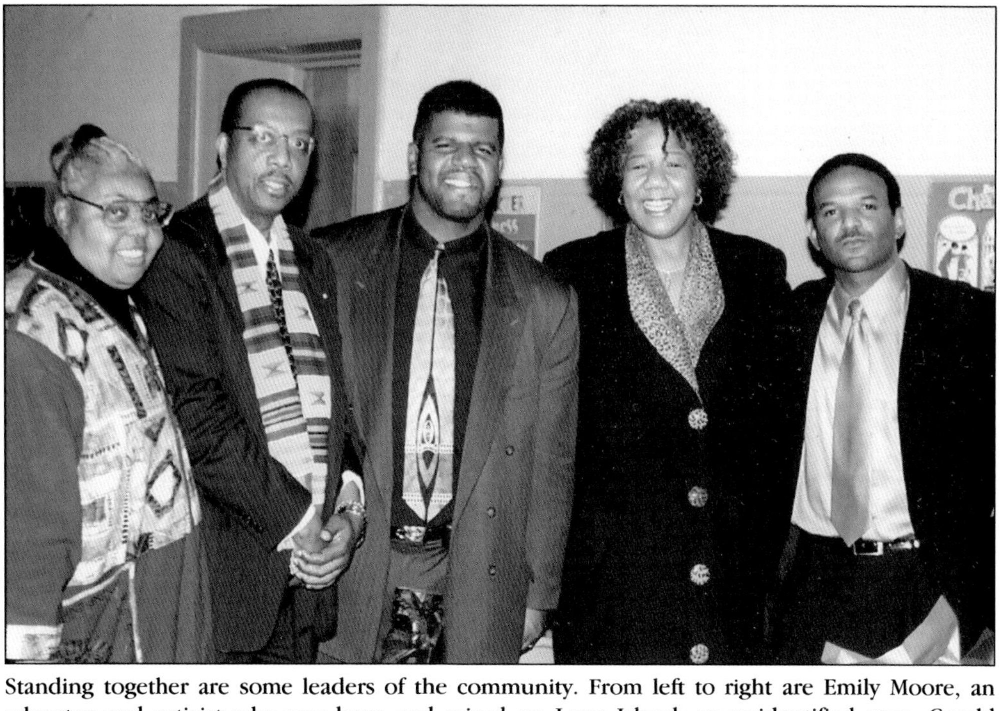

Standing together are some leaders of the community. From left to right are Emily Moore, an educator and activist who was born and raised on Long Island; an unidentified man; Gerald Burnett, executive director of the Burnett Funeral Home, who also was raised on the island; Seretta McKnight, an educator and activist whose family has lived on the island for many decades; and Douglas Mills, the owner of the Burgundy Lounge in Hempstead. (Courtesy of Emily Moore.)

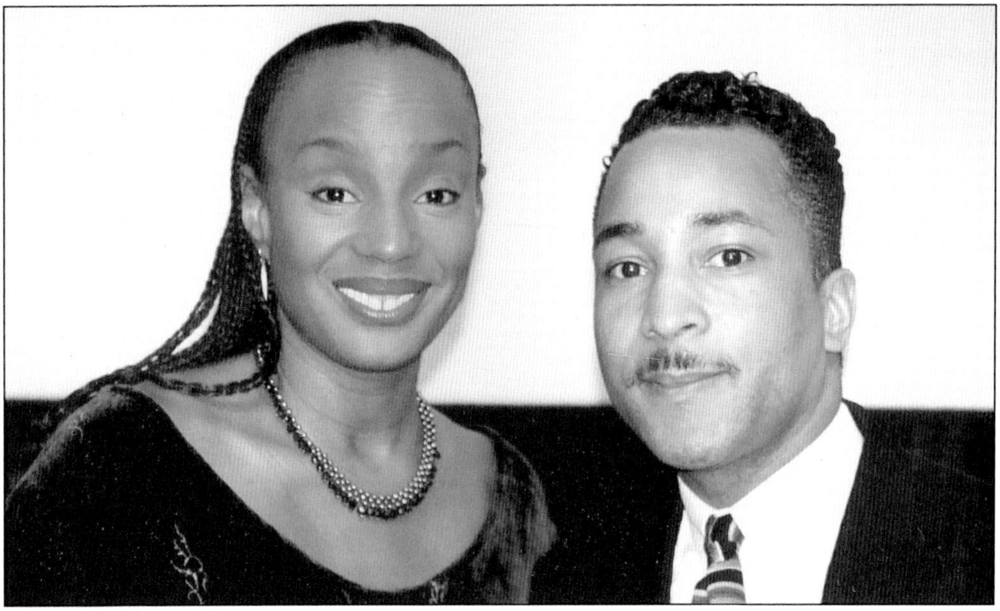

Susan Taylor of *Essence* magazine speaks at Nassau County Community College. With her is Dale Anthony, a member of the White House Presidential Committee against AIDS. (Courtesy of Emily Moore.)

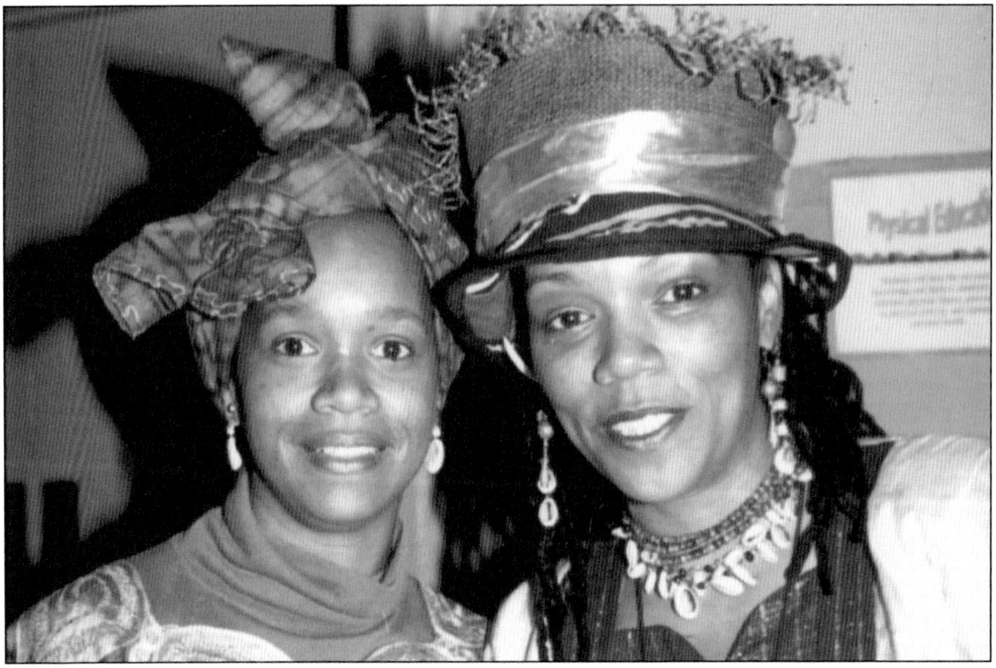

Robin Brazley (right), a professor at Morgan State University, graduated from Hempstead High School, earned a bachelor's degree from Morgan State and a master's degree from Bowling Green, and is currently completing her doctorate at Morgan State. Shelley Brazley Giles (left) lives in Hempstead and is the director of ART in Motion—Africa's Richest Treasures Studio and Cultural Arts Center. The Brazley family has lived in Hempstead since the 1950s. (Courtesy of Emily Moore.)

Dr. Linda Michelle Baron, the poet laureate of Hempstead, recites her work. She is not only a poet but also a performer, an educator, a dancer, and an animator. She trains youth and serves as a reader and entertainer at public functions. (Courtesy of Emily Moore.)

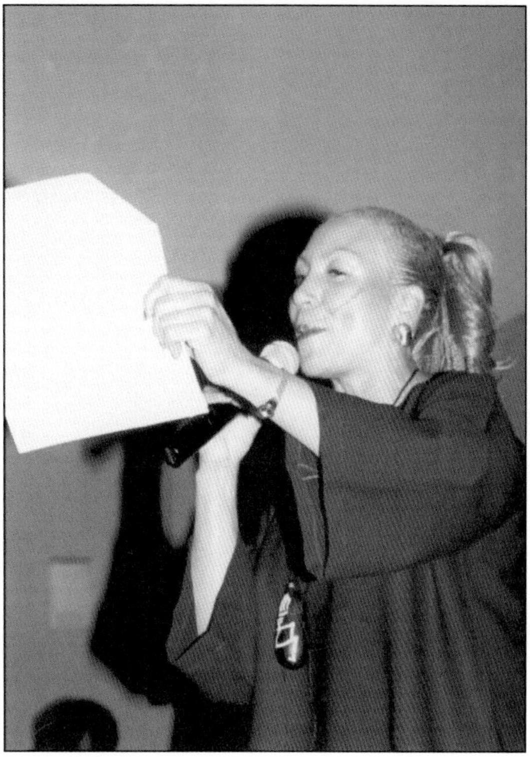

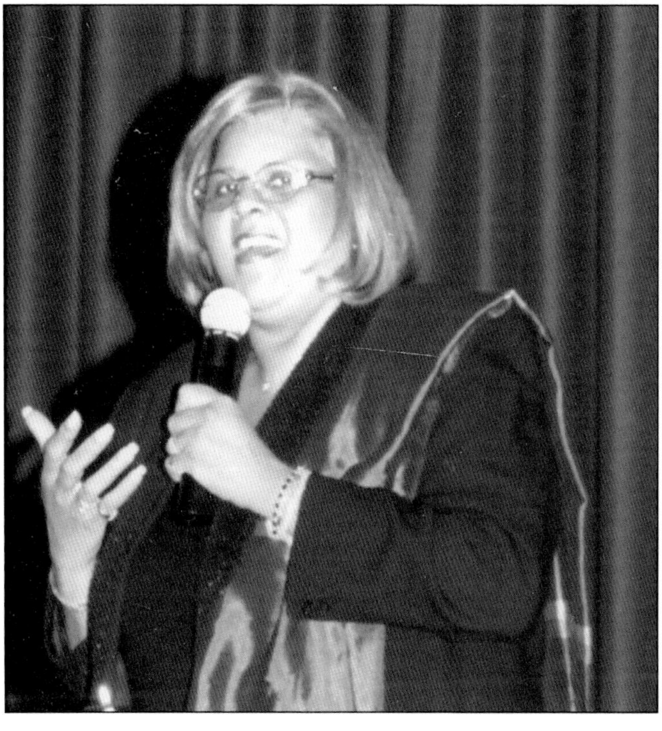

Diane Brown is the principal of Alberta B. Schultze Middle School in Hempstead. She earned a bachelor's degree from Hofstra and a master's from C.W. Post. (Courtesy of Emily Moore.)

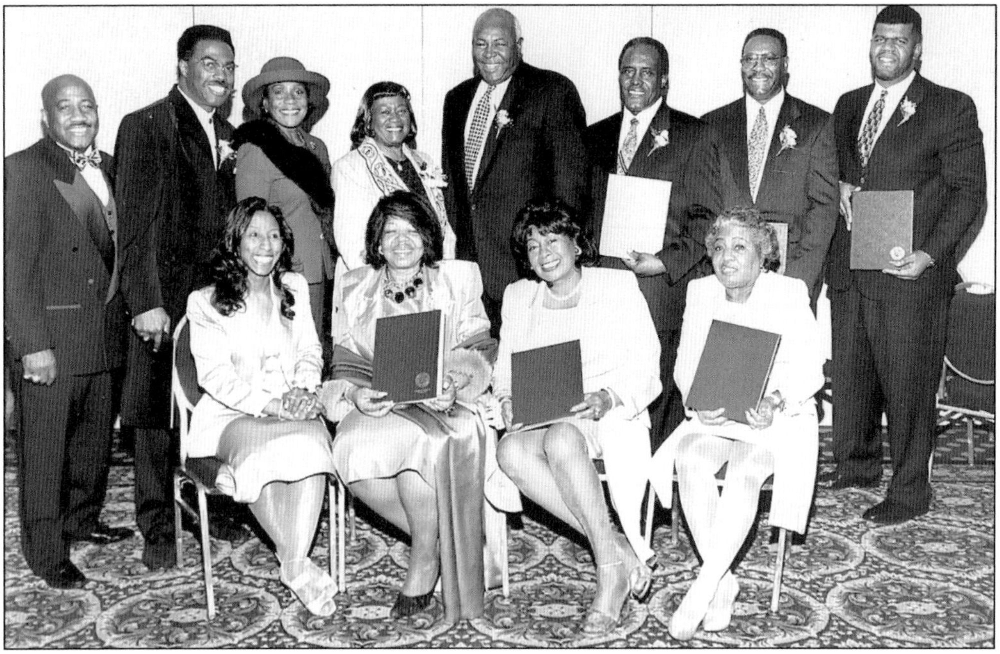

Three women and three men were honored at the first ever Antioch Baptist Church awards luncheon, sponsored by the Antioch Community Development Corporation and the Antioch Housing Fund Corporation. Holding their awards are Betty Cross, Carolyn Simkins, Dixie Hunt, Henry Holly, Isaac Ephraim, and Gerald Burnett. Shown with them, from left to right, are the following: (front row) Sheila Elliot; (back row) unidentified, Rev. Dr. Phillip Elliot, Assemblywoman Earlene Hill Hooper, Hempstead Town Councilwoman Dorothy Goosby, and Hempstead Mayor James A. Garner. (Courtesy of Pastor Elliot and the Antioch Baptist Church.)

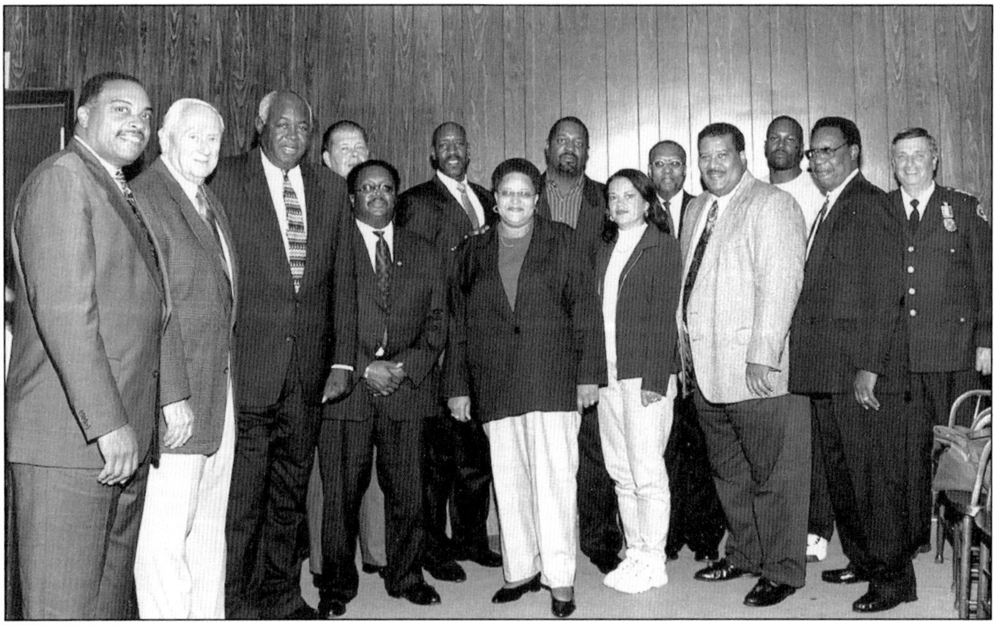

Shown are Hempstead town leaders, who include Mayor James A. Garner (third from left) and Hezekiah Brown (second from right), deputy county executive. (Courtesy of Gary Coley.)

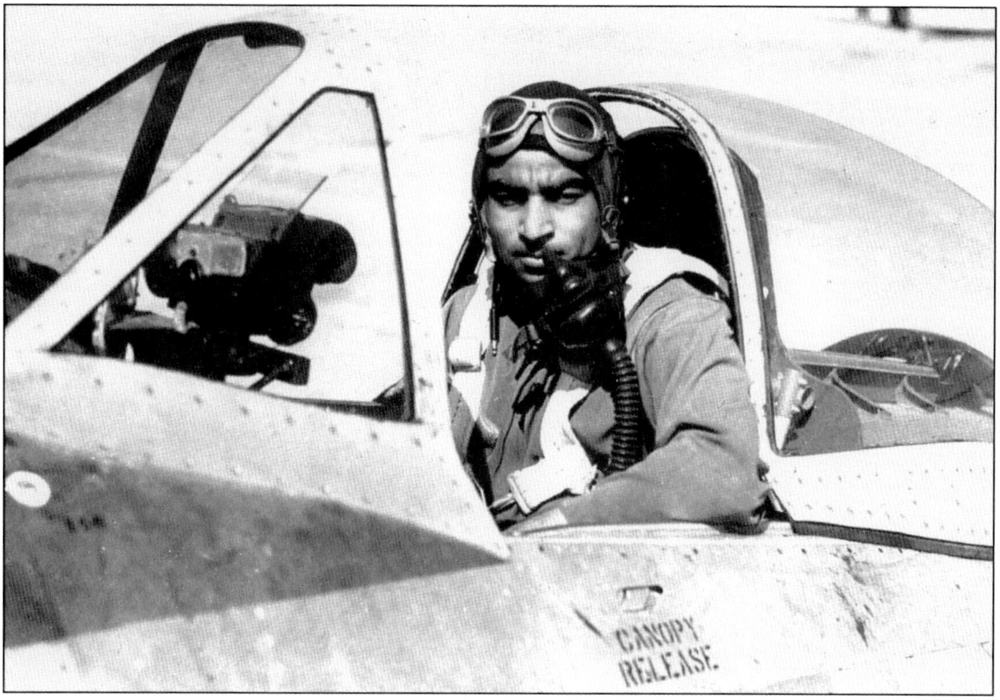

Spam Watson was one of the first Tuskegee airmen. From Westbury, he served as an officer in the group during World War II. (Courtesy of Spam Watson.)

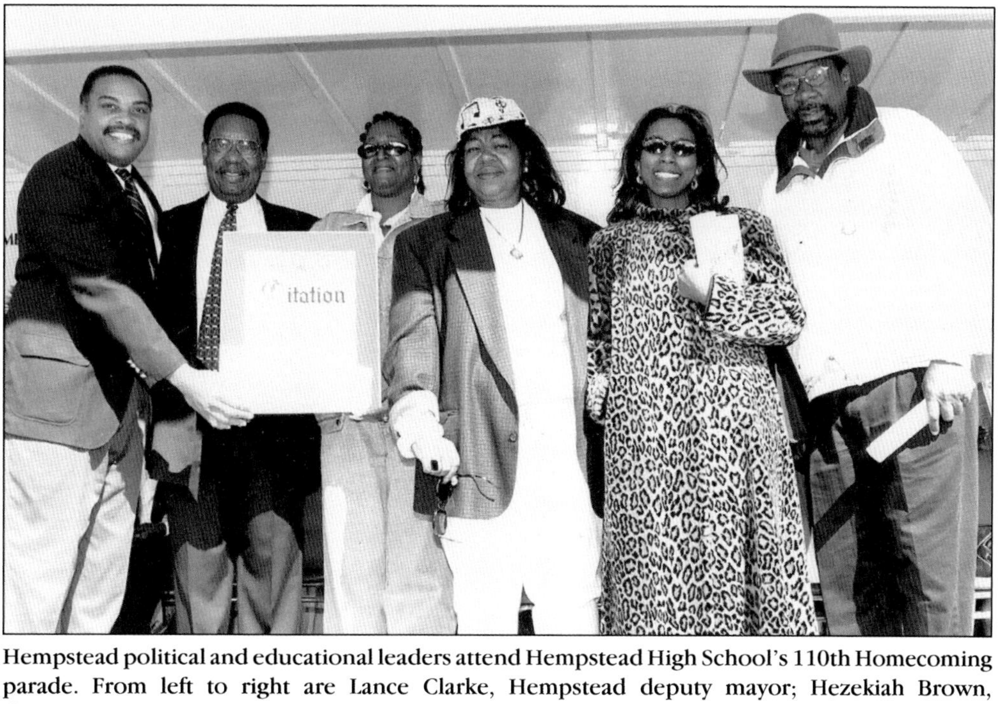

Hempstead political and educational leaders attend Hempstead High School's 110th Homecoming parade. From left to right are Lance Clarke, Hempstead deputy mayor; Hezekiah Brown, deputy county executive; April Jones-White, school board first vice president; Betty Cross, treasurer; Sheila Elliot; and Dan Hester, school board second vice president. (Courtesy of Gary Coley.)

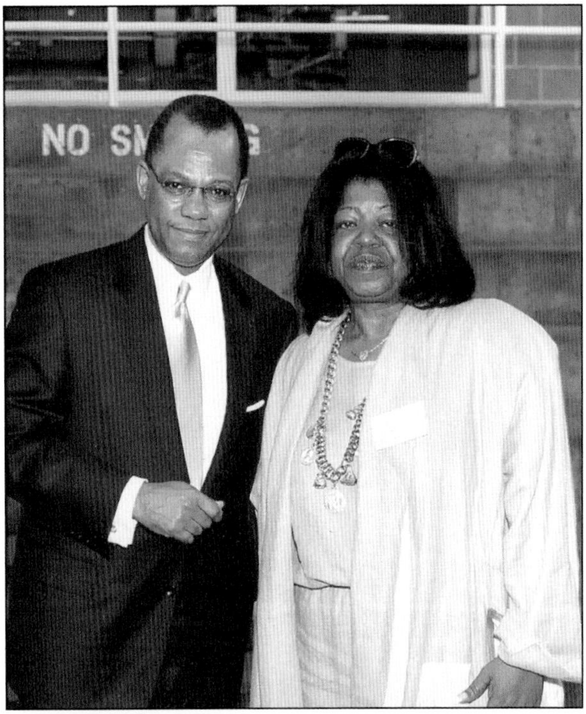

Rev. Dr. Calvin Butts attends a reception honoring his appointment as the new president of the State University of New York at Old Westbury. Among those on hand to congratulate him is Betty Cross, a member of the Hempstead School Board member. (Courtesy of Gary Coley.)

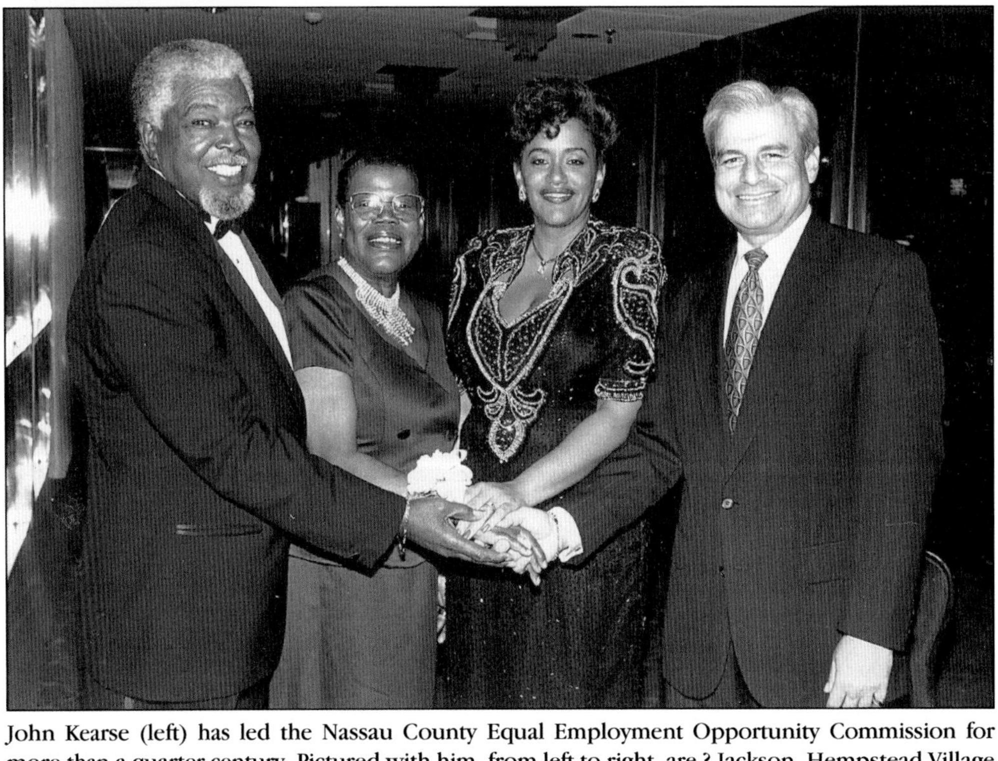

John Kearse (left) has led the Nassau County Equal Employment Opportunity Commission for more than a quarter century. Pictured with him, from left to right, are ? Jackson, Hempstead Village trustee; Cynthia Diaz Wilson, one of the pioneer African American judges in Hempstead; and Tom Gulotta, former county supervisor. (Courtesy of Minority Press Office, Nassau County.)

Darlene Harris (left), the first African American female legislator from the Uniondale district, presents a Nassau County Legislative Citation to Georgia A. Young, (center) on her 26th anniversary year as pastor of Mount Zion Temple Apostolic Church. (Courtesy of Minority Press Office, Nassau County.)

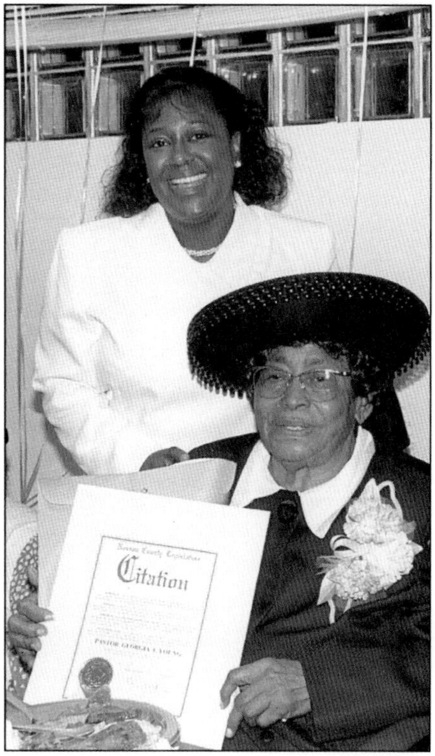

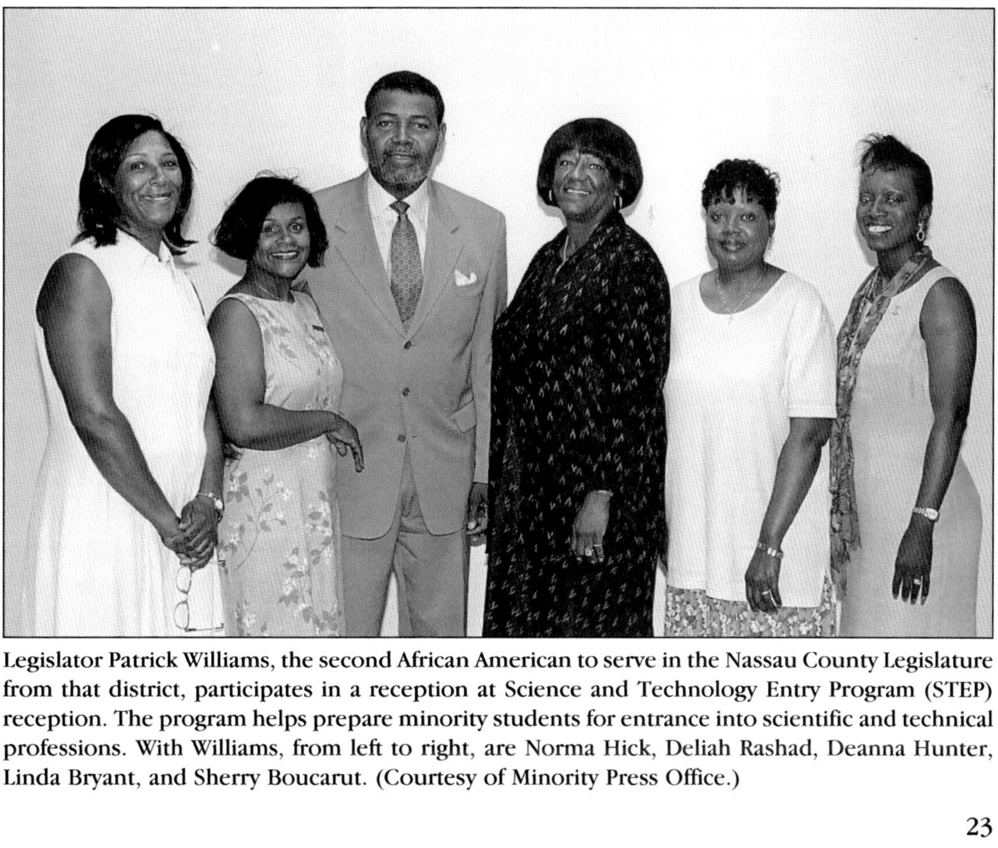

Legislator Patrick Williams, the second African American to serve in the Nassau County Legislature from that district, participates in a reception at Science and Technology Entry Program (STEP) reception. The program helps prepare minority students for entrance into scientific and technical professions. With Williams, from left to right, are Norma Hick, Deliah Rashad, Deanna Hunter, Linda Bryant, and Sherry Boucarut. (Courtesy of Minority Press Office.)

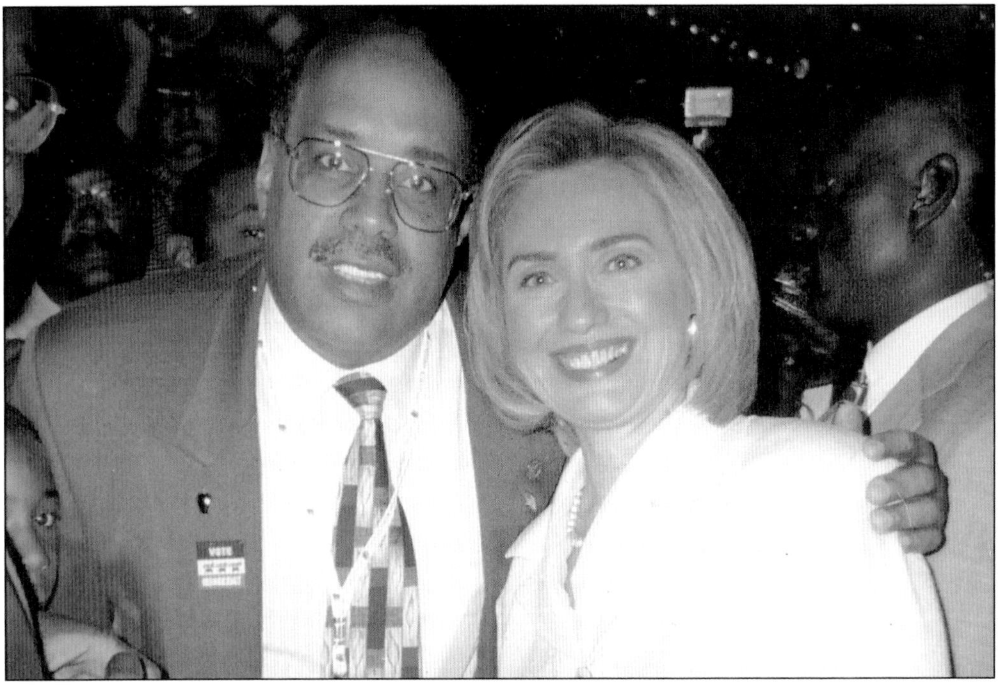

Roger Corbin, deputy presiding officer of the Nassau County Legislature, poses with Hillary Clinton at a local Democratic function. (Courtesy of Majority Press Office, Nassau County.)

Russell Hood, Hempstead community affairs director, presents a Certificate of Recognition to Sally Thompson for her service as principal and teacher at Prospect School. (Courtesy of Russell Hood, the Mayor's Office.)

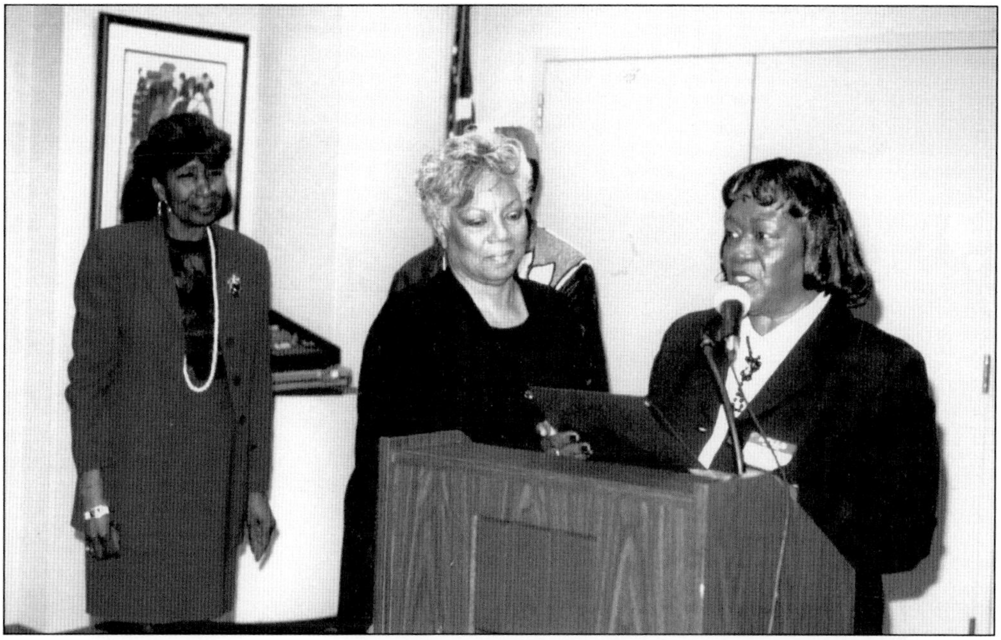

Three Long Island women who have left a mark on the community participate at a Black History Month celebration at the African American Museum in Hempstead. From left to right are retired pharmacist Genevieve Morales, historian and researcher Joysetta Pearse, and Councilwoman Dorothy Goosby. (Author's collection.)

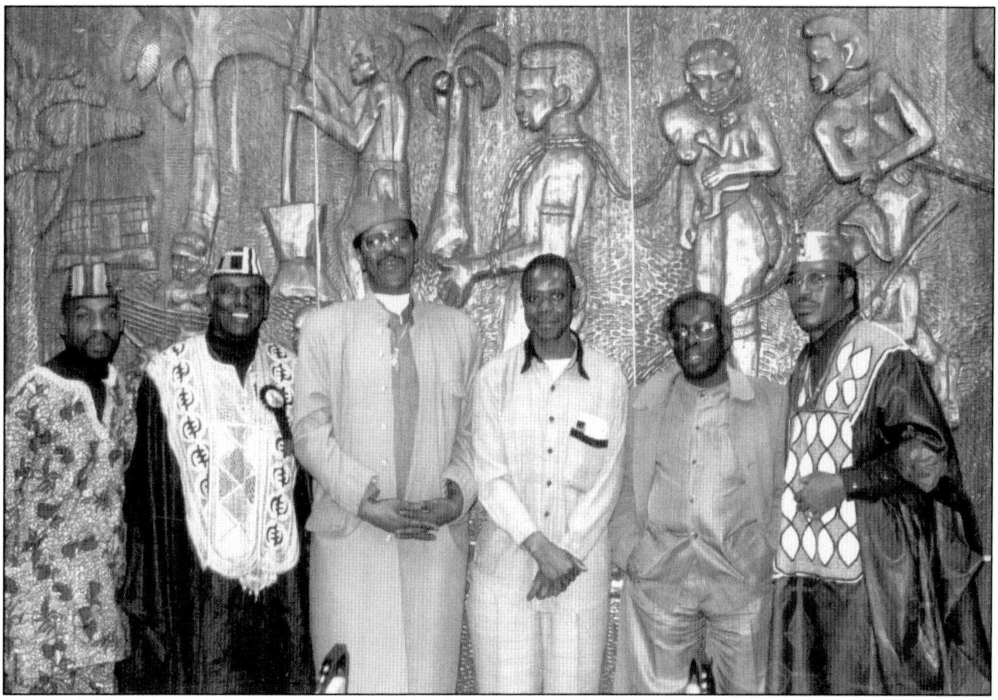

Dr. Leonard Jeffries (second from left) was among those who spoke at the African American Museum during Black History Month. Jeffries is a professor of history and a noted speaker on African American and contemporary issues. (Author's collection.)

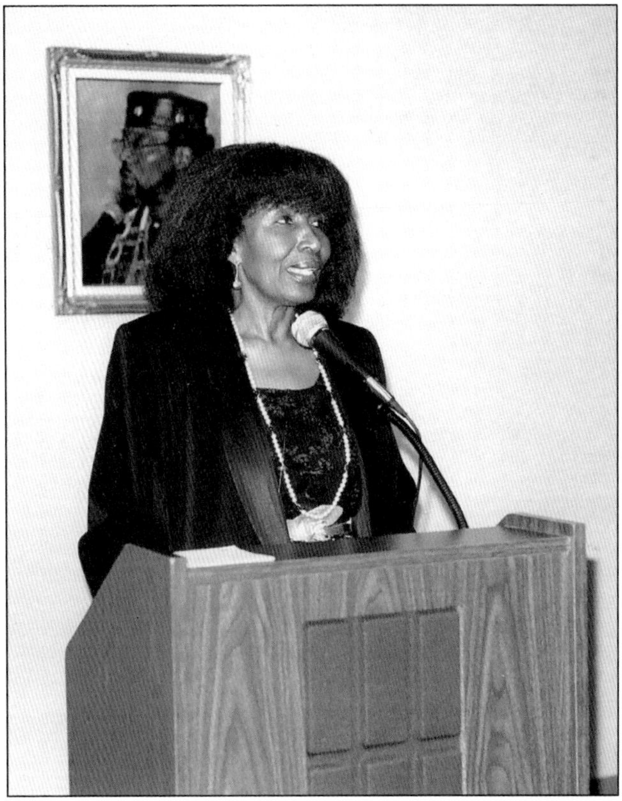

Genevieve Morales is one of the first African American pharmacists in the area. She is a member of the Friends of the African American Museum in Hempstead and of the Genealogical Society of Freeport. (Author's collection.)

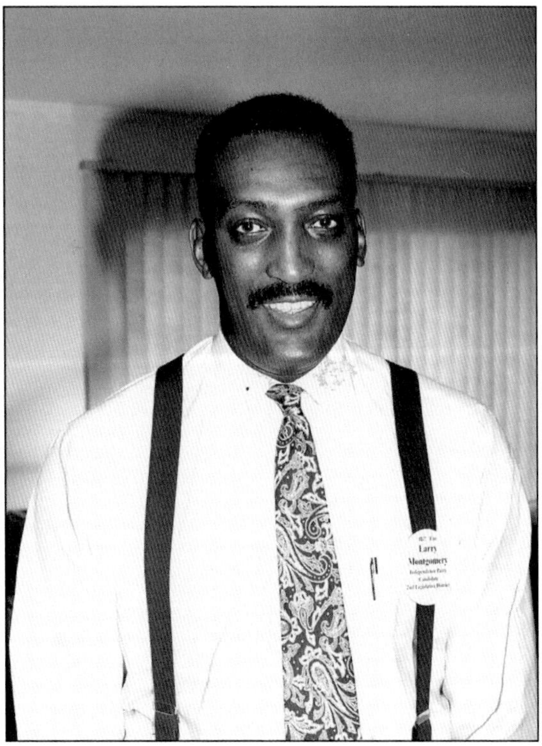

Larry Montgomery, a reporter and commentator, writes for the *Community Reporter* and works for the Nassau County Legislature. (Courtesy of Larry Montgomery.)

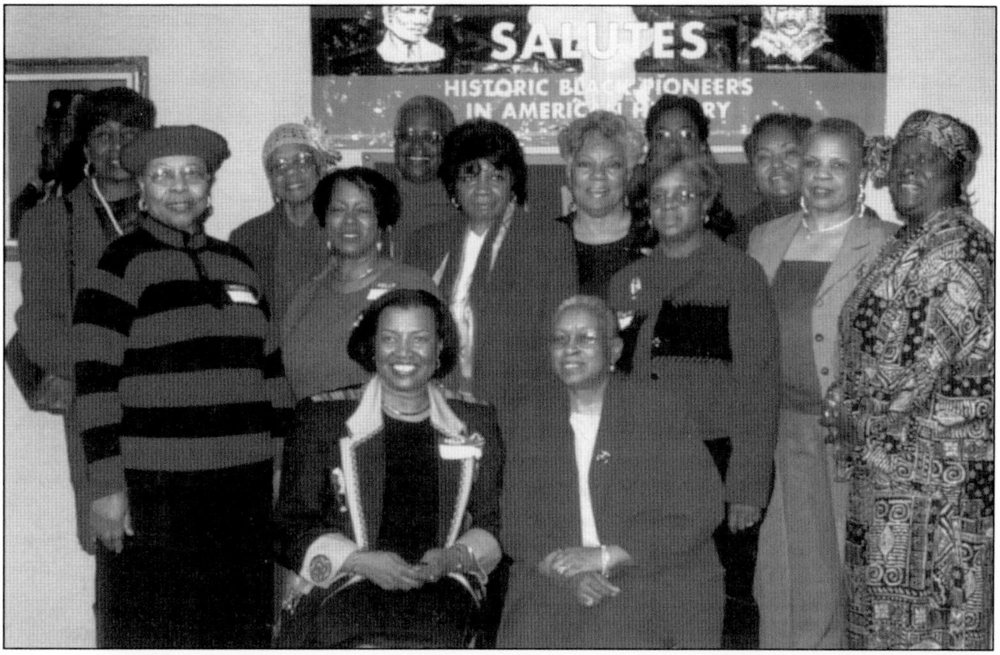

The theme of Black History Month was Historic Black Pioneers in American History. Celebrating their heritage are a group of African American women (above) who have roots in the Hempstead area of Long Island and a gathering of prominent people (below) who offered insight into the African American past. (Author's collection.)

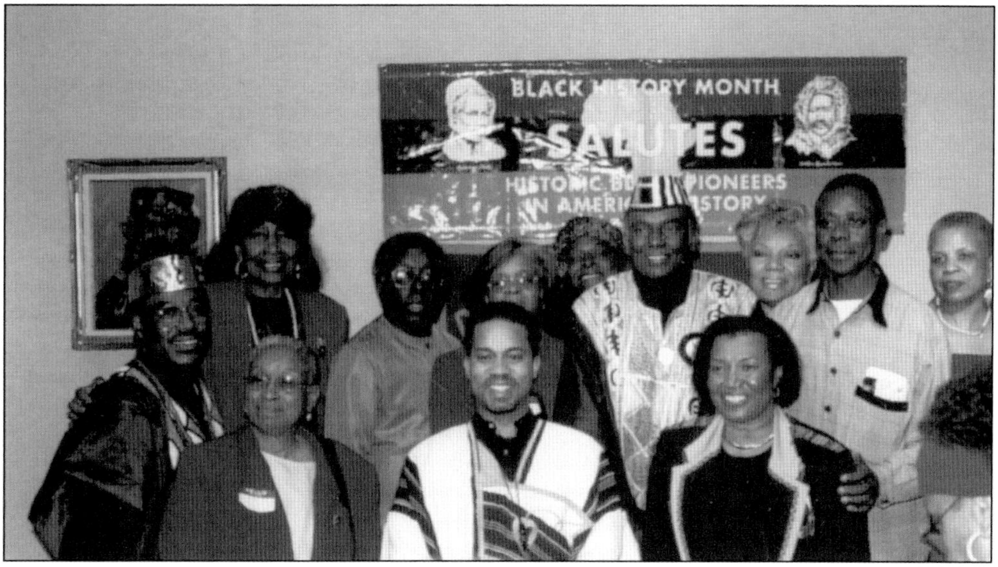

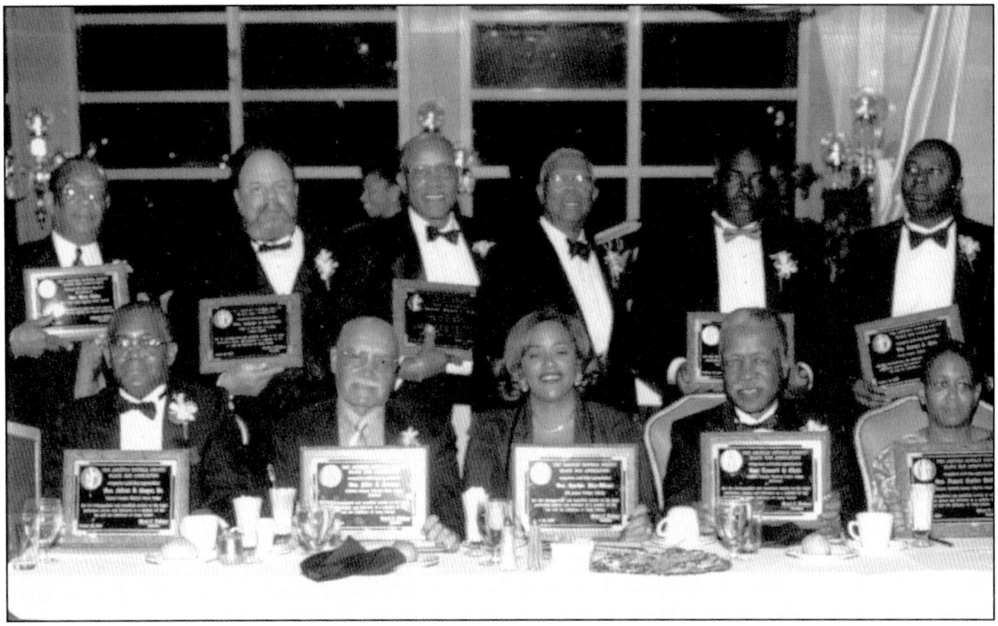

Long Island judges attend the first Amistad Black Bar recognition ceremony. From left to right, they are as follows: (front row) Moxey Rigby Jr., Antonio Brandeveen, Marquette Floyd, Alfred Robins, Jerald Carter, and Carnell T. Foskey; (back row) Alfred D. Cooper, Peter J. Newman, Cynthia Diaz Wilson, Leonard S. Clark, and Francel Trotter Bellinger. (Courtesy of J. Stewart Moore and the Amistad Black Bar.)

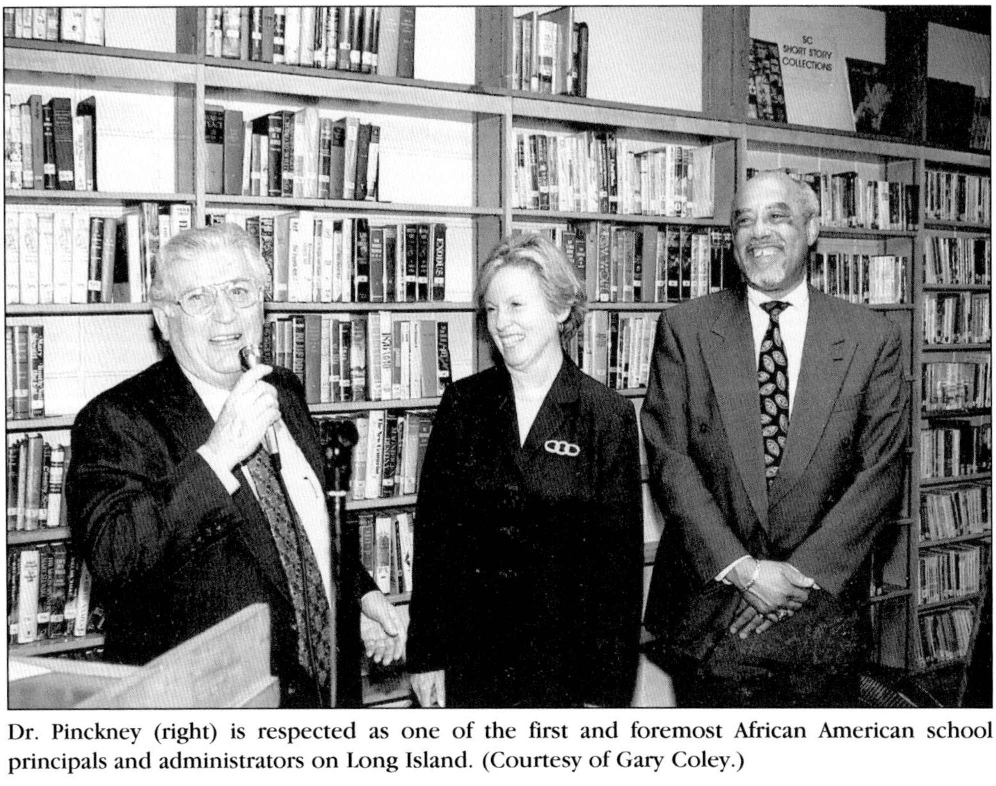

Dr. Pinckney (right) is respected as one of the first and foremost African American school principals and administrators on Long Island. (Courtesy of Gary Coley.)

Two

Roosevelt
Promise and Progress

As with all Long Island communities, it is difficult to establish the date when the first African Americans settled in Roosevelt. However, historians note that 11 men were the first blacks to set foot on what is now called New York to begin the era of servitude. As elsewhere in the country, there might have been a few who were around before the advent of slavery. However, recorded history often traces the genesis of the first African Americans in Roosevelt to the slave epoch.

One black family reportedly lived in Roosevelt's wooded area by the beginning of the 20th century. Several other black families built houses around the first one. Members of these families were employed as domestic servants, road workers, and farm hands. The small black enclave was a recognized part of the community.

Threats from the Ku Klux Klan during World War I reportedly targeted blacks and Jews. After the war, however, a few African Americans started moving into Roosevelt, both from New York City and the South. The rabble-rousers who belonged to the Ku Klux Klan had toned down their rhetoric and, indeed, disappeared from the area.

Like Hempstead, Roosevelt is located near New York City and thus offers opportunities for city and suburban jobs. As a new spirit permeated the area, land developers took advantage of the location and built houses, which they advertised in African American newspapers. The African American population grew and, by the 1950s, it reportedly covered six square blocks. Washington Avenue marked the dividing line between whites and blacks, with whites dominating the north side and blacks residing on the south flank.

As time went on, blacks who moved to Roosevelt came seeking better, less-congested neighborhoods where they could live the American dream of nice houses, clean and neat yards, and suburban schools. However, as soon as they moved to a certain area, the whites who livid there relocated elsewhere. Thus, segregation occurred in Roosevelt either through voluntary departure or natural osmosis. For example, by 1963, the Theodore Roosevelt School was 98 percent non-white. By contrast, Centennial School was 98 percent white. As a result the state education board was compelled to order the desegregation of Roosevelt Schools in the late 1960s.

Over the years African Americans in Roosevelt have faced housing challenges. Although some of the pioneers found it a haven since they could afford housing and other amenities, those on the lower economic rungs battled hard to rent, let alone build houses. Traditional problems of crime, drugs, and discipline in schools surged to the surface, and the state stepped in again, this time to take control of the Roosevelt school.

Today, professionals in the fields of medicine, education, law, engineering, and accounting live in Roosevelt. They came to this promising place, made it their home, and progressed beyond expectations.

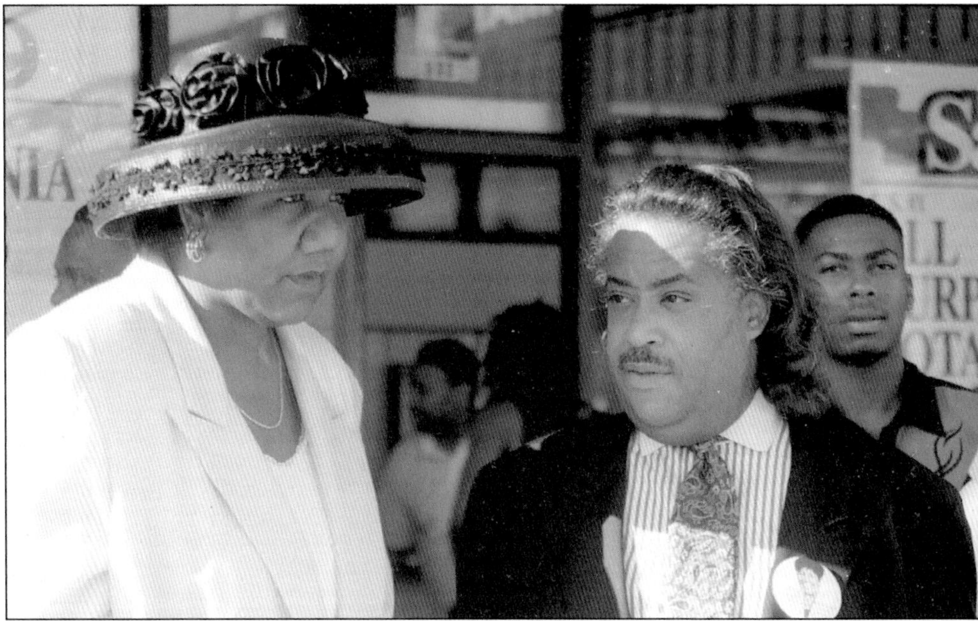

Seretta C. McKnight is one of the first African Americans to become president of a school board. She assumed office in Roosevelt at the historic period when the state took over the local school. Currently president of Sisters in the Struggle, she belongs to an old established families on Long Island. Her parents, Irving and Kathryn McKnight, operated the McKnight Fuel Oil Company. She is pictured with civil rights activist Al Sharpton, a popular guest speaker and commentator. (Courtesy of Emily Moore.)

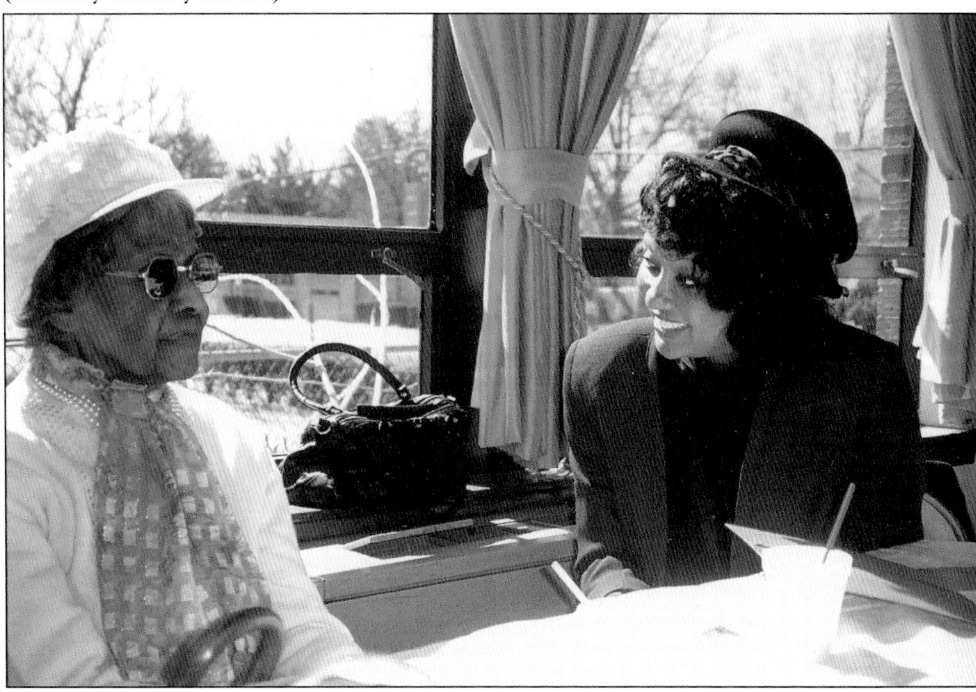

Rev. Maxime Thomas (right) served as a columnist for the *Community Journal.* She was one of the first African American religious writers for a newspaper. (Courtesy of Gary Coley.)

Dr. Aubrey Lewis, a leading Nassau County physician, is the director of the Institute for Community Wellbeing. He focuses on the health of African Americans and excels as an advocate, drawing attention to disparities in health care provision. (Courtesy of Gary Coley.)

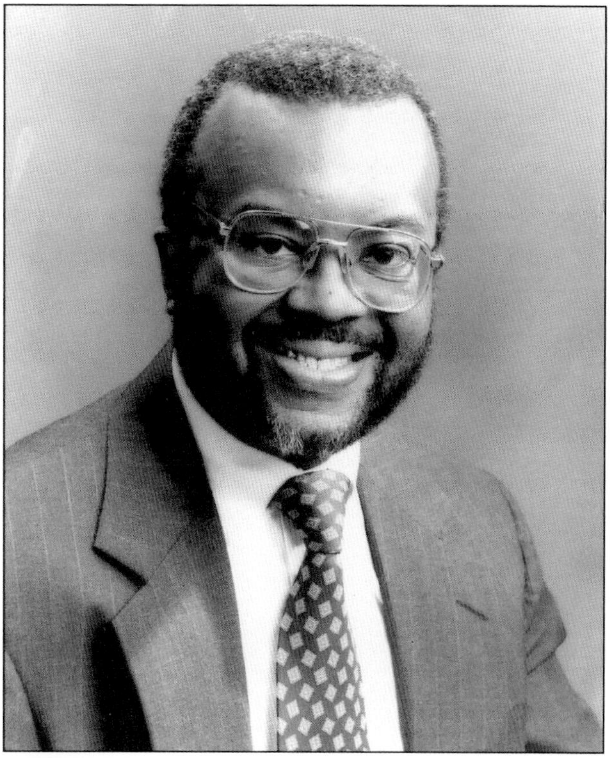

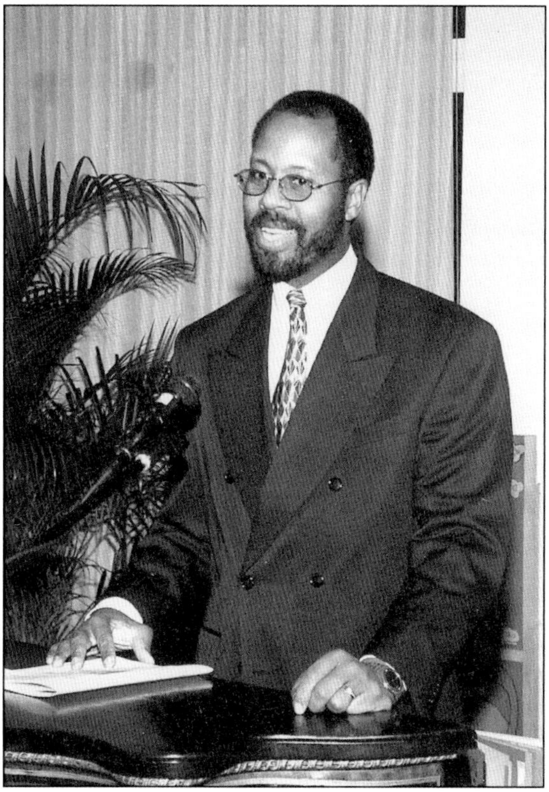

Gary Coley is the founder and publisher of the *Community Journal*. Established in the early 1990s, the *Community Journal* is rated as one of the most influential alternative newspapers in the county. Coley also has served as a board member of the African American Media Network and as chairman of the Roosevelt Chamber of Commerce. (Courtesy of Gary Coley.)

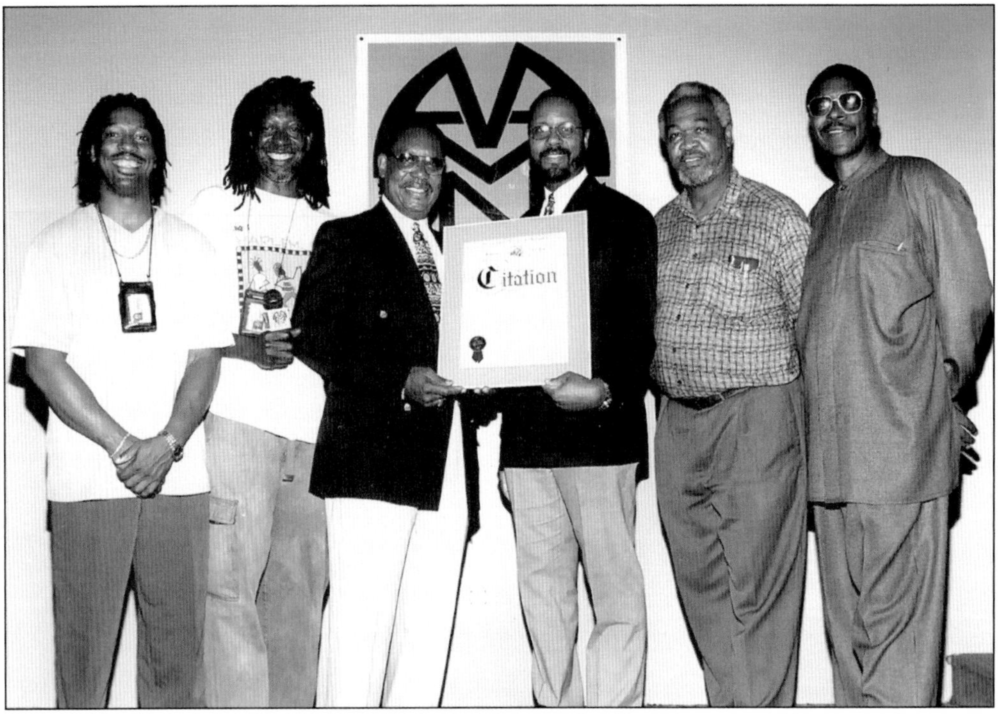

Shown are founders and early members of the Media Center, a leading community institution in Roosevelt. From left to right are Andreaus Guilty, executive director; E. Bailey, media specialist; Hezekiah Brown, then village of Hempstead trustee; Gary Cooley, *Community Journal* publisher; Jack Prophet, African American Media Network administrator; and Hassan Hoskins, Media Network member and host of the show *Shaka's Kraal*. (Courtesy of Gary Coley.)

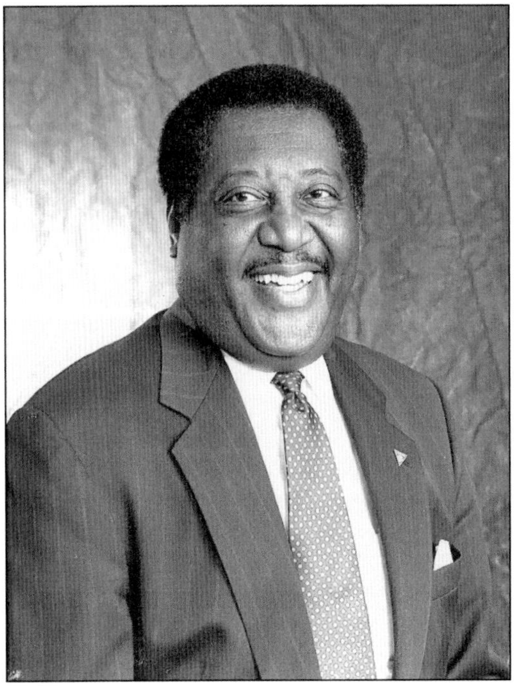

Willie Edlow is one of Long Island's first African American chief executives of United Way. (Courtesy of Gary Coley.)

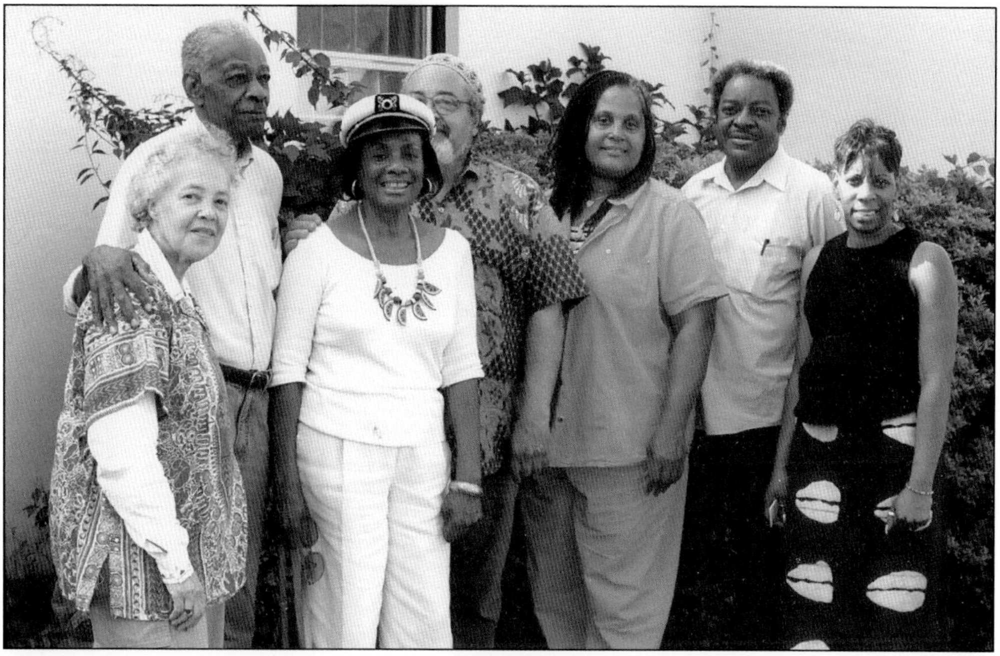

These artists have been associated with the Long Island community for at least 30 years. Among them are sculptor James Count (second from left), Charles Winslow (second from right), and Rhonda Fleishman (right). (Author's collection.)

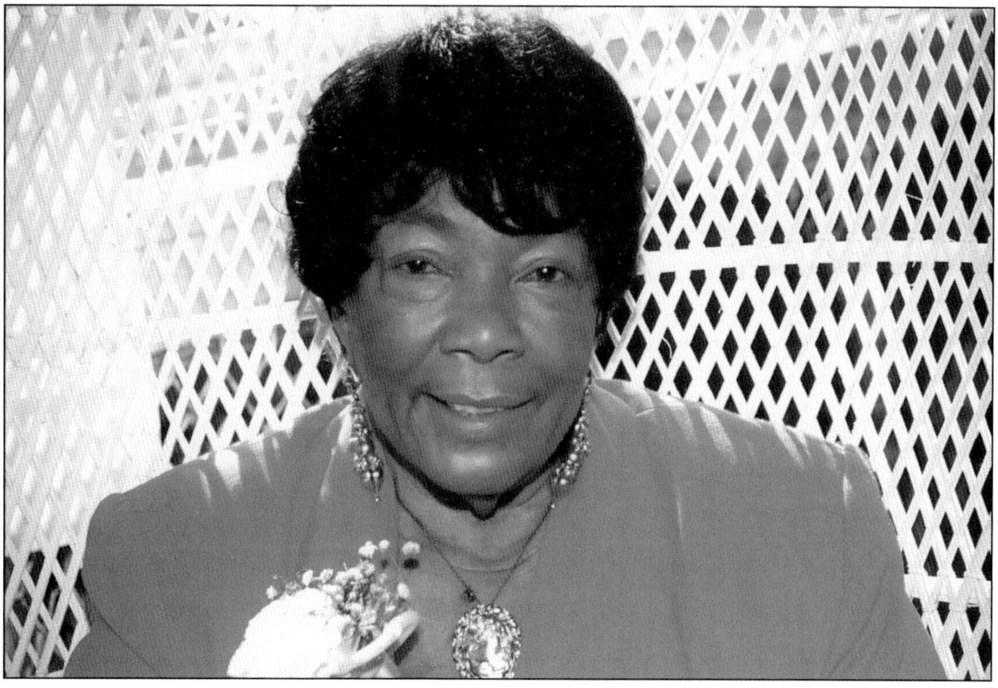

Alberta Gray Schultze has earned great respect for her contributions to the community. An educator and activist, she has served for more than a half century as a teacher and a principal. In recognition, the local middle school is named after her—an honor that very few African Americans on Long Island have received. (Courtesy of Gary Cooley.)

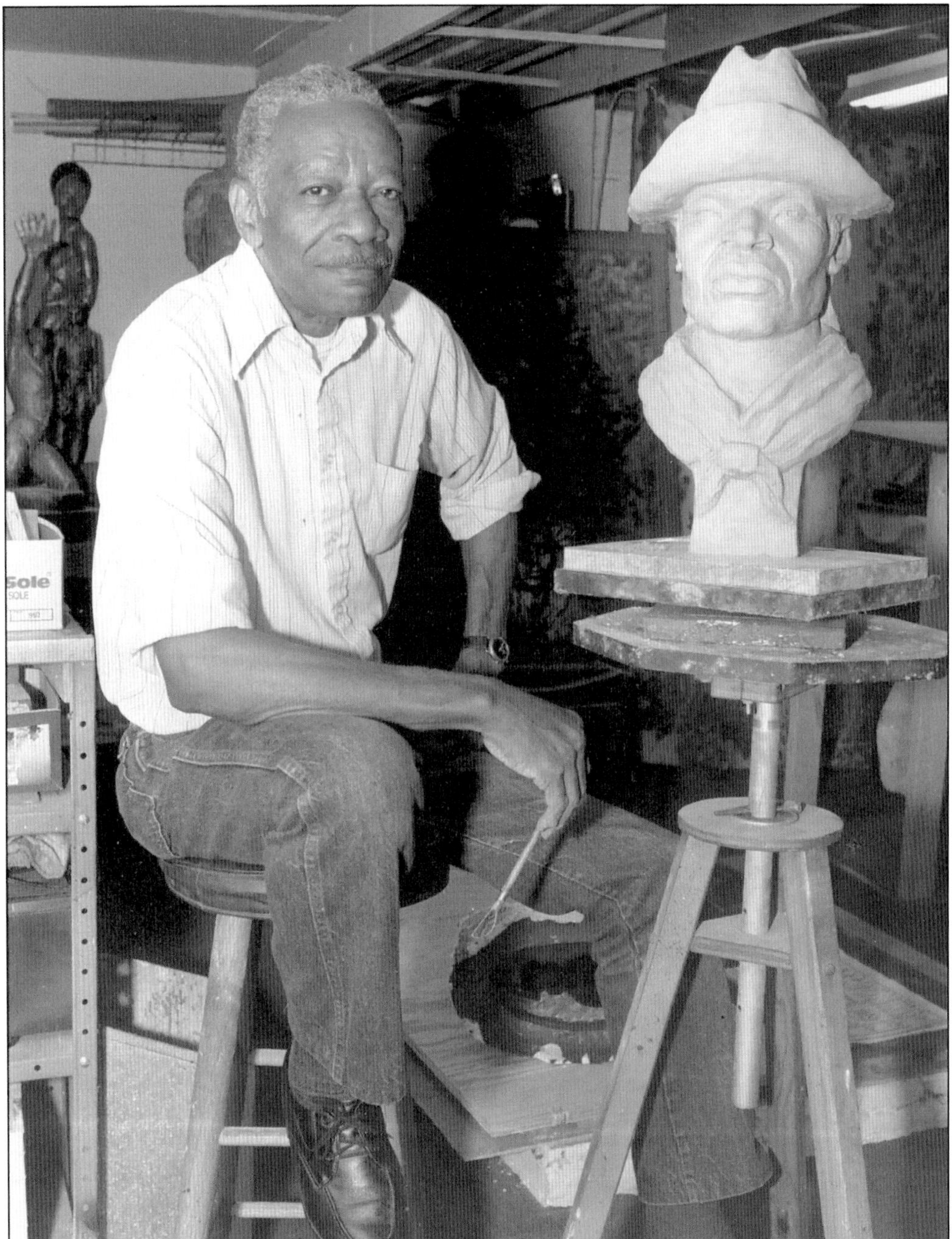

James Counts is one of the foremost African American sculptors on Long Island. His works of art date back to the 1950s. Among them are busts of current Hempstead Mayor James A. Garner and of Dr. Martin Luther King Jr. (Courtesy of Gary Cooley.)

Rev. A.L. Mackey Sr. served as pastor of Mount Sinai Cathedral. A community leader, he participated in major projects that affected the area. (Courtesy of Joe Turner and Pastor Mackey Jr.)

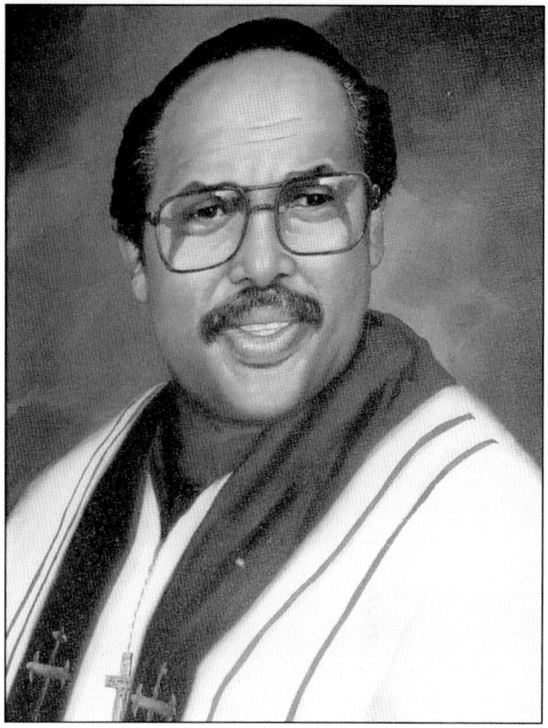

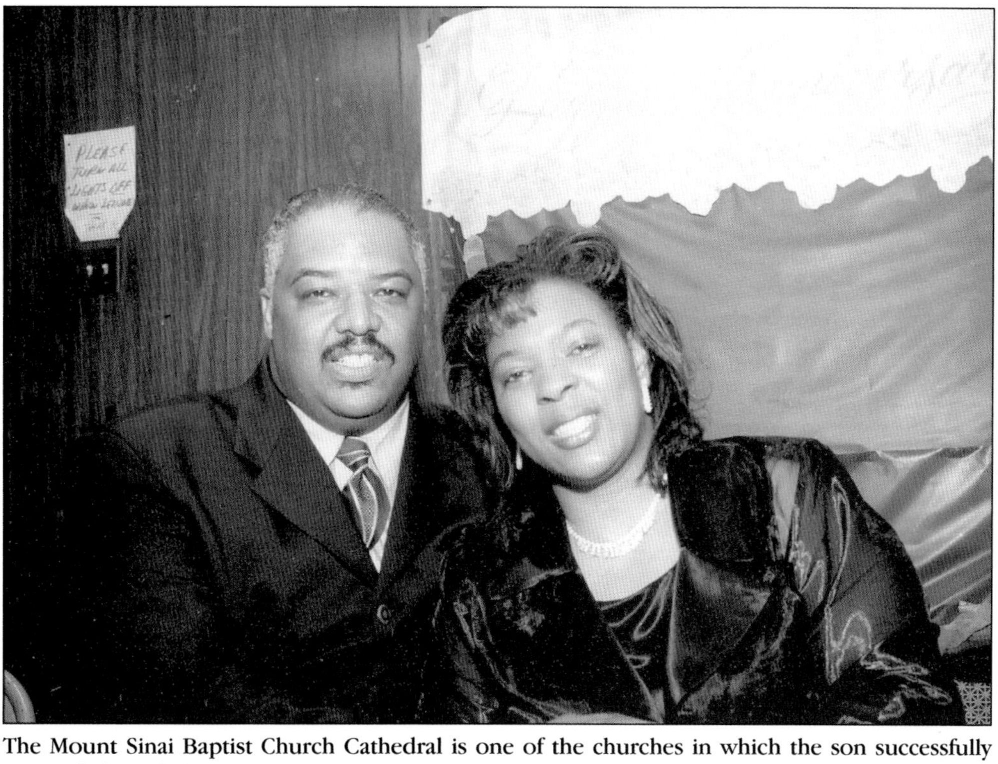

The Mount Sinai Baptist Church Cathedral is one of the churches in which the son successfully succeeded the father as pastor. Rev. Arthur L. Mackey Jr. and wife, Brenda Mackey, took over the church after the pastorate of Rev. A.L. Mackey Sr. (Courtesy of Joe Turner and Pastor Mackey Jr.)

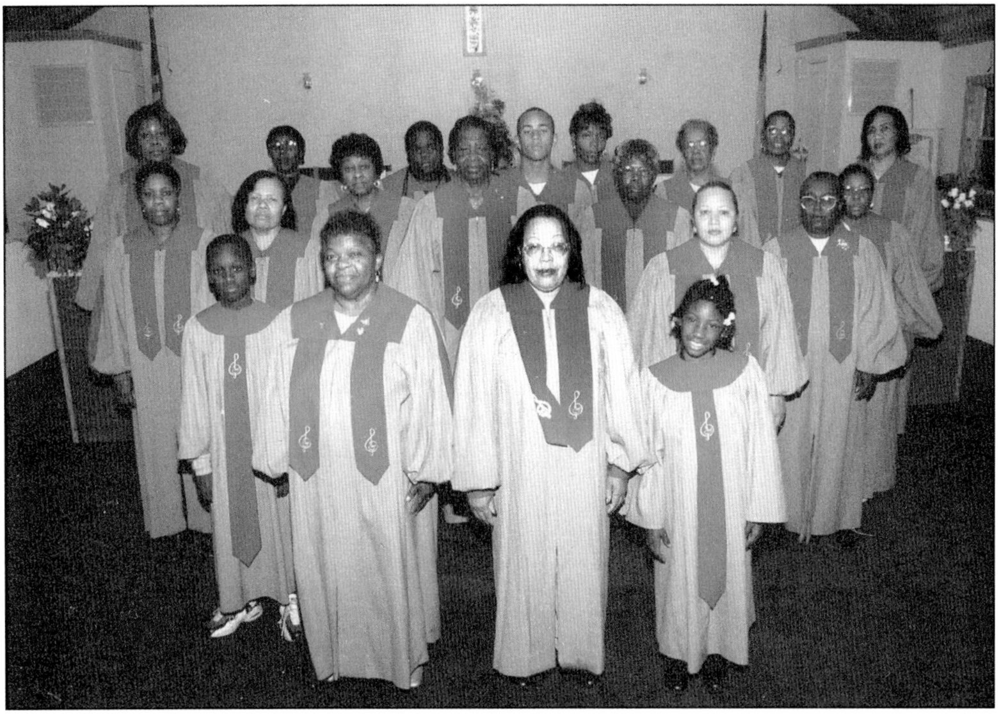

The Mount Sinai Cathedral Choir in Roosevelt has long been admired for its excellent music. Directed by Alice Hill, the group sings with rhythm and motion. (Courtesy of Joe Turner and Pastor Mackey Jr.)

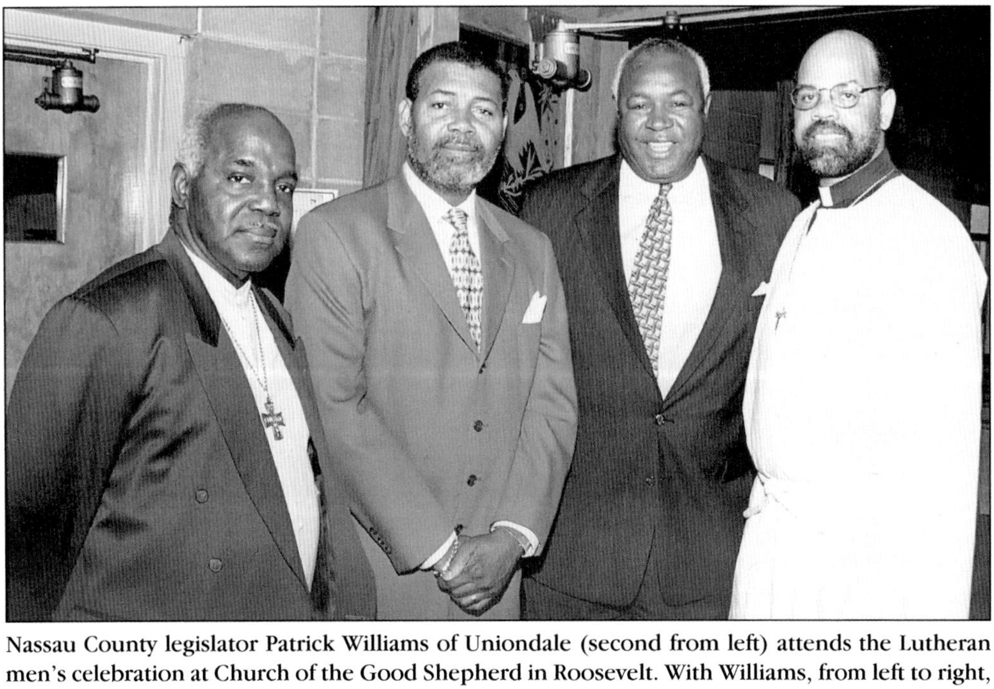

Nassau County legislator Patrick Williams of Uniondale (second from left) attends the Lutheran men's celebration at Church of the Good Shepherd in Roosevelt. With Williams, from left to right, are Archdeacon Donell Becoate, Hempstead Mayor James A. Garner, and Pastor Jerome Taylor. (Courtesy of Gary Coley.)

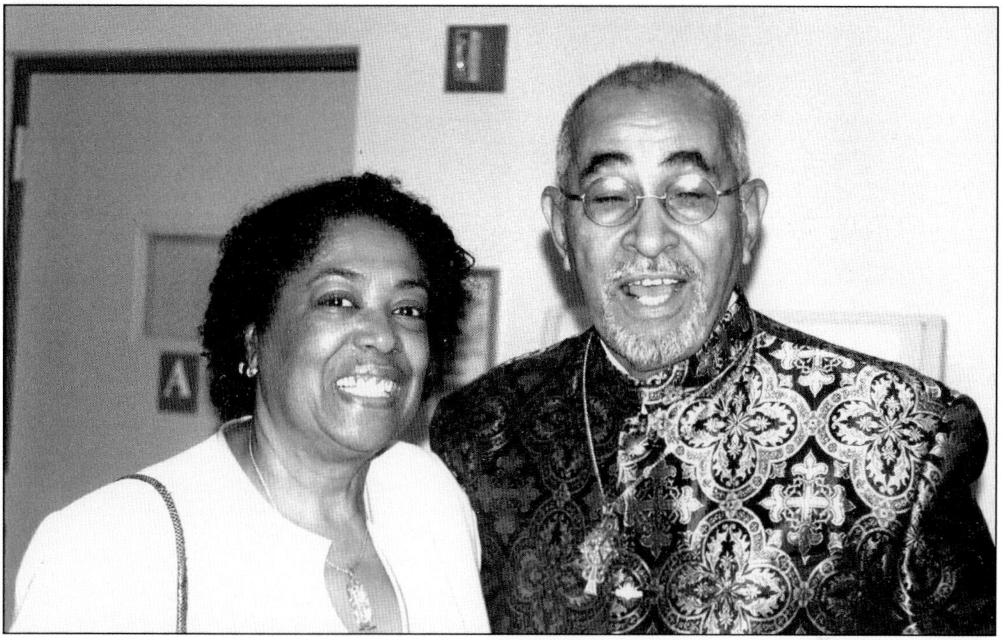

Lillian Loggins Watson, Roosevelt school principal, shares a laugh with the popular Rev. Wyatt T. Walker. One of the leaders of the civil rights movement, Walker is a New York City pastor and frequent Long Island visitor. (Courtesy of Emily Moore.)

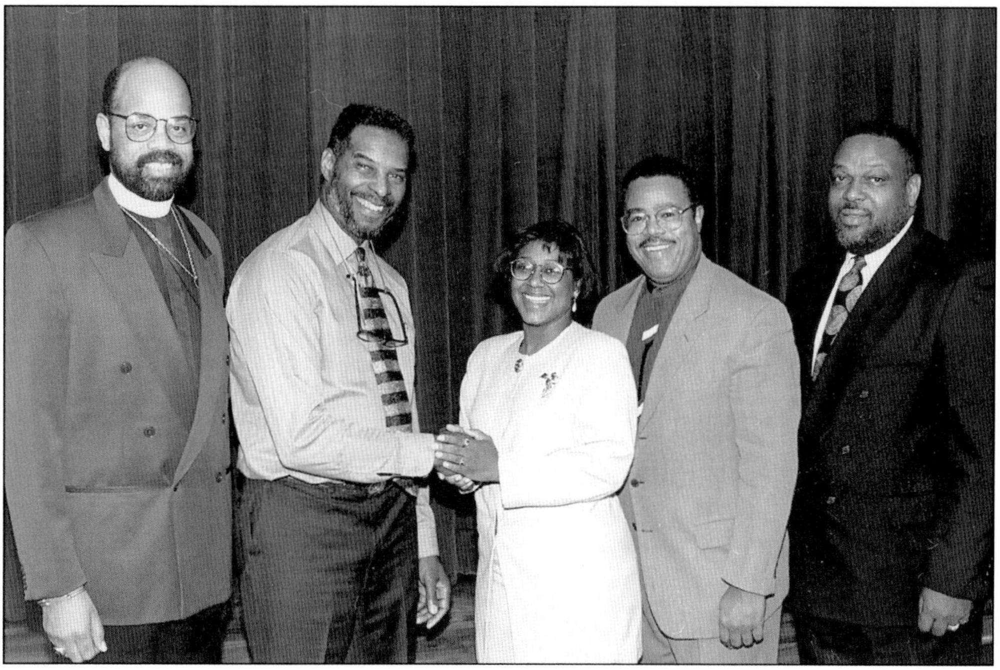

Nassau County legislator Darlene Harris (center) is pictured with some of her constituents, who include former Pastor Tuggle (second from right). (Courtesy of Gary Coley.)

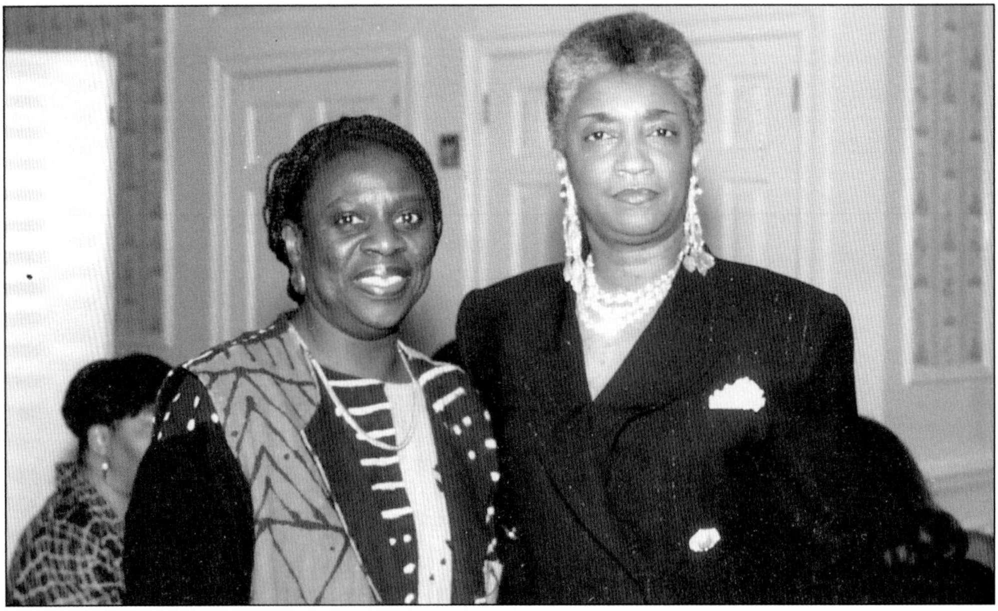

Dolores Small (left) is a counselor at Nassau Community College, where she has served for over two decades. With her is Patricia Catherine, one of the few African American school principals in the area. The principal of Harry Daniels Elementary School, she helped organize the Max program, which traces the history of African American soldiers. (Courtesy of Gary Coley.)

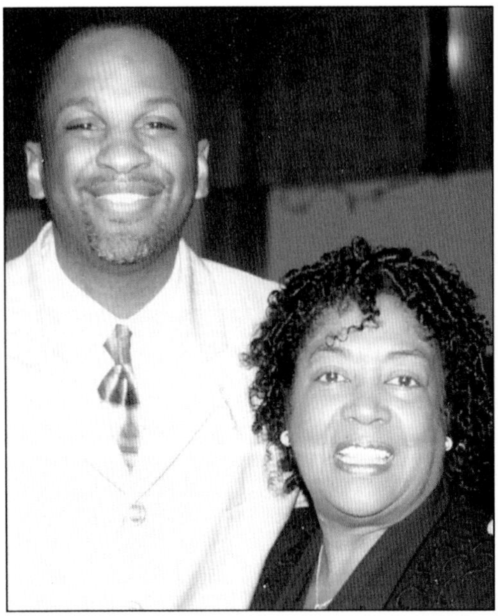

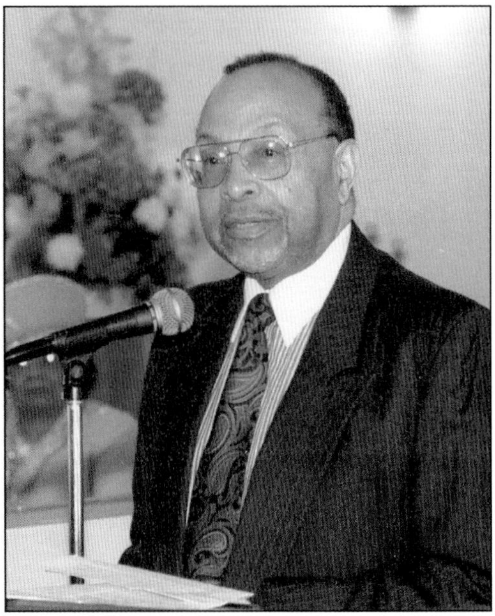

Lillian Coddines-Watson of Roosevelt is the principal of Ulysses Byas Elementary School. On New York State tests, the students of her school score extremely well, a tribute to her educational policies, which include taking young people on special trips. With her is Donnie McClurkin (left), well-known Long Island pastor and gospel singer. M. Watkins (right) was one of the first African American principals of Roosevelt High School. A leading educator since the 1970s, he currently serves as a consultant and adviser on issues related to the education of African American youth. (Left, courtesy of Emily Moore; right, courtesy of Joe Turner and M. Watkins.)

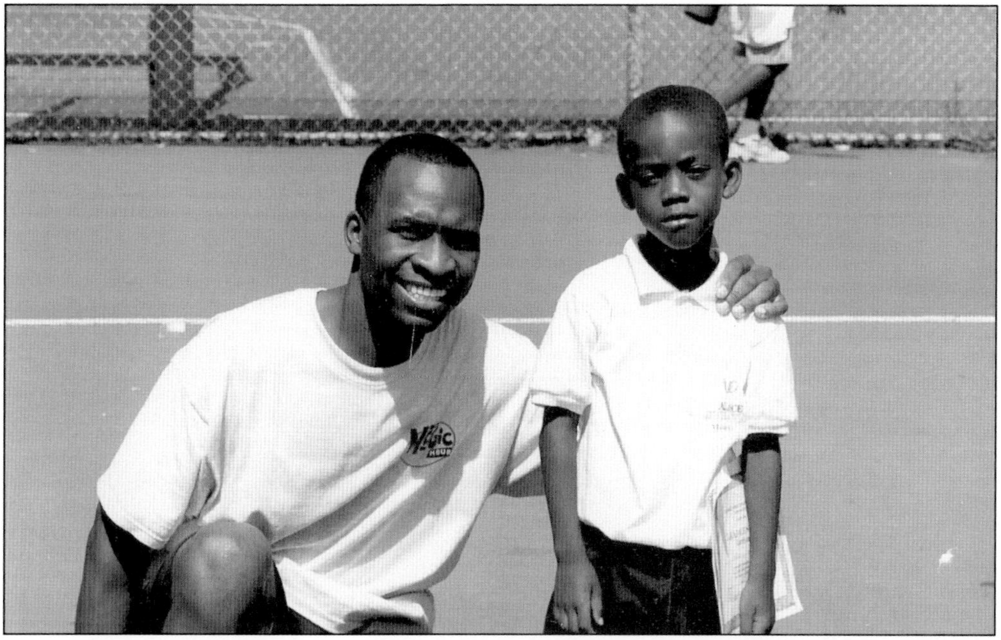

Comedian and actor Steve White (left) takes time to motivate young people in the Roosevelt area. A graduate of the Roosevelt school system, he is pictured with Omotayo Adedeji. (Courtesy of Emily Moore.)

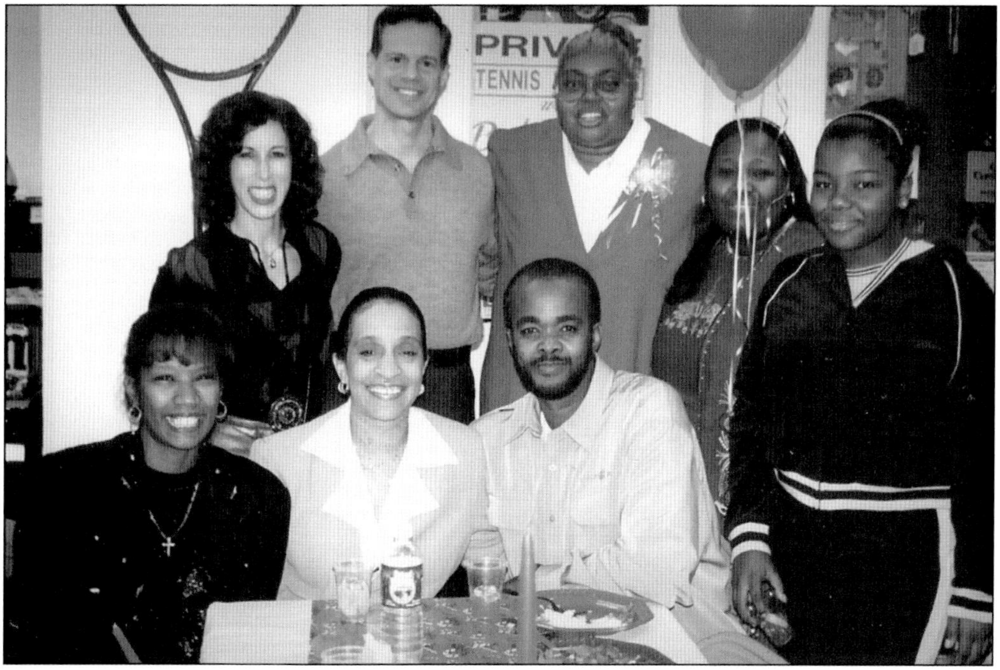

For more than three decades, the Alliance Junior Tennis Training and Development Camp in Roosevelt Park has trained and motivated Long Island youth. The camp was founded and directed by Emily Moore (back center). Shown with her, from left to right, are the following: (front row) unidentified, and Mr. and Mrs. St. Claire; (back row) Mr. & Mrs. Saltzman and J. Evans and her daughter B. Evans. (Courtesy of Emily Moore.)

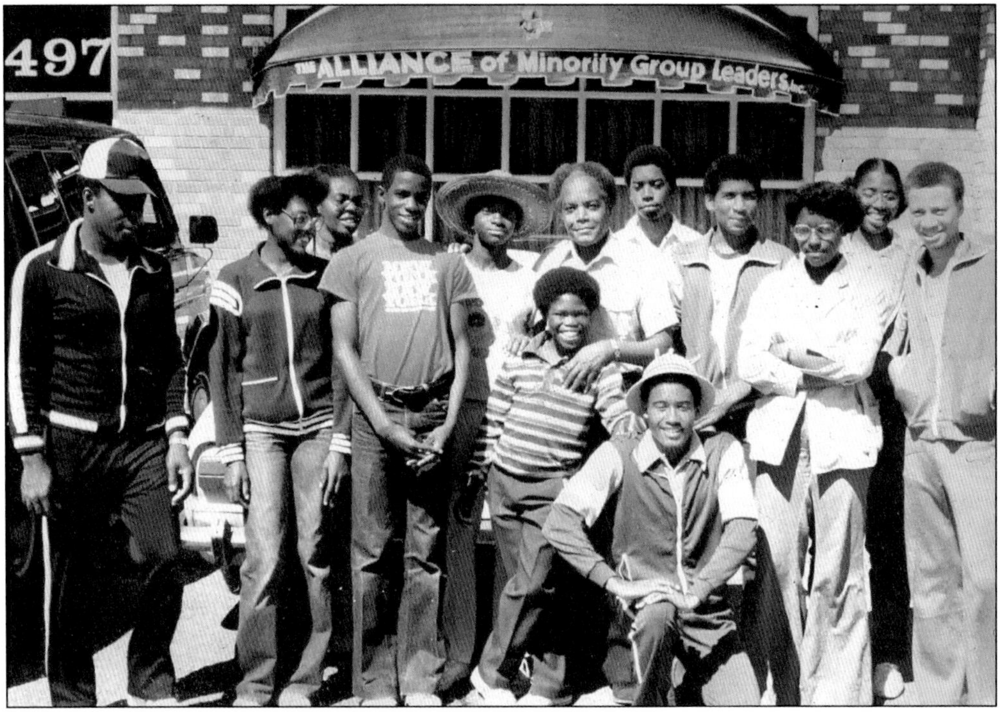

Former CORE director Lincoln Lynch (with his hands on the boy's shoulders) came to the Alliance Junior Tennis Training and Development Camp in Roosevelt Park to support the young tennis players who were on a trip to Long Island in the 1970s. Among these tennis players are many who went on to earn college degrees, including two physicians and two lawyers. (Courtesy of Emily Moore.)

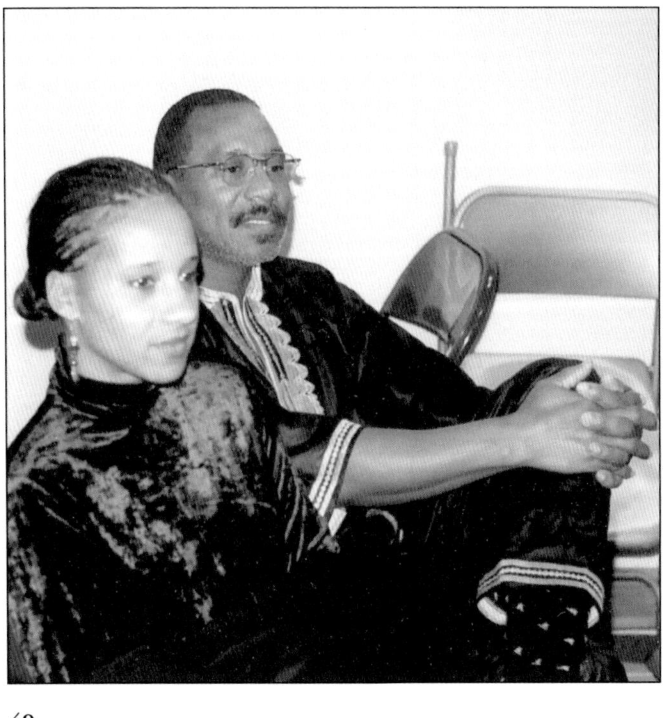

Dr. John Mitchner (right) has a medical practice in Roosevelt. A Vietnam veteran, he earned his medical degree from the State University of New York at Stony Brook. His daughter Lolita Mitchner (left) has a degree in psychology. (Author's collection.)

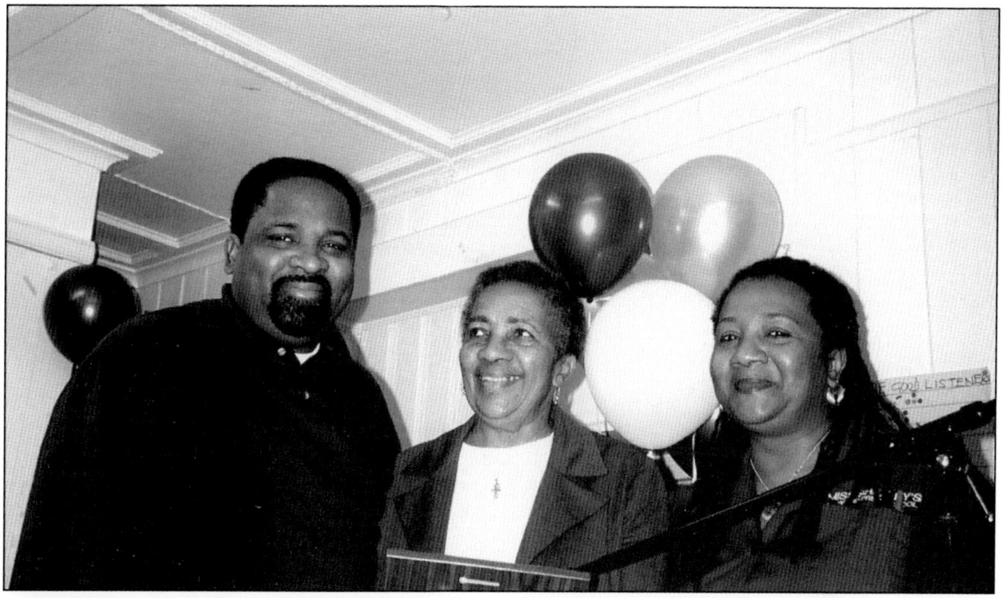

Three Roosevelt residents pause to reflect on life. From left to right are John Moore of the Moore Funeral Home, Bernice Moore, and Mrs. Shelley. They have been active in community affairs for the past three decades. (Courtesy of Gary Coley.)

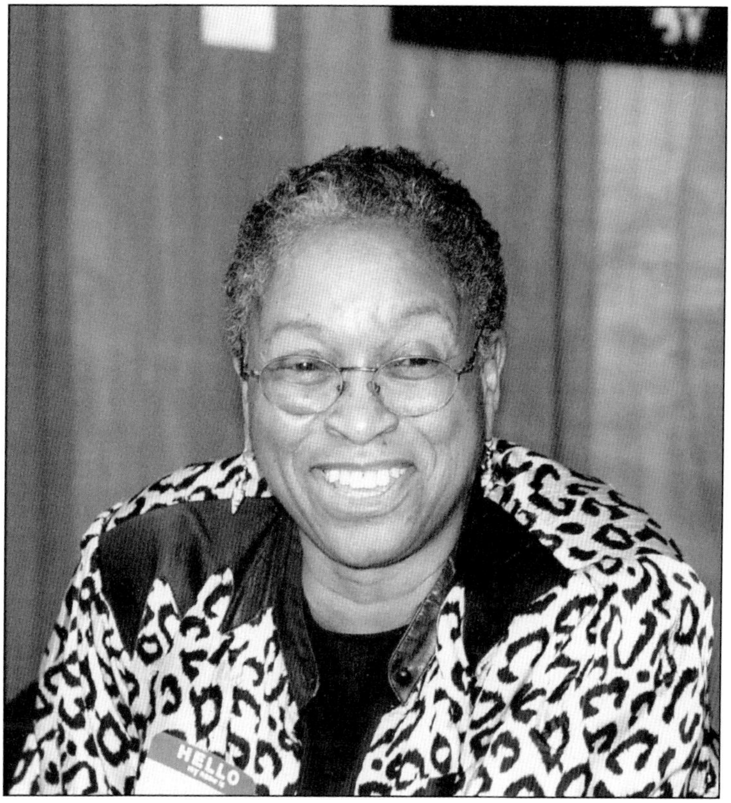

Dr. Carlether Burwell has served as president of Long Island's Business and Professional Women, Nassau Central Club. This organization is an affiliate of the National Association of Negro Business and Professional Women's Club. (Courtesy of Emily Moore.)

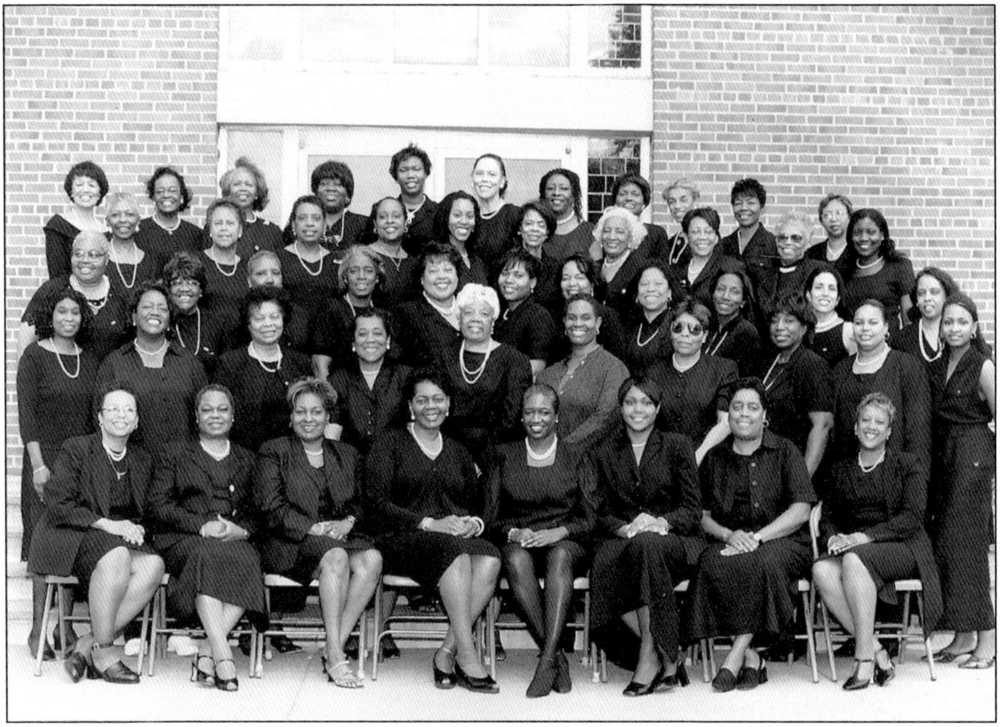

The Delta Sorority is a group of professional women who excel in various careers and pursuits. Shown are some of the leading Long Island members. (Courtesy of Emily Moore.)

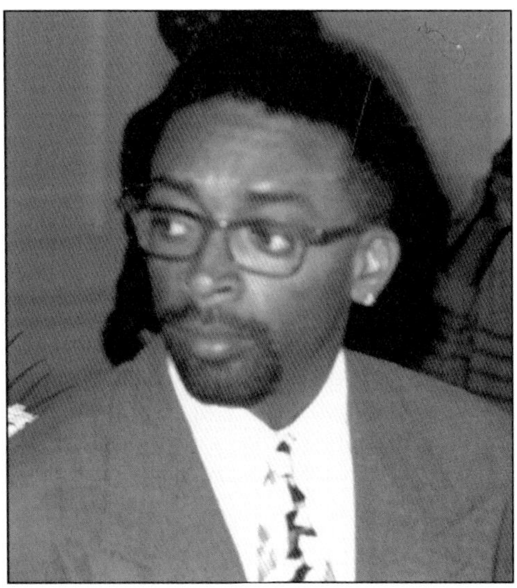

Actor Spike Lee has roots in Roosevelt and frequently visits the area for community and social events. (Courtesy of Emily Moore.)

Three

FREEPORT
PRESENCE AND PRIDE

African Americans have long had a presence in Freeport. Precisely when the first African Americans arrived in the area is a still matter of discussion. Some historians and researchers believe that there may have been African Americans living in the early settlements during the age of exploration. Some lived here in the 1800s as slaves. After the Civil War, many moved up from the South in quest of a better life.

The Jackson and Jarvis families were among the early settlers in Freeport. They were reportedly farmers and entrepreneurs. The Jarvis family managed a scavenger business until the 1930s. These pioneers helped found the Bethel African Methodist Episcopal Church, the first such church in the area, in 1902. Currently under the pastorship of Dr. Harry White II, the church is located at 420 North Main Street. Among the early members of the church were the Toomer, Baker, Wilkerson, Daly, Tate, and Singleton families.

As more people came from North Carolina, South Carolina, and Virginia—initially as seasonal workers and later as residents—new churches were founded: Freeport Church of God in Christ in 1918, Little Zion in 1941, and the Greater Baptist Church.

Freeport became the home of some noted African American families. The Alers, Monroes, Whites, Hales, and Pearses lived in Freeport. Additionally, writers, musicians, and athletes made Freeport their home. The first African American judge, Moxly Rigby, was raised here. Dr. Curtis T. Skeete served as the first African American medical doctor in 1927. The jazz artist Hale Smith and novelist Alers resided here, as did Barbara Patton, the first African American commissioner for elections.

Today, Freeport is home to landscapers and laborers, civil servants and educators, medical workers and small businesspeople. Owing to its proximity to New York City, Freeport is also home to many who commute there to work.

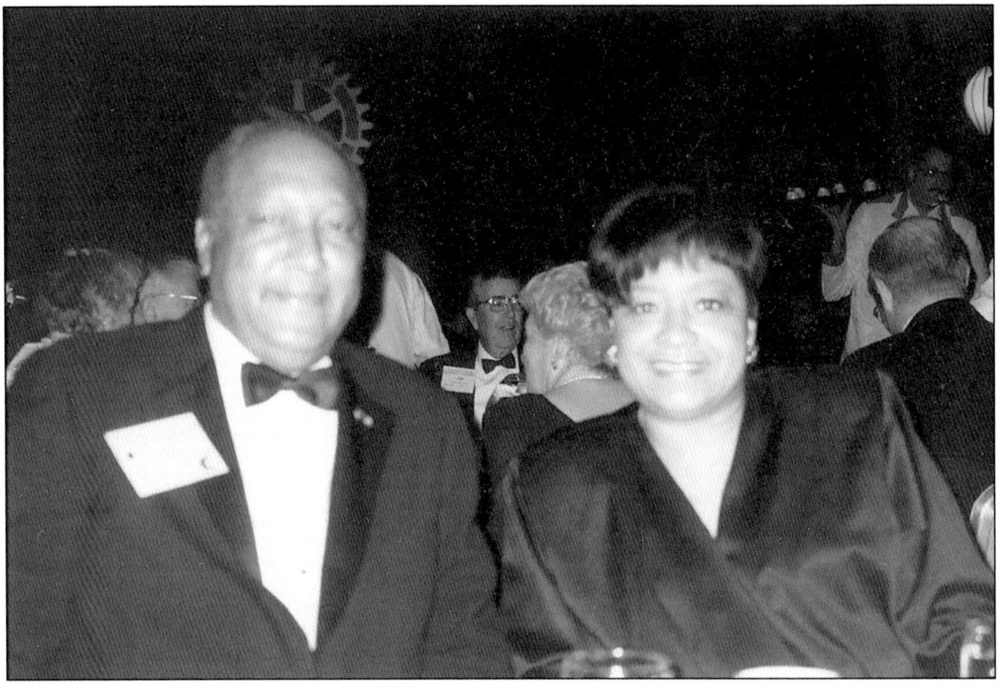

Both Edward D. Monroe and his wife, Betty Monroe, served on the Freeport Board of Education. Edward Monroe was also the first African American to run for mayor in Freeport. During his career, he was assistant vice president and adjunct faculty adviser at Nassau Community College in Garden City and vice president and director of College Facilities at Teacher's College, Columbia University. After retiring from the educational field in 1990, he founded Plumbing Service and Environmental Engineering Management Associates. (Courtesy of Ed and Betty Monroe.)

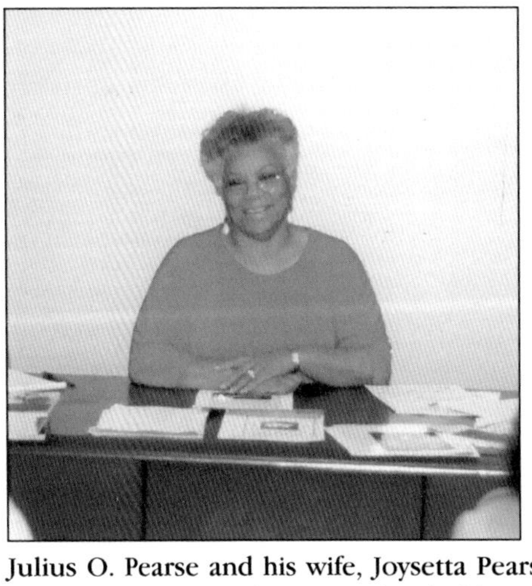

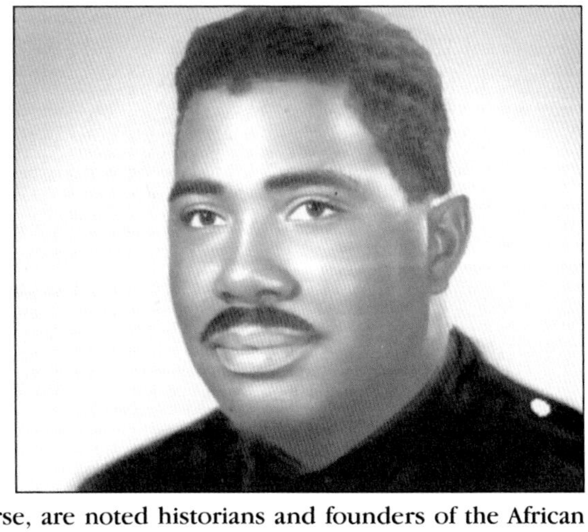

Julius O. Pearse and his wife, Joysetta Pearse, are noted historians and founders of the African Atlantic Genealogical Society. They hold monthly meetings for the discussion of African American history and genealogical techniques, and they have a radio talk show. In addition, they organize workshops, seminars, and excursions to noted historical sites and locations throughout the country. A retired detective, Julius Pearse was the first African American police officer in Freeport. (Courtesy of Julius and Joysetta Pearse.)

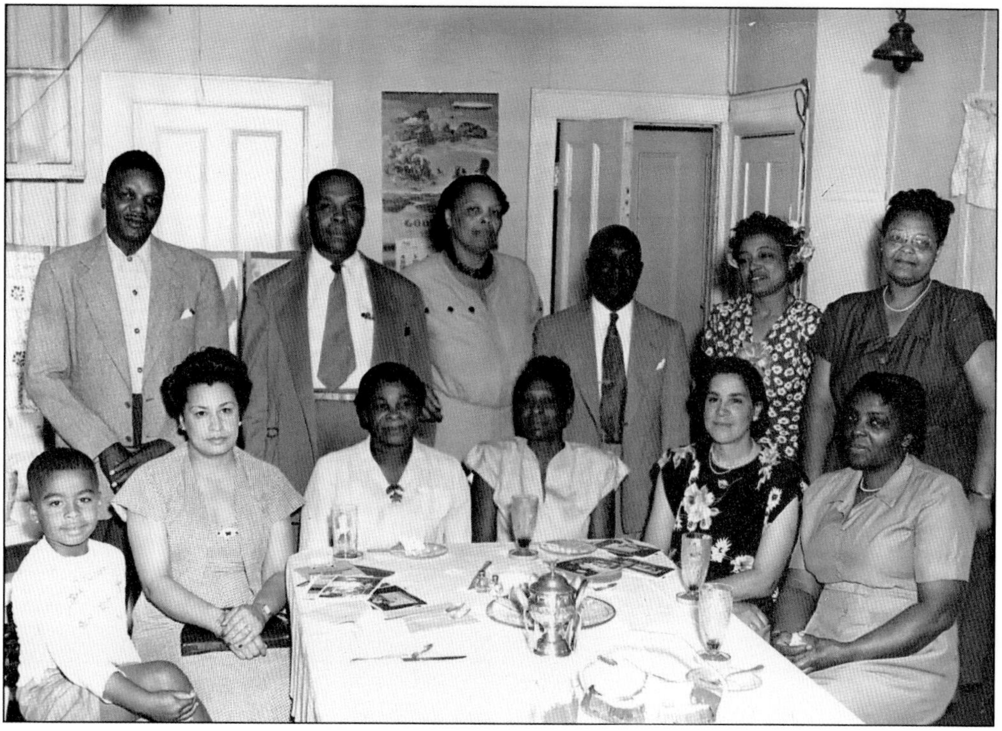

Dr. Curtis T. Skeete (standing, second from left) was one of the first African Americans to practice medicine on Long Island. Born in Barbados, British West Indies, he attended Kings University in Kingston, Ontario, from 1916 to 1918 and graduated from Tufts University Medical School in 1925. Three years later, he opened an office in Freeport and became the first African American to practice medicine in Nassau County. The husband of Myrtle Skeete (sitting, second from left), he was also a civil rights leader. (Courtesy of the Skeetes.)

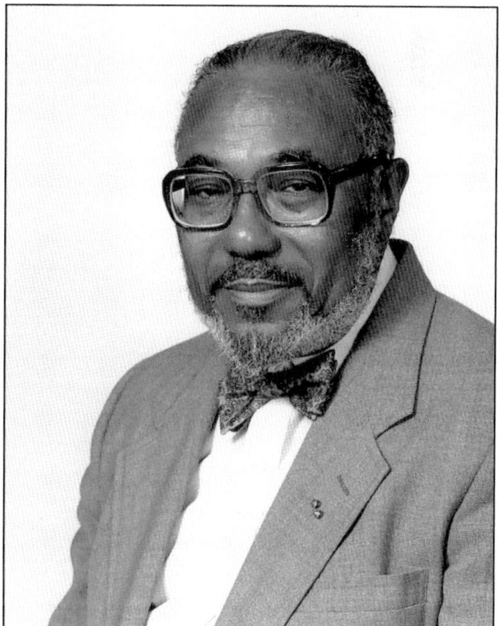

Hale Smith of Freeport, a distinguished musician and composer, has received several awards, including two from the American Academy of Arts and Letters and the National Black Music Caucus. He holds bachelor's and master's degrees in composition and has taught at C.W. Post Long Island University and the University of Connecticut. An arranger and director, he has also contributed to music publications as a critic and editor. (Courtesy of the Hale Smith family.)

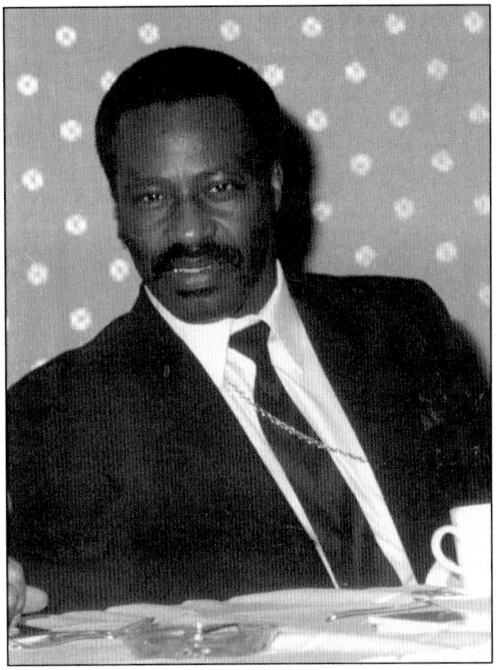

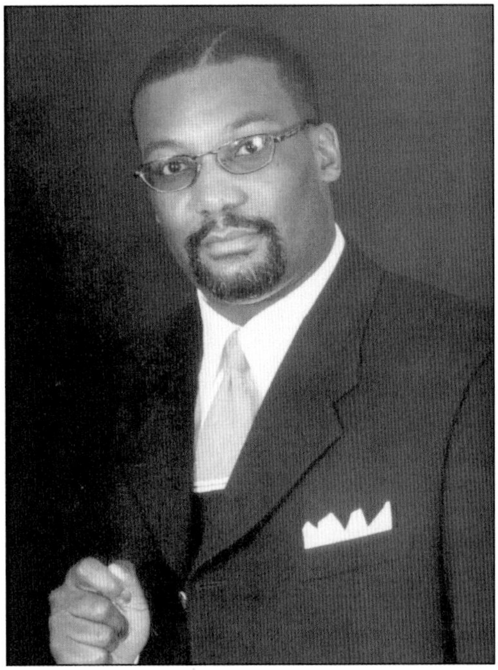

Bishop Frank O. White (left) has led the Little Zion Church of God in Christ in Freeport since 1972. As bishop of the Third Ecclesiastical Jurisdiction of Eastern New York, he guides churches in that area. He was born in South Carolina and raised in Freeport. His son Rev. Dr. Frank Anthone White (right) is currently associate pastor of Little Zion Church and pastor of King's Chapel in Southampton. In addition to being an articulate preacher and an amiable pastor, he is an accomplished pianist, choir leader, and organizer. (Courtesy of Bishop Frank O. White.)

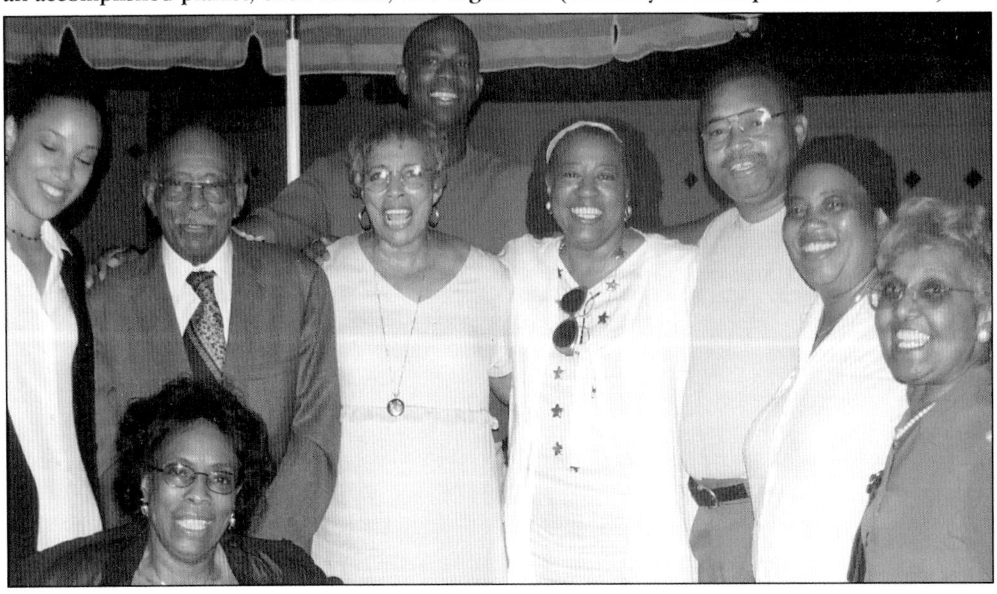

The Gillespie family was one of the first African American families to move to Freeport. From left to right are Serious Gillespie, who worked for Republic Airlines; his wife, Marie Gillespie; his niece Marcia Gillespie, the first African American editor of *Essence* magazine and currently the editor of *Miss Magazine;* and other members of the family. (Courtesy of Emily Moore.)

Dr. Constance R. Clark is one of the first female African American school superintendents of the Westbury School District and one of just two African American women serving in that position in Nassau County. She has forged alliances with the community and major universities and has earned the award of Educator of the Year from Hofstra University. Formerly deputy school superintendent in Washington, D.C., she is a member of the Long Island Links group. (Courtesy of Dr. Constance Clark.)

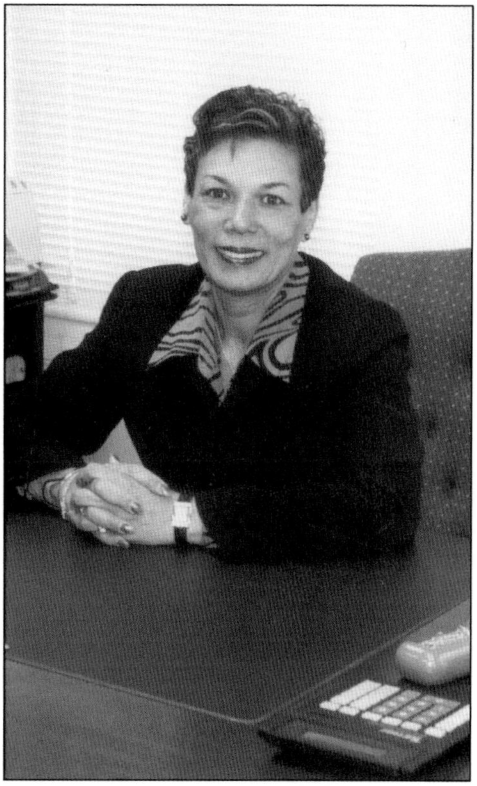

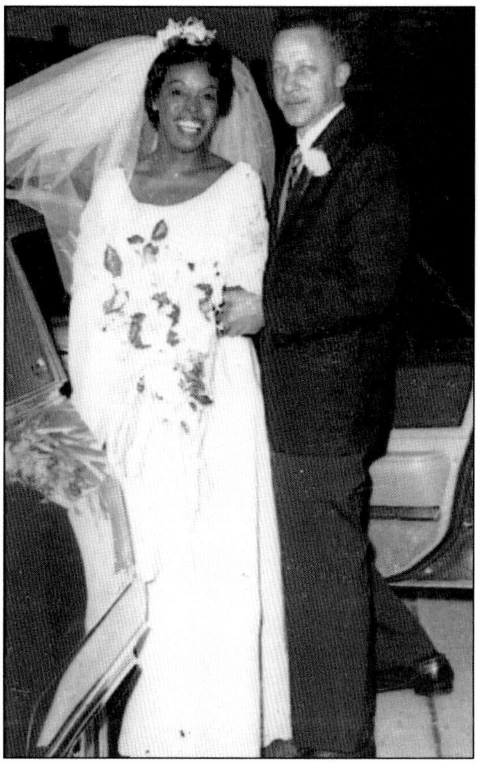

Shown are Louis and Jeanette Meggett on their wedding day. Jeanette Meggett is an active member of the African Atlantic Genealogical Society in Freeport. She earned a master's degree in guidance and counseling from Hunter College and served at Queens College for nearly four decades. Louis Meggett graduated from South Carolina State University and was a postal supervisor. (Courtesy of Louis and Jeanette Meggett.)

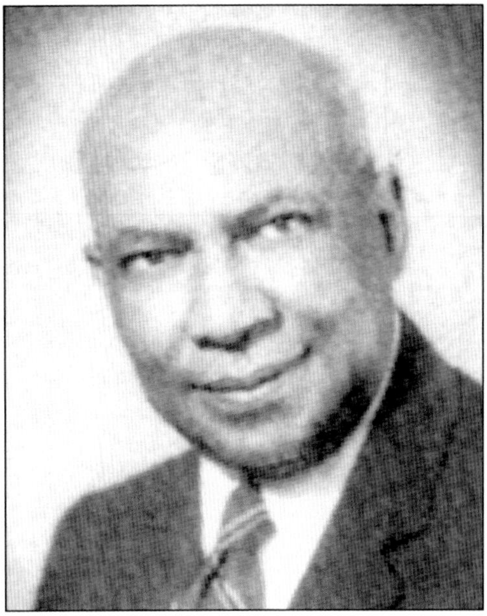

Judge Moxly Rigby (1892–1962) was the first African American appointed to the Nassau County bench. He served as assistant district attorney of Nassau County. Later, he was appointed to the local housing authority and, in 1951, to administer neighborhood rehabilitation and low-cost housing. (Courtesy of J. Stewart Moore, Amistad Black Bar Association.)

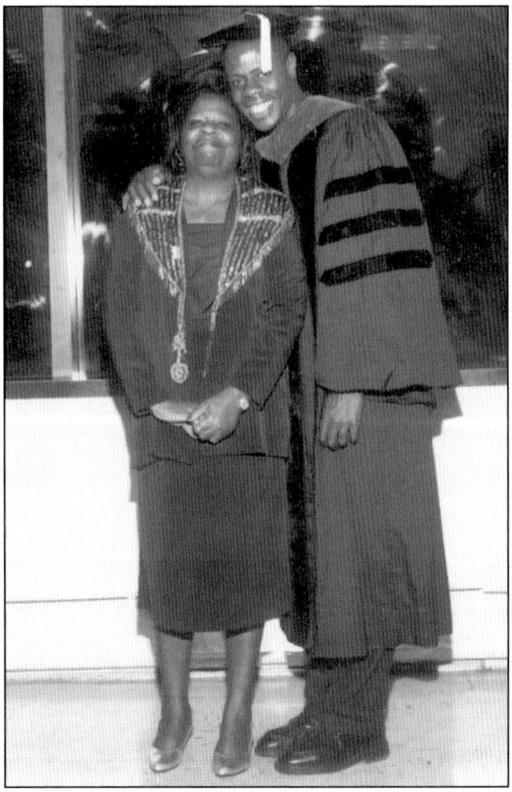

Mildred Clayton, a historian, researcher, and minister, came to New York in 1960. An African American Museum founding member, she teaches and lectures on African American history. Her son Larinzo Clayton was born and raised on Long Island and graduated from Hofstra University Law School in 1995. (Courtesy of Mildred Clayton.)

The Honorable Renaire Frierson was the first African American female ever elected in the village of Freeport's 105-year history. She was also the first appointed to serve as deputy mayor in 1997, and the first to serve as full-time deputy village attorney. Born in 1960, she and her family moved to Freeport when she was two. She graduated from Freeport High School in 1978, earned a degree from Hofstra University Business School, and graduated from Boston School of Law in 1985. She is a member of the Greater Second Baptist Church in Freeport. (Courtesy of Nassau County Press Office.)

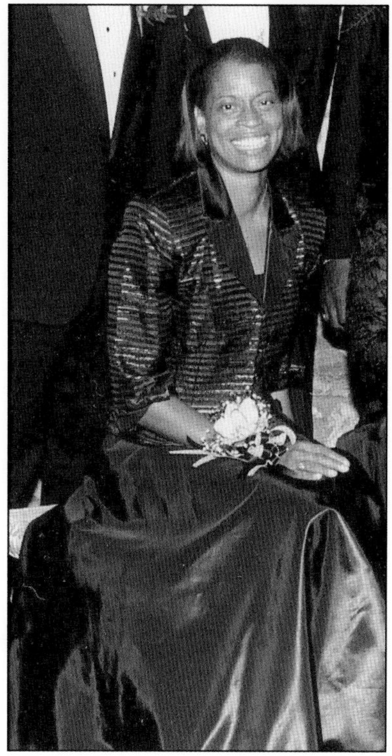

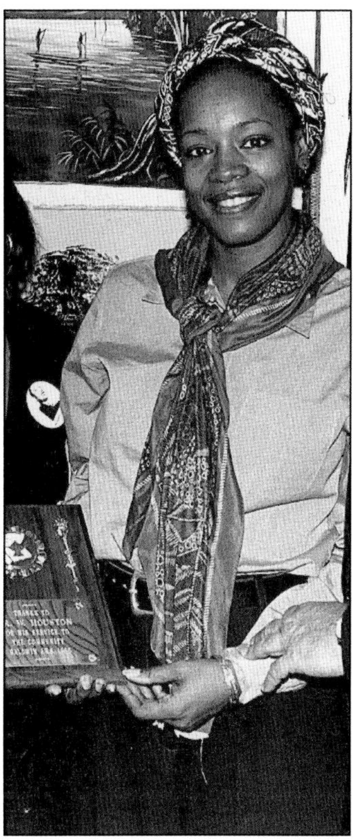

Emerencia Funderburke of Freeport is the director of the African American Dance troupe Imani. (Courtesy of Willie Houston the African American Museum.)

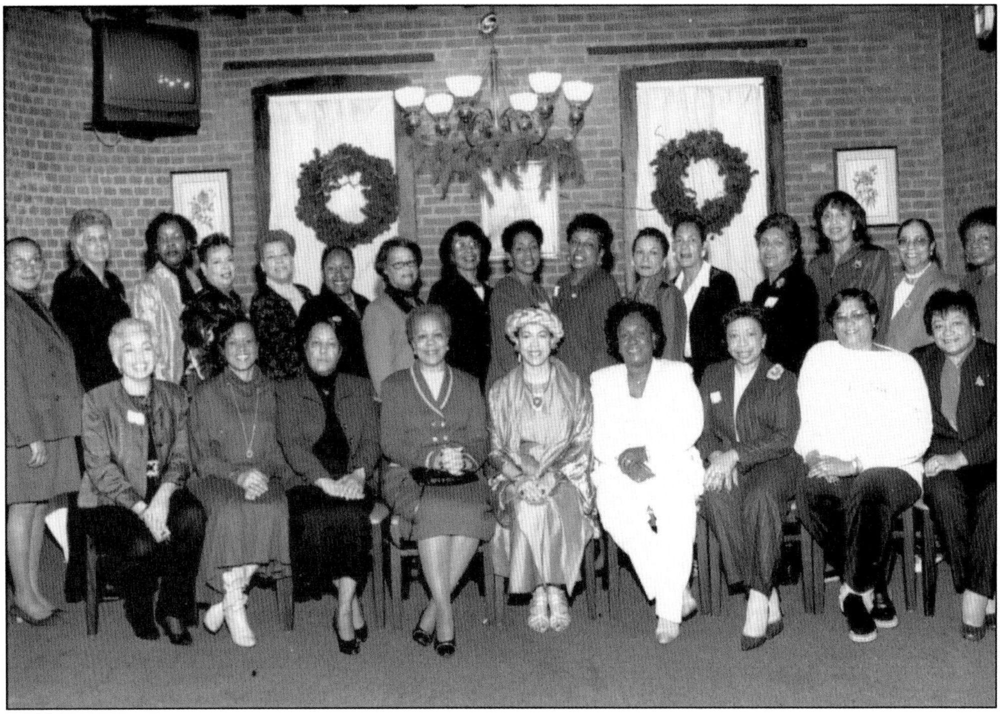

The Long Island chapter of the Links Inc. was chartered on October 27, 1962. It is one of 274 chapters with more than 11,000 chapters in the United States and the world. Chapters focus on the arts, trends, services, and youth affairs. The Long Island Links chapter celebrates its 40th anniversary in 2002. It currently has 33 members, with Marcia White as president. Members organize events, mentor youth, and sponsor international humanitarian programs. As one of the leading women's clubs on Long Island, it attracts a wide range of professional women. (Courtesy of Marcia White and Long Island Links Inc.)

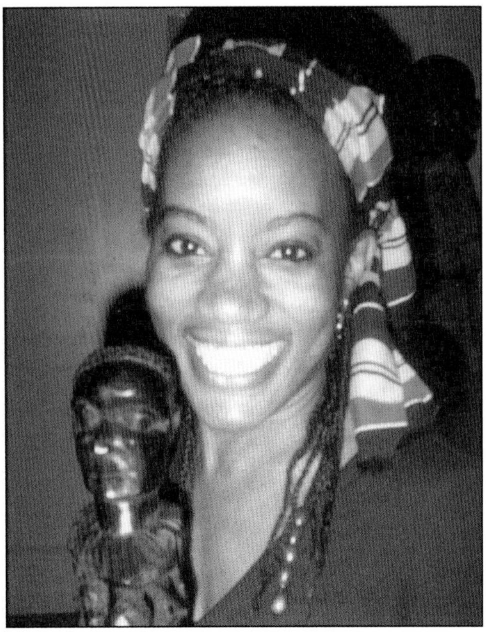

LaVada Felder is a business entrepreneur who works with children. Born and raised in Freeport, she graduated from Hofstra University and started her business project at age 24. She is the founder and chief executive of the ETS Youth Division. With a staff of 25, ETS operates a summer computer camp and a childcare program in three locations. It offers before-school and after-school care, a cultural arts program, Kid's Café, and Youth-in-Training, a talent search recruitment. (Courtesy of LaVada Felder.)

Four

Huntington
Struggle and Success

A strategic and confluence town, Huntington attracted slave owners who brought a number of slaves to the area. A majority of the African Americans served as domestic servants, laborers, farm hands, factory workers, and landscapers. Huntington may well have been a transition point for the Underground Railroad, the informal network that abolitionists used to help slaves reach freedom. After the Emancipation Proclamation in 1864, African Americans moved north, settled in Huntington, and ultimately made it their home. Upon arrival, they met Indians, slaves, and freed slaves who lived in established communities.

The birth and development of churches signifies evolutionary patterns in African American societies. In 1910, as the northward migration continued, the need for churches arose. Families got together and formed Evergreen Baptist Church. The Bethel African Methodist Episcopal Church, which had emerged in 1843, included families such as the Crippens, Plummers, Allens, Powells, Trabues, Smiths, Edwards, Seamans, Balltons, and Points. The church, then as now, was their center for not only praise and worship but also social, political, economic, and cultural exchange. Currently under the leadership of Pastor Clarence John, the church has survived for over 150 years. Indeed, one of Huntington's illustrious sons is Bishop Decatur Ward, whose children and grandchildren contributed to Huntington's development.

Huntington drew other prominent African Americans—reformers such as pastor and orator Henry Garnet, musician Louis Armstrong, and prayer warrior Sojourner Truth—who stopped by the city during their campaigns.

Today, beneath Huntington's serenity, charm, and architectural splendor, lies African American struggle and modest success. Driving through this beautiful community of undulating hills and lovely and lavish beaches, visitors stumble on African Americans. As the home of Touro Law School and a fanciful mall, it attracts people from all parts of the world. Both indigenous and migrant African Americans from other areas of the country now serve the city as pastors, teachers, nurses, lawyers, and doctors. Many who obtain their education in the city relocate to pursue their careers elsewhere. Success stories arise, but there is still much room for development and expansion.

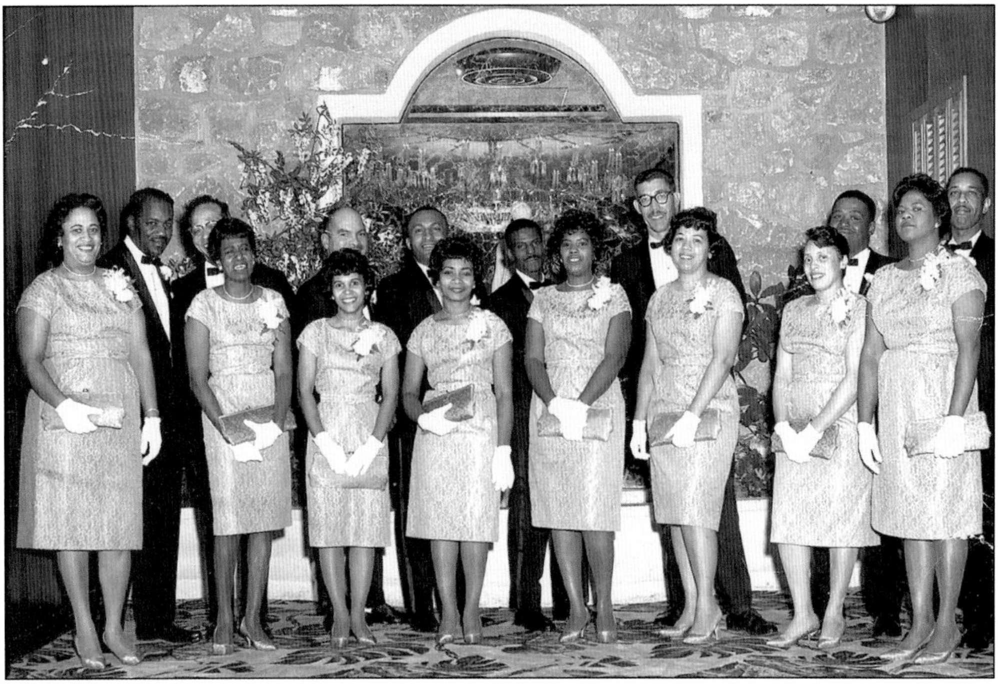

Founded in 1959, the Silhouettes of Huntington organized cultural, recreational, and educational programs for young people. Women of the group are pictured celebrating with their husbands. From left to right are Mary and Alvin Edwards, Ida and Peyton Bowler, Sadie and Arthur Allen, Dolores and Royal Thompson Jr., Arlene and Leo Roulhac, Emily and Warren Bunn, Norma and Raymond Thompson, and Jennie and Joseph Starkes. (Courtesy of Dr. Rev. William Robert Spencer.)

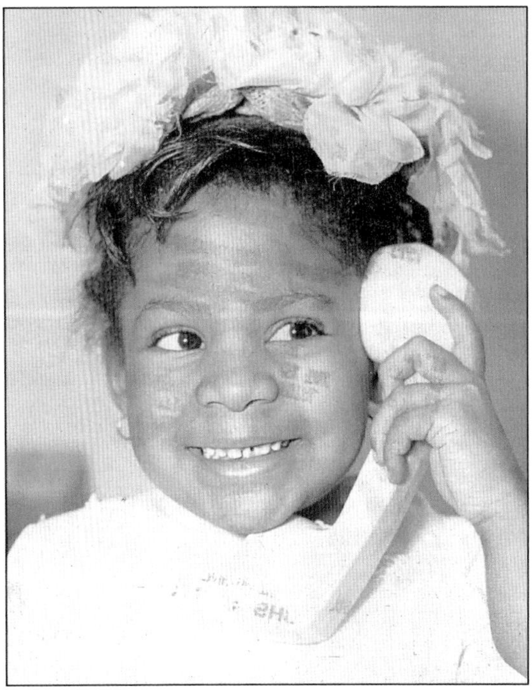

Tracey Edwards chats on the telephone in Shepherd Day Nursery School in 1965. A 1978 graduate of John Glenn High School in Northport, she currently chairs the Huntington Planning Board and is the executive director of diversity at Verizon. She and her husband, Walter Edwards, have three children. (Courtesy of Dolores Thompson.)

Ordained as a minister in 1993, Dr. William Robert Spencer Jr. is both a doctor and a pastor. He earned a B.A. in chemistry from Wesleyan University and served his internship and residency in surgery at St. Vincent's Hospital and Medical Center in New York City. He is licensed in medicine and surgery in New York and Florida. (Courtesy of Dr. Rev. William Robert Spencer.)

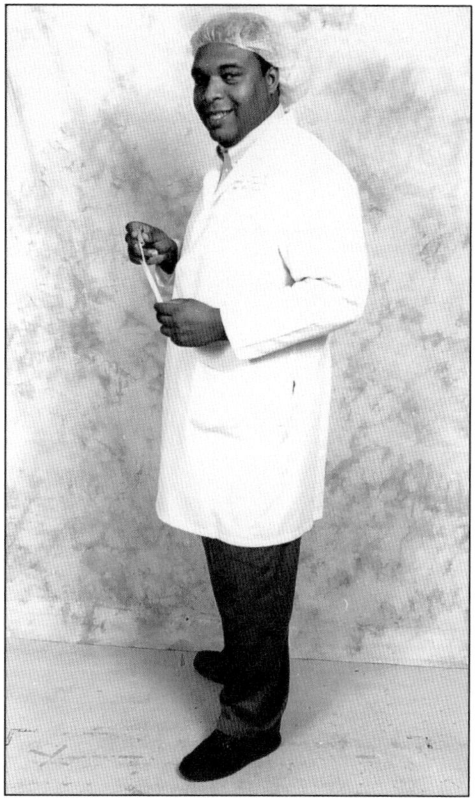

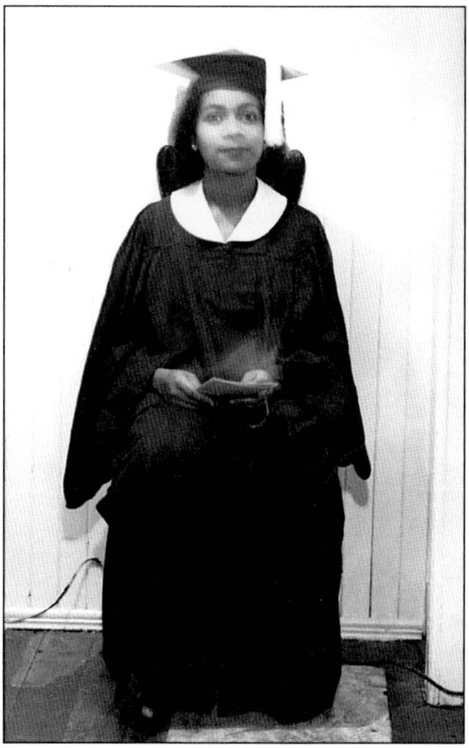

Dolores Thompson is currently the president of the Huntington branch of the National Association for the Advancement of Colored People (NAACP). She served as manager of operational services for 30 years, retiring in 1984. She then founded the Huntington Station Enrichment Center and became a trustee of the Huntington Hospital. She graduated from Huntington High School in 1948. Her father, Aaron Jarvis, worked for Kodak and her mother, Ruth Jarvis, was a homemaker and organist for Bethel African Methodist Episcopal Church from 1940 to 1965. (Courtesy of Dolores Thompson.)

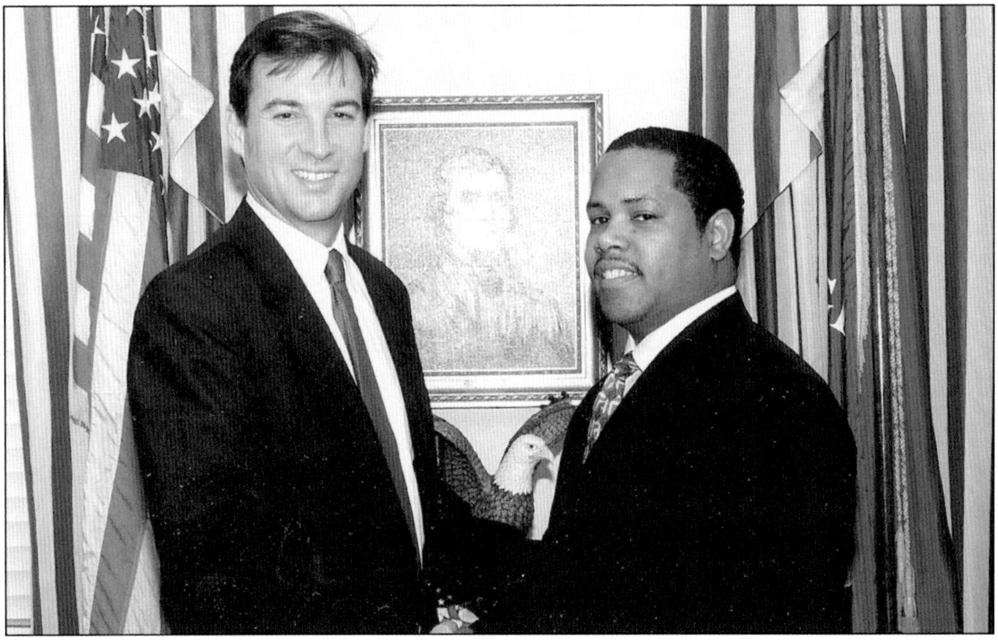

Rev. Jerry L. Turner Sr. (right) is pastor of Salem Baptist Church, which in a short time has grown from 35 to more than 250 parishioners. He meets with Thomas R. Suozzi, Nassau County chief executive and former Glen Cove mayor, to discuss the challenges facing the people in his community. (Courtesy of Joe Turner.)

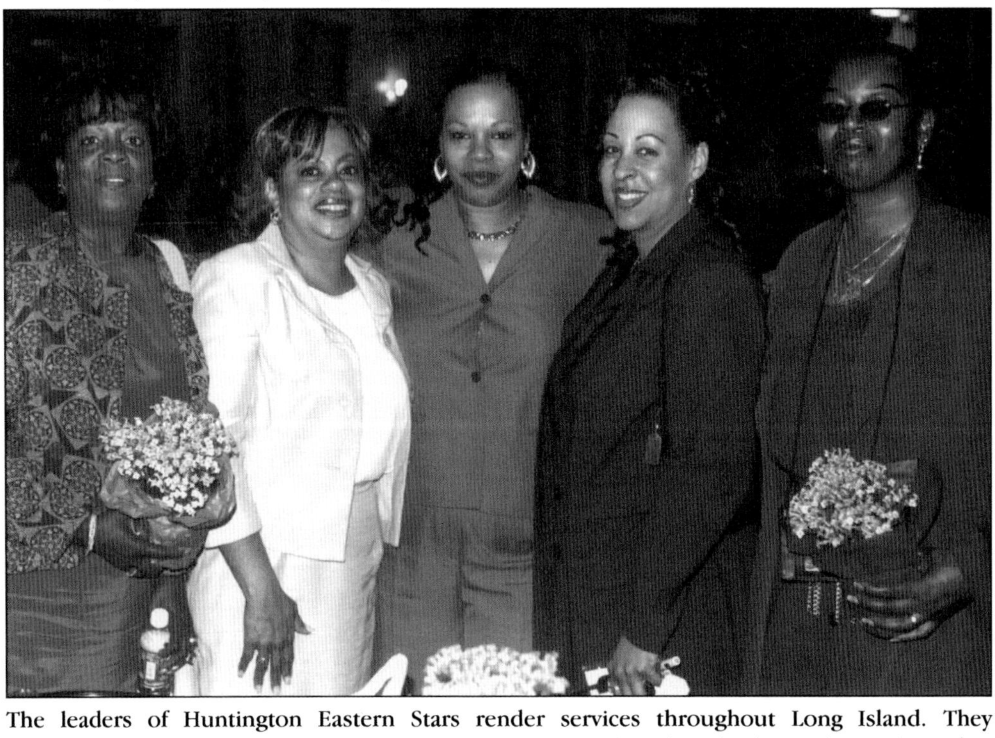

The leaders of Huntington Eastern Stars render services throughout Long Island. They are professional women who have roots in the area that date back to the early 1940s. (Author's collection.)

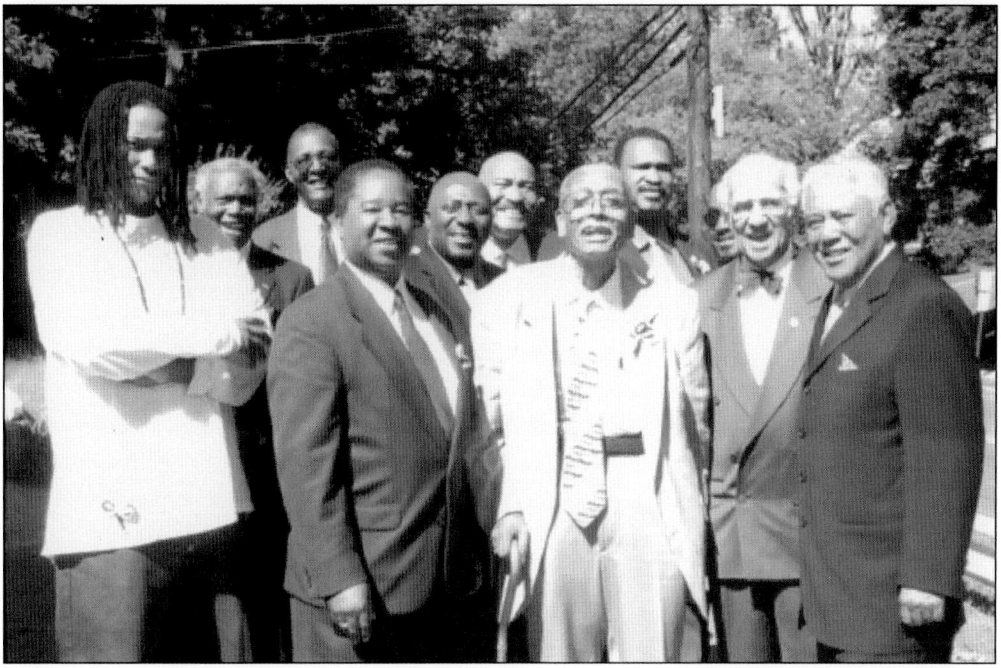

Bethel African Methodist Episcopal Church in Huntington was incorporated in 1843. From left to right are church members Pierre Stallings, John McMillan, Jerry Reilly, Ulysses Spicer, Gilford Prince, Rev. George Spearman, Howard Gamblin, Kevin Spearman, Leonard Motley, Bill Brazier, and Stanley Allen. (Courtesy of Rev. Clarence Johns, Mrs. Johns, and Bethel AME Church.)

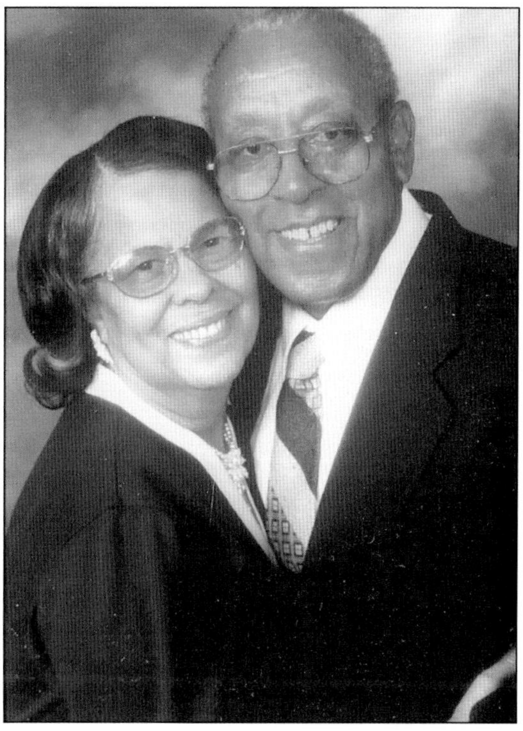

Rev. Clarence Johns heads Bethel African Methodist Episcopal Church in Huntington. He was previously the pastor of St. Paul AME Church in Rockville Center. Both he and his wife graduated from Hampton University, in 1949 and 1951, respectively. At the university, she was a four-letter athlete and he was wrestling champion for four years—the first to accomplish that feat. (Courtesy of Rev. Clarence Johns, Mrs. Johns, and Bethel AME Church.)

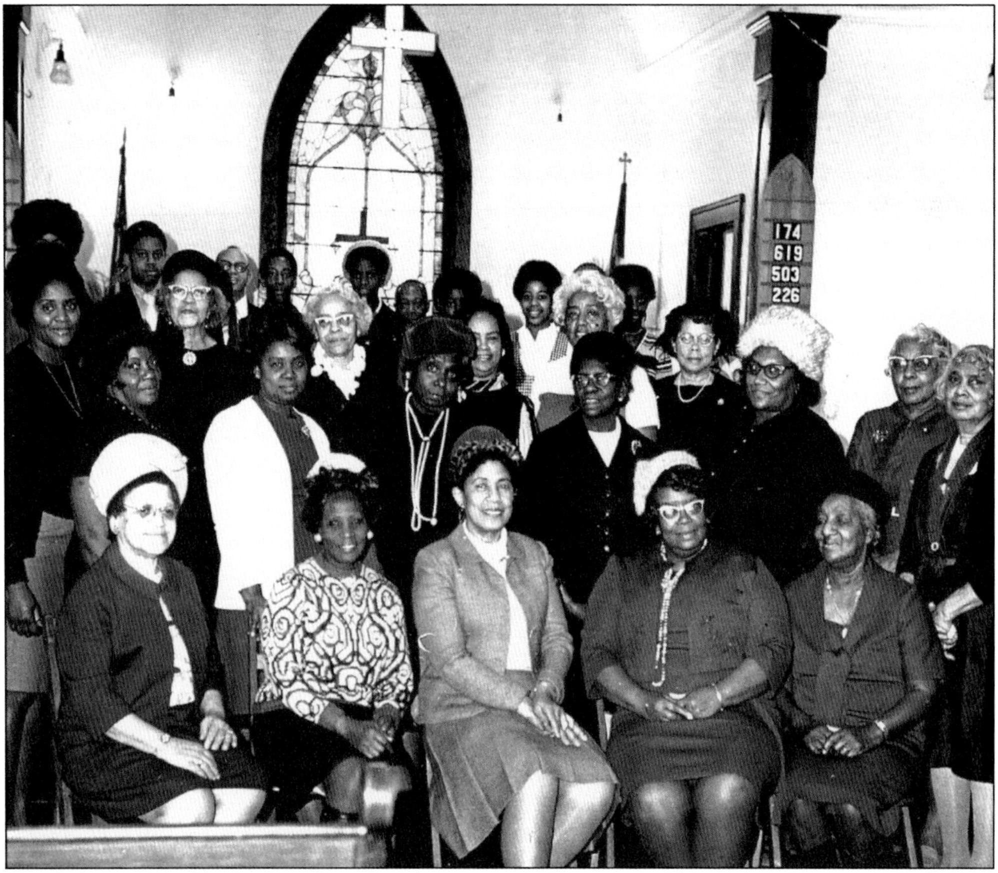

This was the celebration of Missionary Day at Bethel African Methodist Episcopal Church in Huntington. The photograph was taken *c.* 1970. (Courtesy Estate of Edna F. Point and the Huntington Historical Society.)

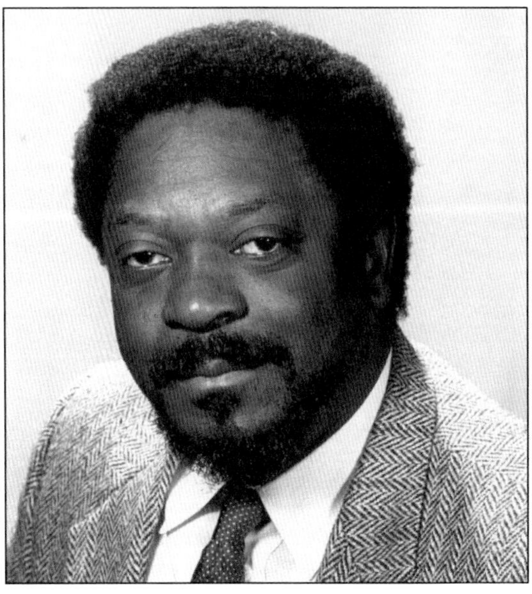

Les Payne, a Pulitzer Prize-winning reporter, is associate managing editor for national, science, and international news at Newsday and is a columnist for the Los Angeles Times syndicate. Payne is responsible for the paper's Queens edition. His news staffs have won every major award in journalism, including the Pulitzer Prize. He joined Newsday in 1969 and has covered Long Island migrant farmworkers, involuntary sterilization, and illegal aliens. He has reported from Africa, Asia, the Caribbean, and the United Nations. (Courtesy of Les Payne.)

For the past 21 years, Rev. Kenneth L. Nelson (center) has served as pastor of the African Methodist Episcopal Zion Church in Oyster Bay. A member of the Montauket tribe, he was born on Long Island, the youngest son of Harry Nelson and Eunice Bess Nelson. He earned degrees from Suffolk Community College and St. Joseph's College. He is shown with family members who include grandchildren Rachel Nelson and Paidraig Sullivan. Dr. Eunice Nelson Sullivan (right) holds a law degree from Wayne State University and is a practicing attorney in the Boston area. Next to her is her husband, Mark Sullivan. Kenneth W. Nelson (left) owns and operates Montauk Computers, a computer repair business in Oyster Bay. (Courtesy of Rev. Kenneth Nelson and family.)

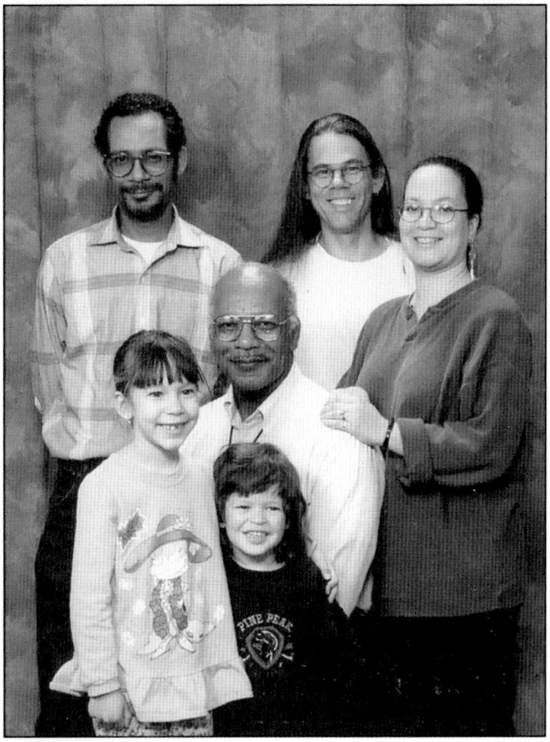

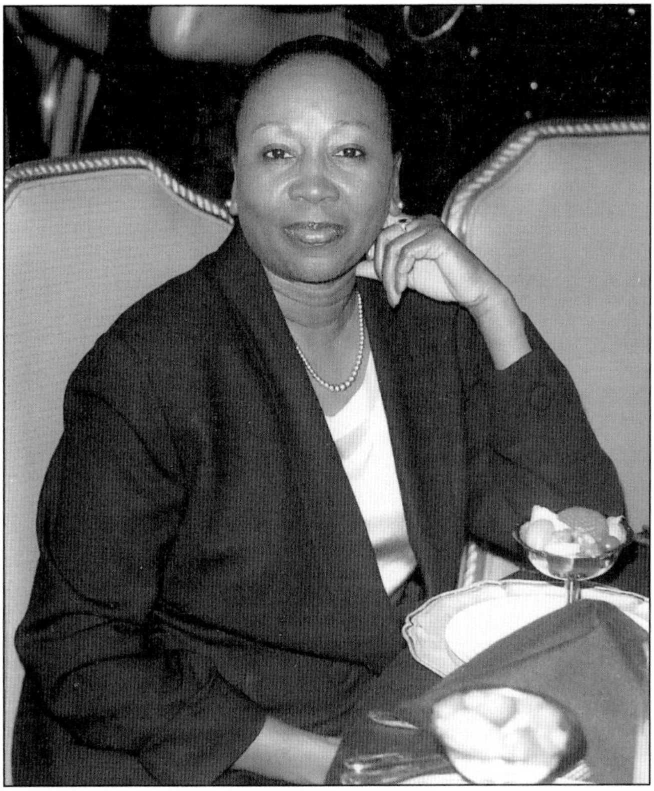

Betty Miller is a lawyer and advocate. Active in the community, club, and church affairs, she serves as director of minority affairs in the town of Huntington. (Author's collection.)

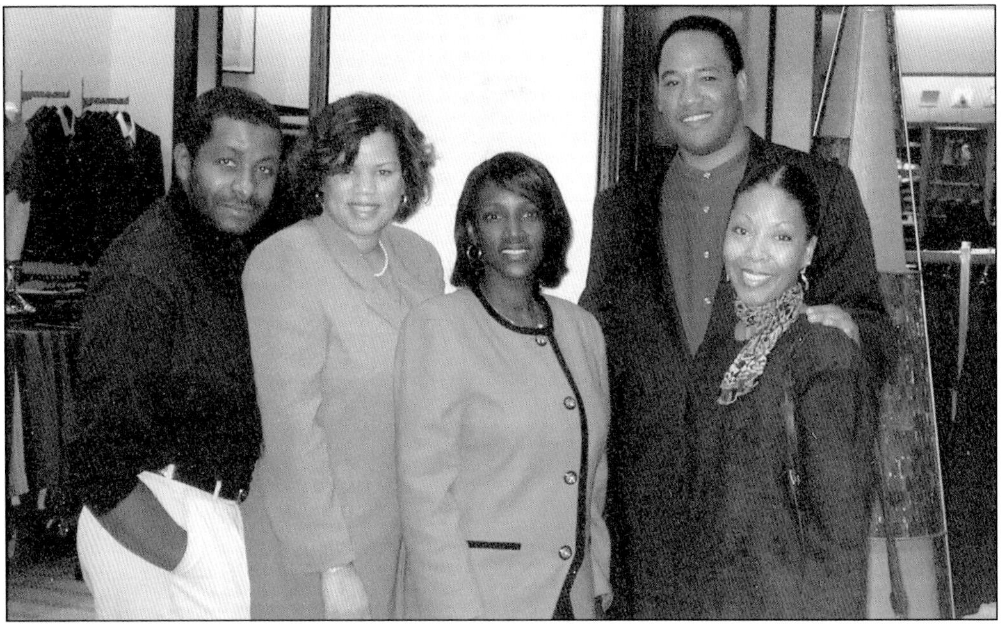

Shown are some of the leaders of the community. From left to right (above) are Fred Ainsley, Victoria Gumps, Michelle Woodard (the first African American female lawyer to serve as a Supreme Court judge), Jordan Wilson, and Denise Wilds. From left to right (below) are attorney Genya Grant, Michelle Woodard, Paul Johnson (former Huntington NAACP president), Valerie Howard, and Dee Smith. (Courtesy of J. Stewart Moore.)

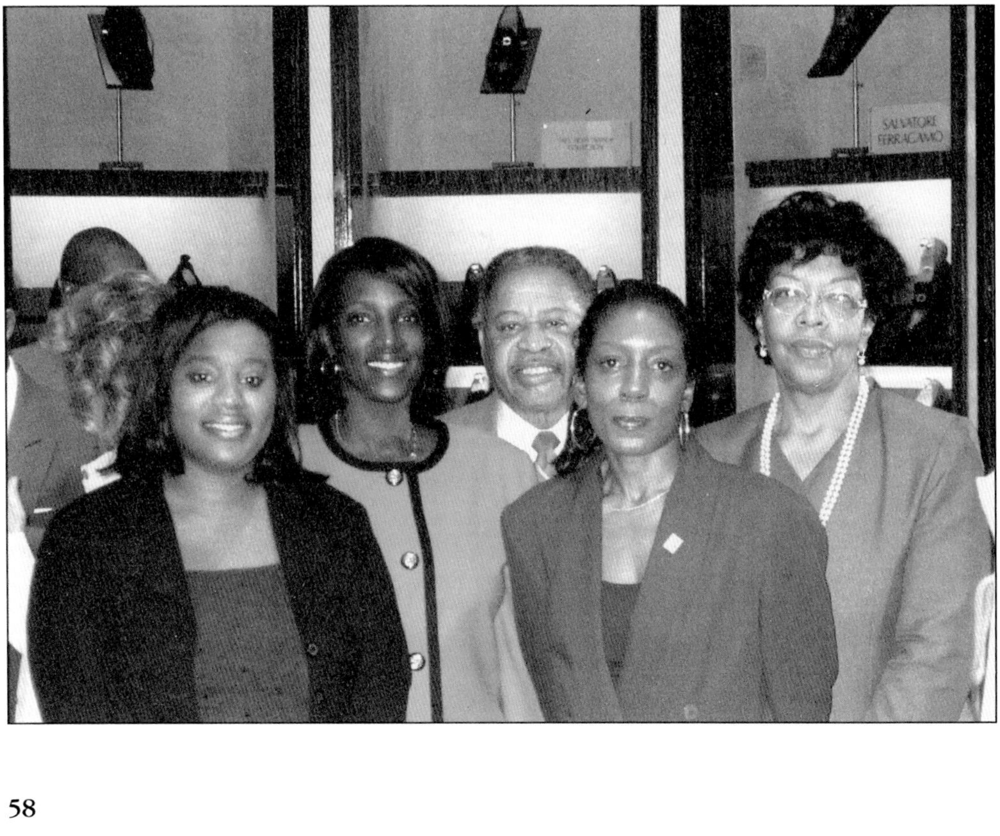

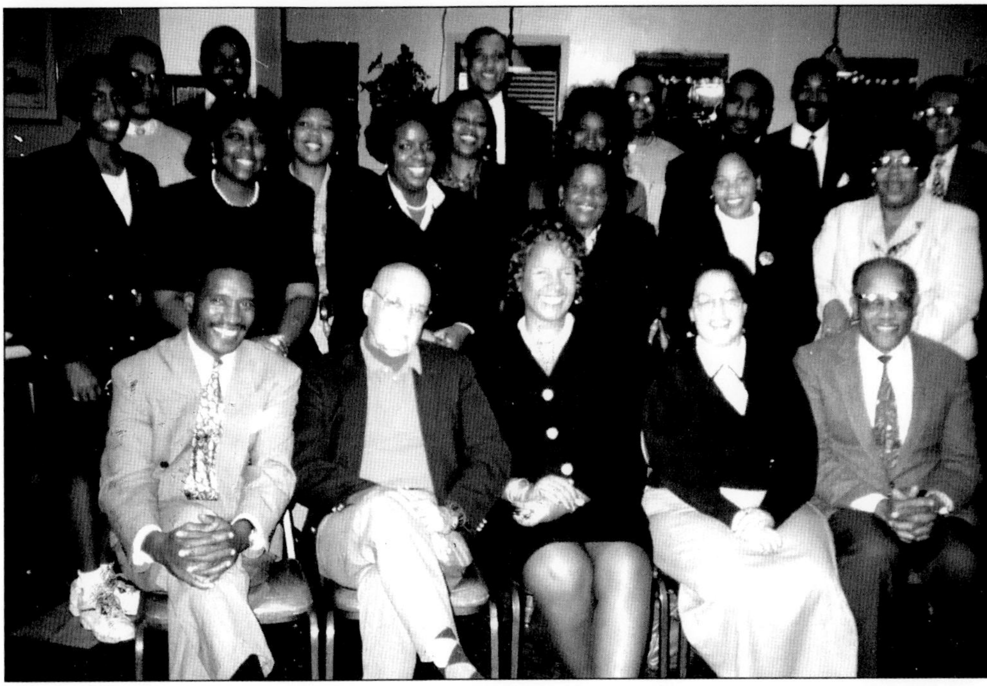

The Amistad Black Bar Association groups African American attorneys on Long Island. Through special events, members advance excellence and professionalism and encourage young people to consider a career in law. Association founder Stewart Moore (front left) is executive director. (Courtesy of J. Stewart Moore.)

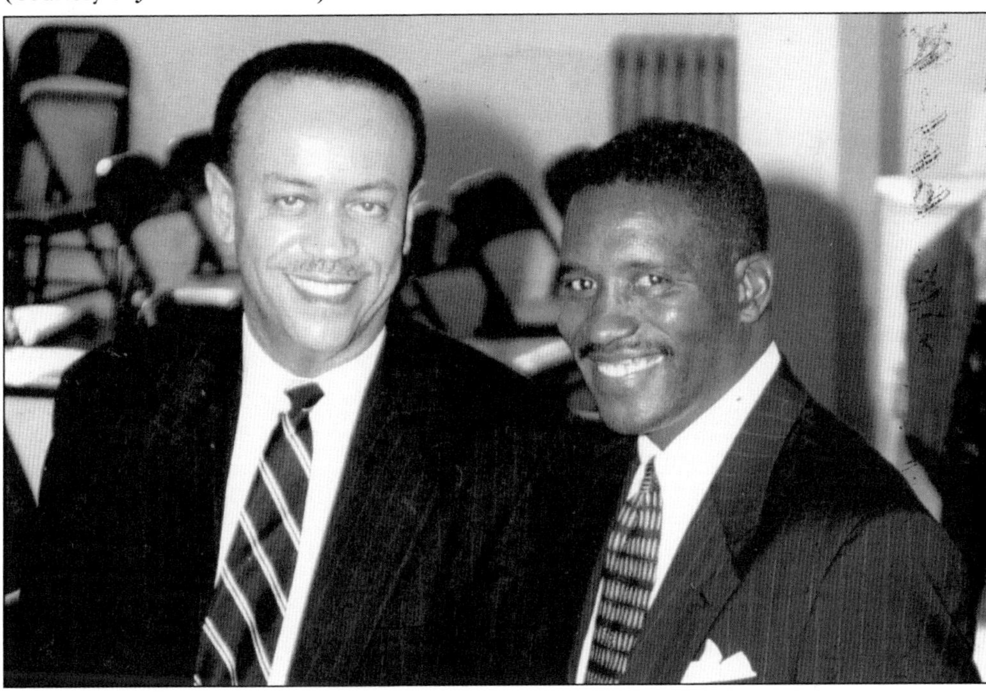

Kevin Mayo (left) and Stewart Moore exchange notes at an informal meeting. Mayo is from Riverhead, and Moore was born and bred in Huntington. (Author's collection.)

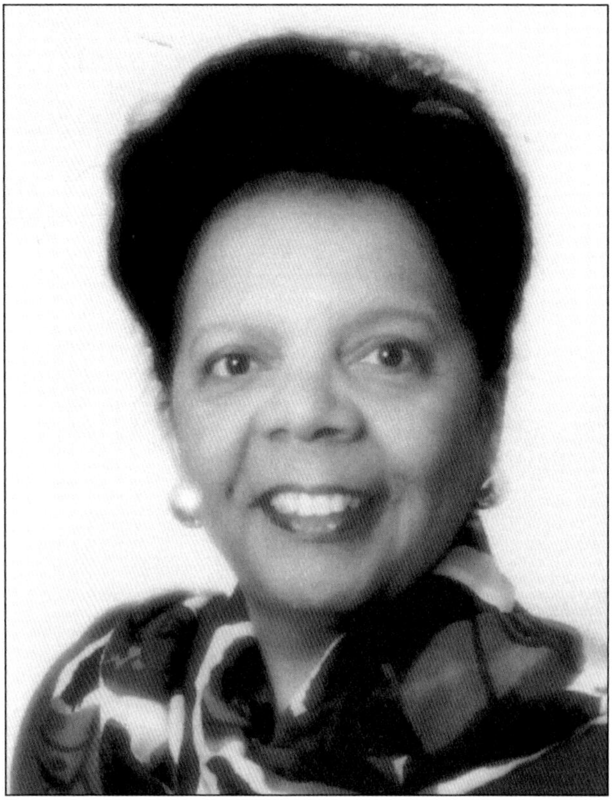

Dr. Patricia Hills Williams is one of the foremost African Americans in higher education on Long Island. Three U.S. presidents have appointed her to national committees, and she has received awards for volunteerism, community service, and excellence. As vice president for external affairs at the State University of New York in Farmingdale, she excels in human relations and international connections, especially involving development in Latin America and the Caribbean. Previously, she served as assistant to the university president. She is a charter member and past president of the 100 Black Women of Long Island. (Courtesy of Dr. Patricia Williams.)

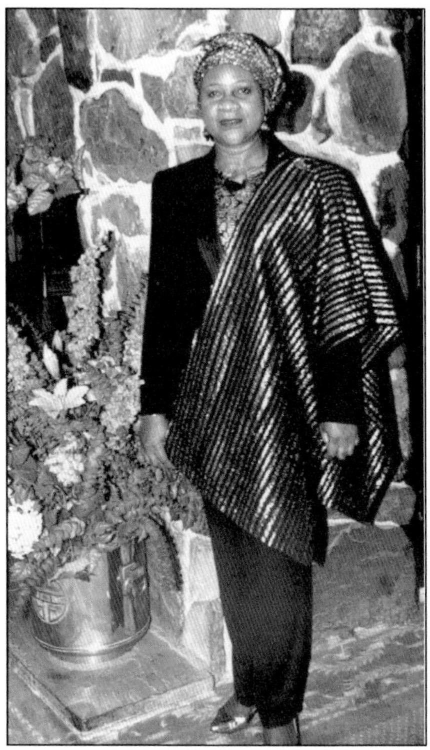

Dr. Veronica Henry is a leading educator on Long Island. She is one of the faculty deans at the State University of New York in Farmingdale. (Courtesy of Joe Turner.)

Five

Babylon to Amityville
Effort and Effect

African Americans came to Long Island in the 1700s and settled in Wyandanch, Amityville, and North Babylon. The names of some of the first families include Fowler, Miller, Squire, and Devine. In 1815, African Americans and Montauket Indians founded Bethel African Methodist Church in Copiague, which some historians claim to be the first African American church on Long Island. Others suggest that the African Methodist Episcopal Church in Setauket was probably the first congregation, established in 1811.

The trend in Babylon followed what happened throughout the island: many African American remained as slaves until the Emancipation Proclamation in 1865, after which some migrated from the South, especially after World War II, when migrant workers finally started making the area their home. At the same time, affluent blacks looking for a place to raise their families away from New York City migrated to towns such as Amityville. Although they may not have resided in the best part of town, they gained some peace and space, which the city lacked. Babylon itself offered the prospect of jobs and thus became one of the strategic spots.

Babylon developed as a town with people from backgrounds originating in many regions of the world. It has lovely parks, safe neighborhoods, and bustling shopping centers. Because the challenges of race and segregation posed initial obstacles for settlement in Babylon, African Americans chose to live in places that did not pose restrictions on them, such as North Amityville, Wyandanch, Roosevelt, and Hempstead. Even there, however, it was not a smooth ride. Problems surfaced and civil rights leaders such as Dr. Reed, Jean Dember, and Irwin Quintyne negotiated and fought hard to improve the situation.

Today, African Americans have made lasting bequests in all sectors of life. In Babylon's long history, the first elected African American official emerged in 1999: Janice Tinsley-Colbert, as town clerk—a big stride forward. Others have excelled as teachers, pastors, lawyers, and accountants. A new day has dawned, but the door is still wide open for improvement.

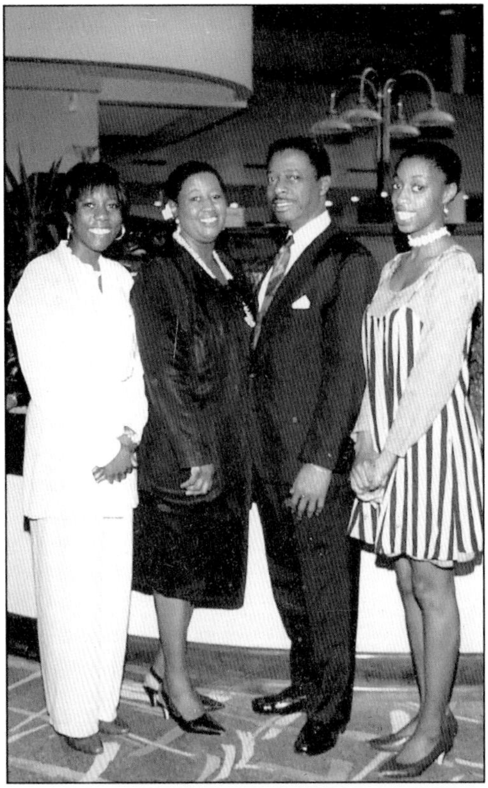

The Stewart family lives in Wyandanch. Delano Stewart (third from left) is the founder and publisher of the African American newspaper *Point of View*. In addition, he formulated and published five master plans for the city of New York, founded and directed an African American theater group, initiated and promoted medical scholarships and tax incentives to attract New York doctors to special communities, and served as Long Island campaign coordinator for Jesse Jackson's presidential campaign. An alumnus of Columbia University, he is married to Anne M. Stewart (second from left), a Nayak College graduate who has served as human services commissioner for the town of Babylon and with the Economic Opportunity Council of Suffolk County. Their daughters are Anika Stewart (left), who earned a degree in English from the State University of New York in Stony Brook and works in public relations for Grossman Strategies, and Dara Stewart (right), an editor with Penguin Putnam Publishing.

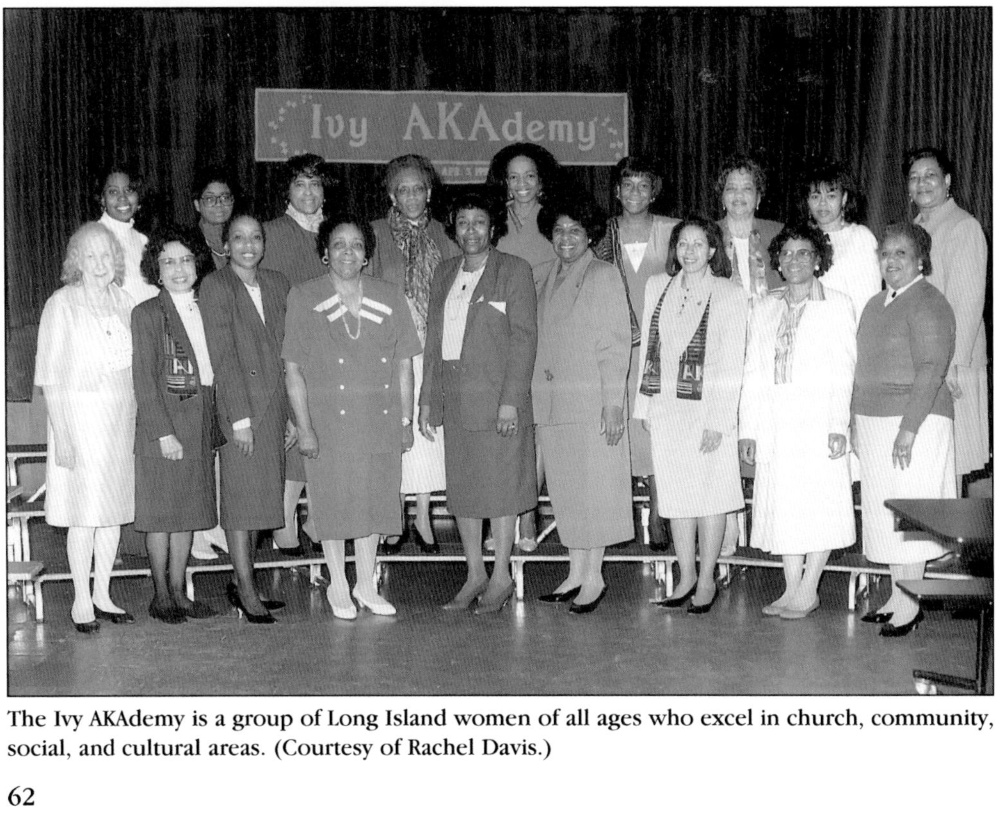

The Ivy AKAdemy is a group of Long Island women of all ages who excel in church, community, social, and cultural areas. (Courtesy of Rachel Davis.)

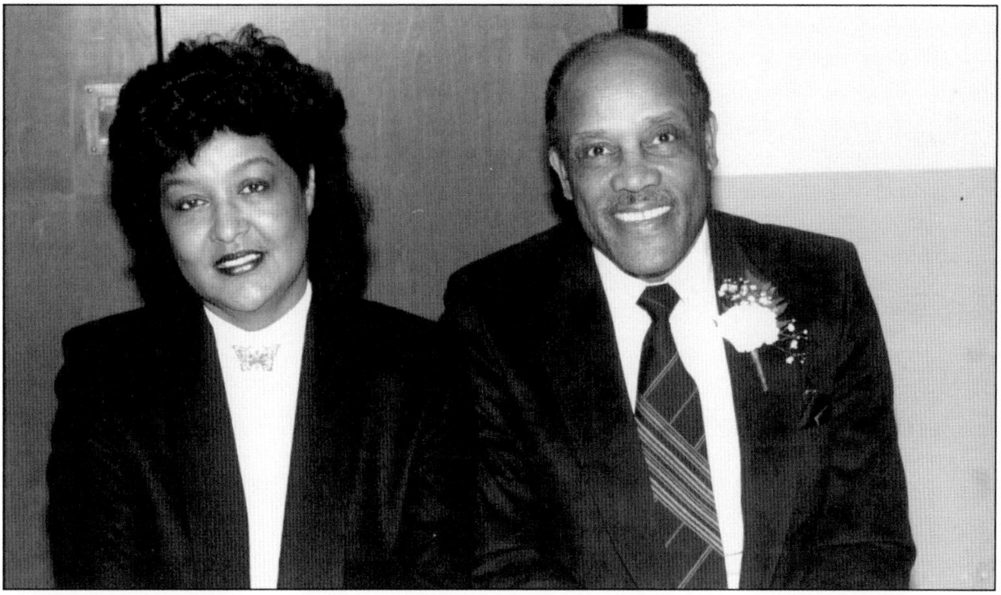

Marquette L. Floyd, pictured with his wife, was the first African American elected to Suffolk County District Court. A longtime resident of Babylon, he was born in 1928 and graduated from White Plains High School, New York University, and Brooklyn Law School. In 1986, he was appointed to the county court and, in 1989, won election to the state supreme court, where he presides over civil cases. (Courtesy of Joe Turner.)

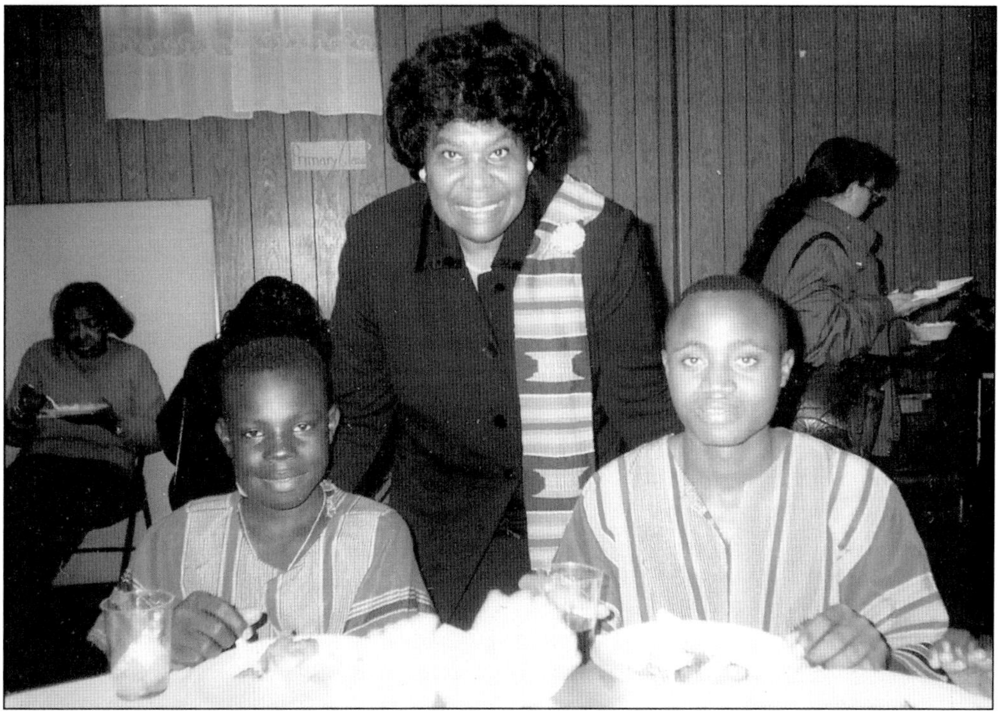

Rachel Lee Davis taught school for more than three decades and served as president of the Long Island Links group. She has won awards for her many contributions to the community. She is pictured with two visitors from Uganda who were on a 1998 Tour of Light organized by Links.

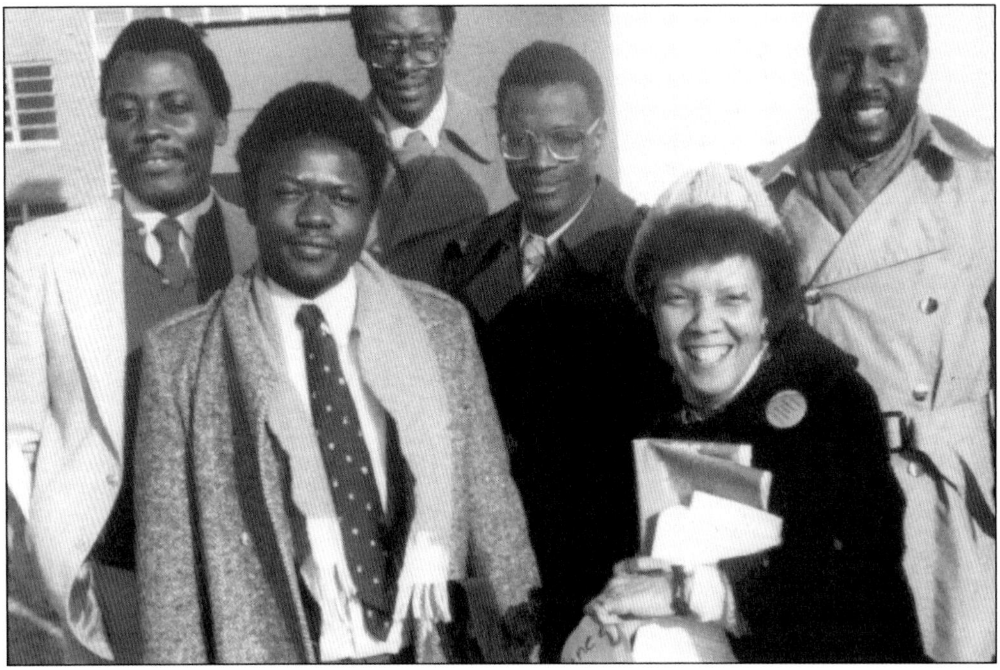

Jean Dember (front right) is a national and international advocate and civil rights leader. At 75, she is still as militant and dedicated as before. She participated in the civil rights protest and has long championed the cause of the weak and oppressed, the homeless, and the physically and mentally impaired. She has radio and television shows, organizes workshops, facilitates discussions, and serves as a mentor, teacher, guide, and, above all, a spokesperson for people. A mother of 10, she has outstanding abilities and success at urging youth to embrace education and forge ahead. (Courtesy of Jean Dember.)

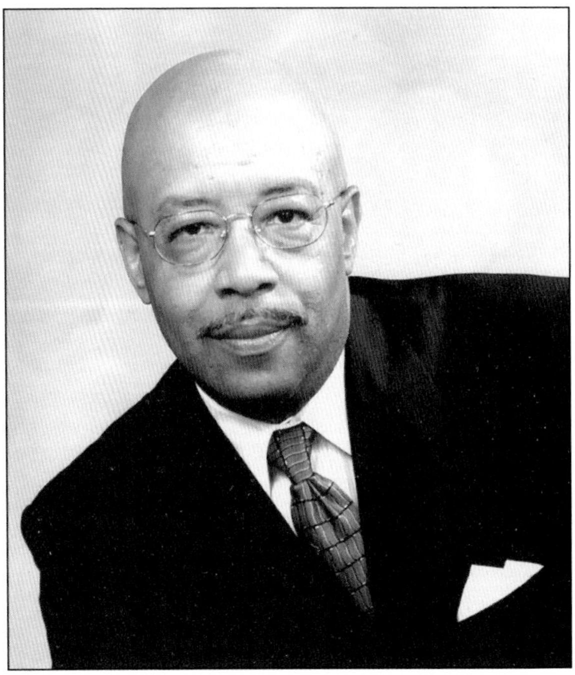

Derek Robinson, a founding member and president of the Amistad Black Bar Association, is the principal assistant county attorney in the Suffolk County attorney's office. A North Amityville resident, he graduated from Howard University and the Antioch School of Law in Washington, D.C. He was also a founding member and chair of the Suffolk County Dr. Martin Luther King Jr. Commission. (Courtesy of Derek Robinson.)

The Honorable Janice E. Tinsley-Colbert, the town clerk of Babylon, is the first African American elected to office in the 127-year history of the town. A lawyer, she earned a bachelor's degree in political science and a law degree from Brooklyn Law School. She has served in both the public and private sectors. (Author's collection.)

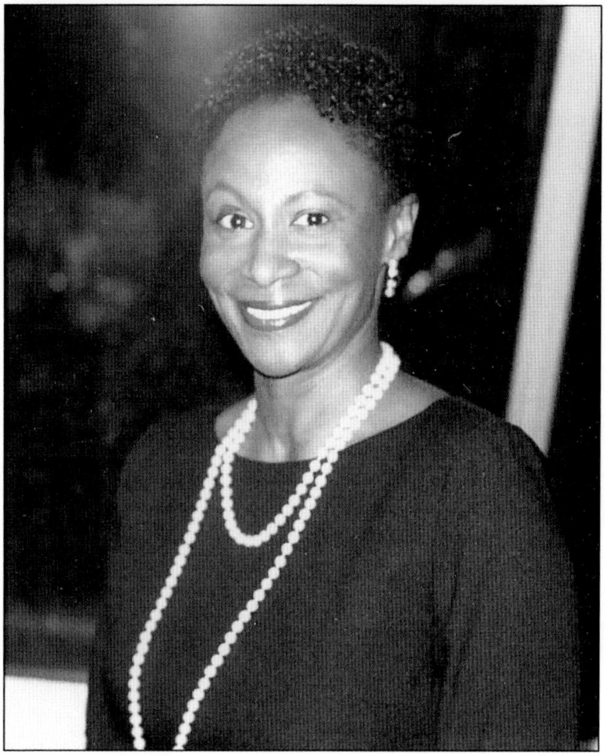

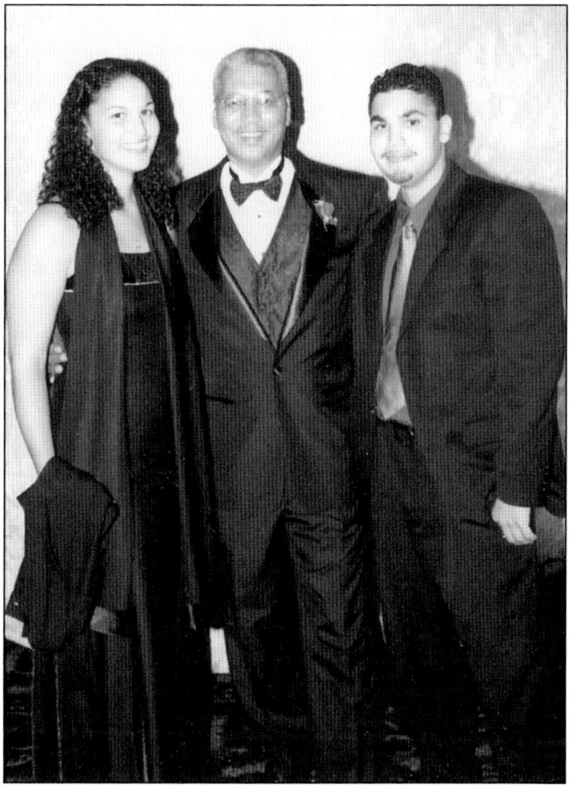

Robert B. Cox Jr. (center) earned an economics degree from Tufts University and graduated from Touro Law School in 1993. A practicing attorney, he is also first vice president and founding member of the Amistad Black Bar Association and a barber. Shown with him are his daughter Aliya, who graduated from the University of Massachusetts, Lowell, with a B.S. in health education, and his son Jamal, who holds a bachelor's degree from the University of Connecticut in business finance. (Courtesy of Robert Cox.)

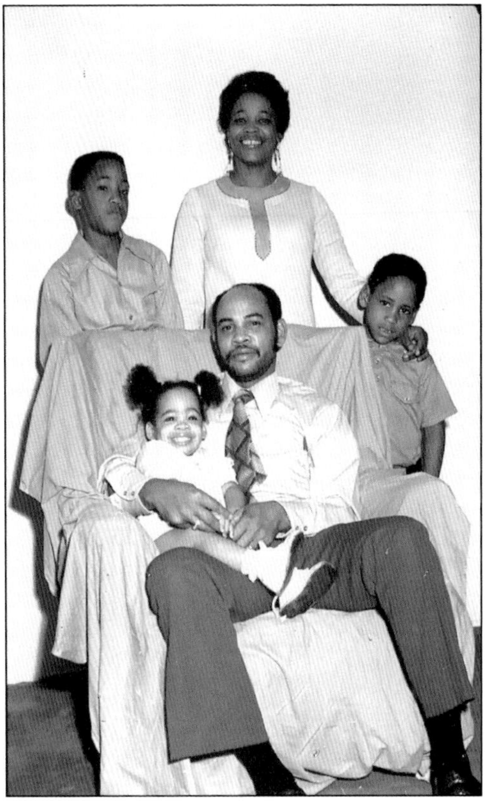

The Jordan K. Wilson family of North Babylon moved to Long Island from Durban, North Carolina, in the 1960s. Jordan Wilson (front) was one of the first African American teachers in the area. Beginning in 1966, he taught mathematics in Plainview for more than 30 years. His wife, Dorothy Wilson (back), was also a teacher, in Babylon. In 1984, Jordan Wilson became one of the first African Americans to run for the legislature. He is active in the Democratic party, the National Association for the Advancement of Colored People (NAACP), the church, and other civic organizations. Also pictured are a daughter and two sons—Janene, Kermit, and Jeffrey—who were raised in North Babylon. (Courtesy of Jordan Wilson.)

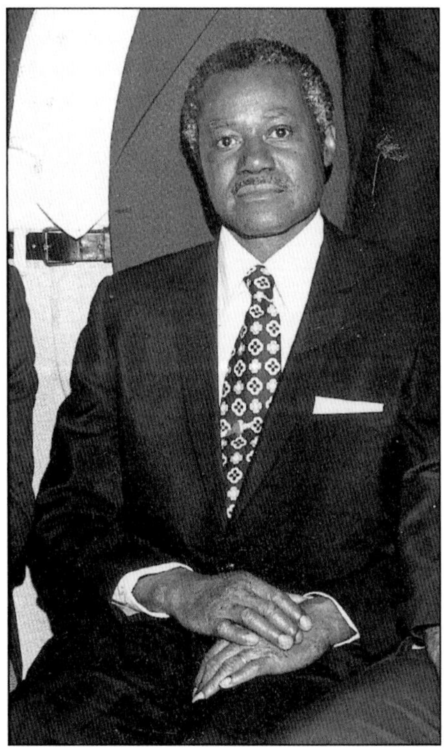

Oney Spencer has lived in Babylon for more than half a century. As senior building inspector for the town of Babylon, Spencer made his mark by becoming one of the first African Americans to serve in the local government. After graduation from Sladeville High School in 1940, he served with the U.S. Navy from 1941 to 1945. In 1949, he earned a trades and industries diploma from Hampton Institute. (Courtesy of Oney Spencer.)

From the late 1940s to the present, Dolores and Irwin S. Quintyne have strived for civil rights. Today, those rights make a difference in the lives of African Americans. (Courtesy of Joe Turner and the Rccord.)

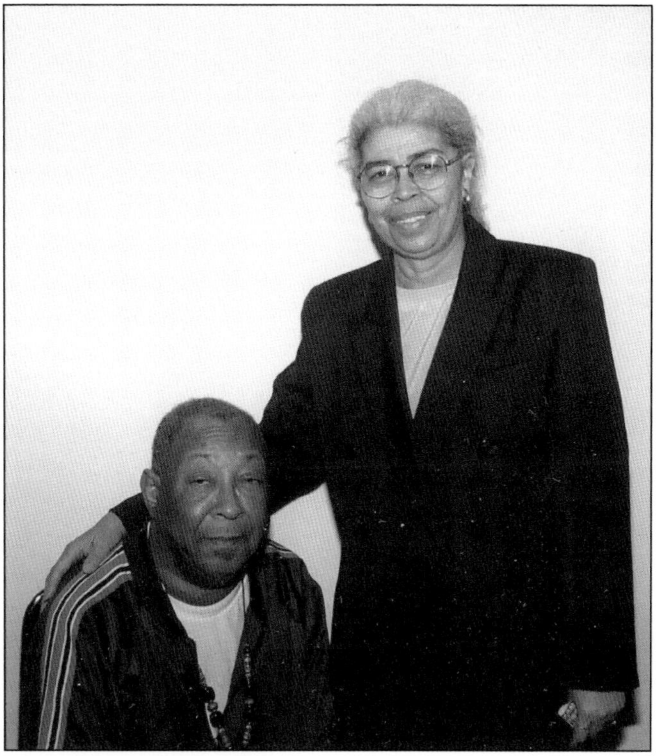

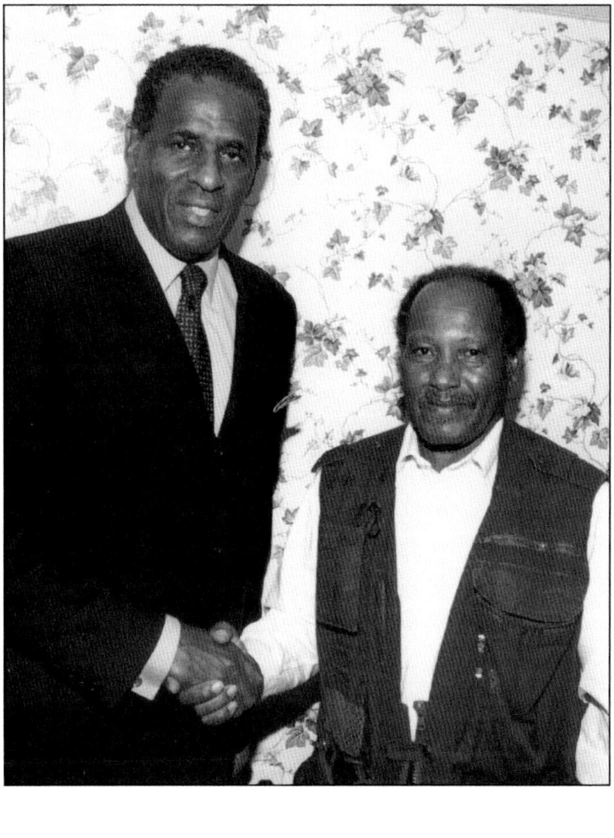

Joe Turner (right) of Amityville shakes hands with New York State comptroller Carl McCall. Turner is a photographer, journalist, businessman, and historian. He hails from Virginia and may be related to Nat Turner, who led the slave insurrection in Virginia in 1831. (Courtesy of Joe Turner and family.)

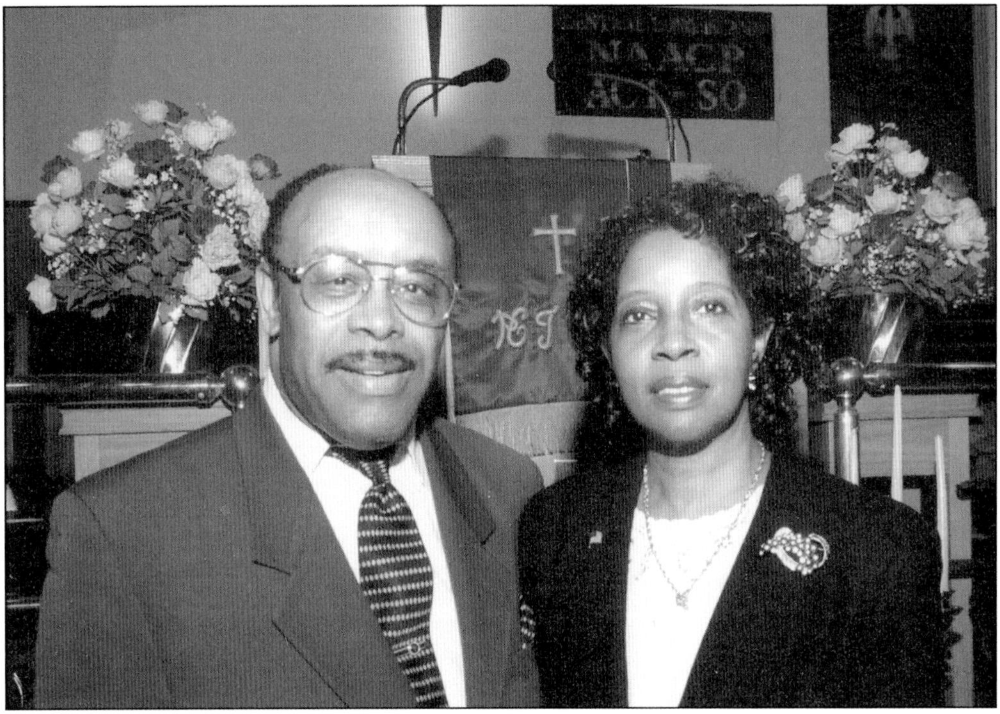

Rev. Dr. Robert D. Abbott and his wife, Eva Abbott, lead Holy Trinity Baptist Church, on Albany Avenue in North Amityville. They have also served the local community on boards and other agencies. (Courtesy of Joe Turner and Rev. Abbott.)

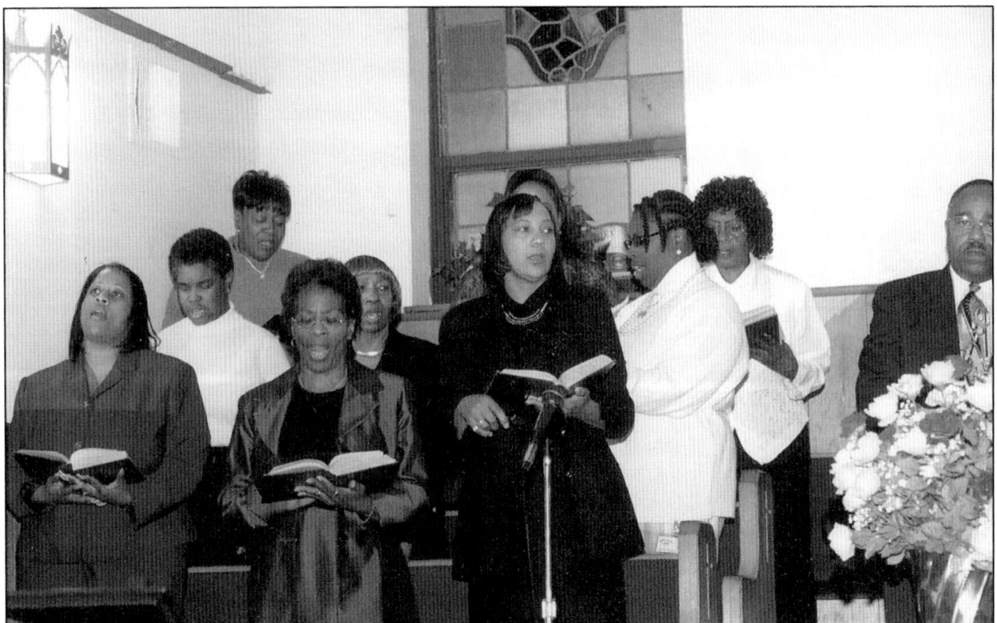

The choir at Holy Trinity Baptist Church in North Amityville sings during the 55 Freedom Fund program organized by the central Long Island branch of the National Association for the Advancement of Colored People. (Courtesy of Joe Turner and Rev. Abbott.)

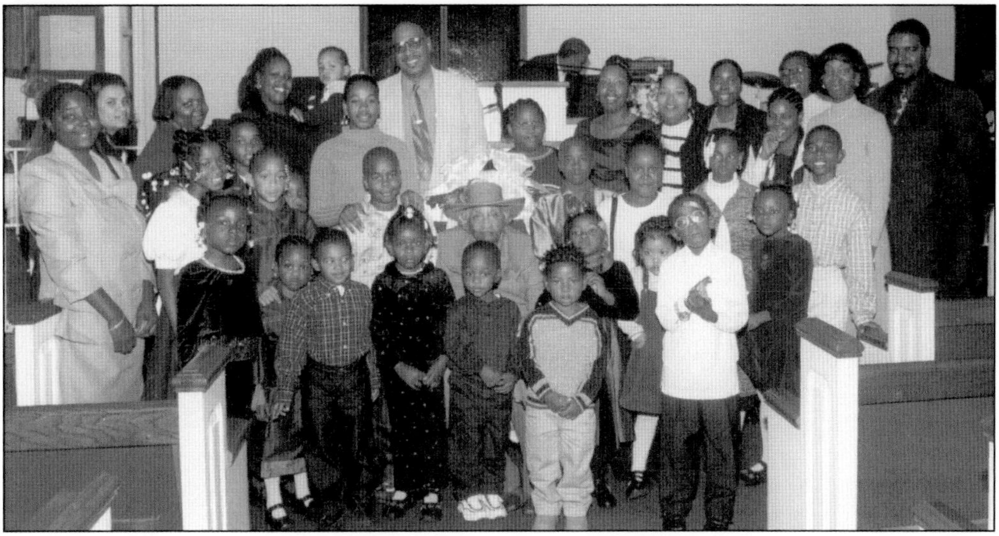

Five generations of the Battle family gather at Prayer Tabernacle in North Amityville for the 80th birthday of Mother Mamie Battle (center, with hat). (Courtesy of Joe Turner and Rev. Walter Willie.)

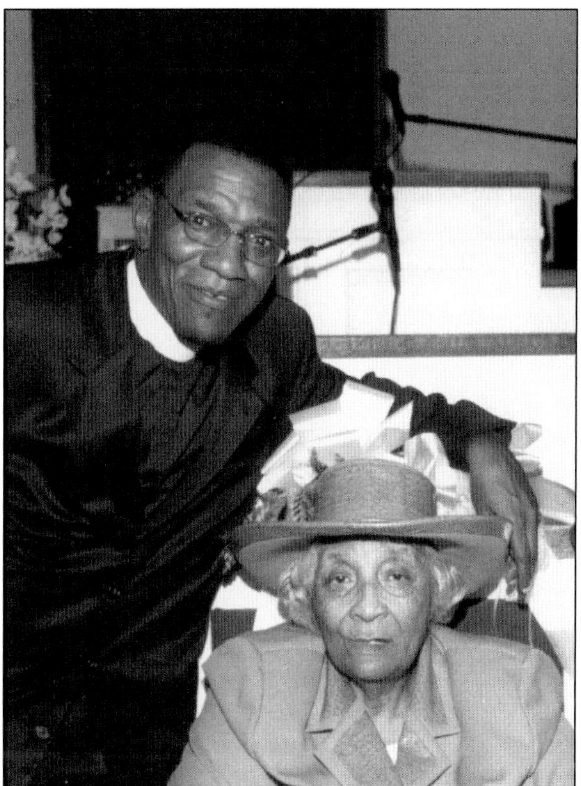

Rev. Dr. Walter C. Willie Jr. celebrates the 80th birthday of Mother Mamie Battle at Prayer Tabernacle, 3550 Great Neck Road, North Amityville. Mother Battle is a devoted mentor and church leader. (Courtesy of Joe Turner and Rev. Walter Willie.)

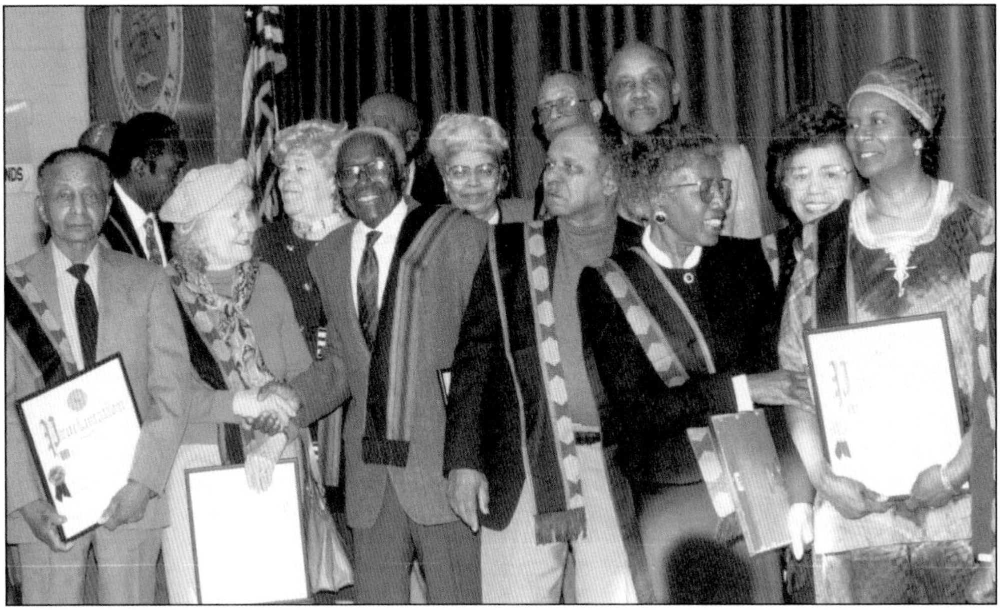

Members of the Babylon community come together to observe the eighth annual Black History Month. (Courtesy of Joe Turner.)

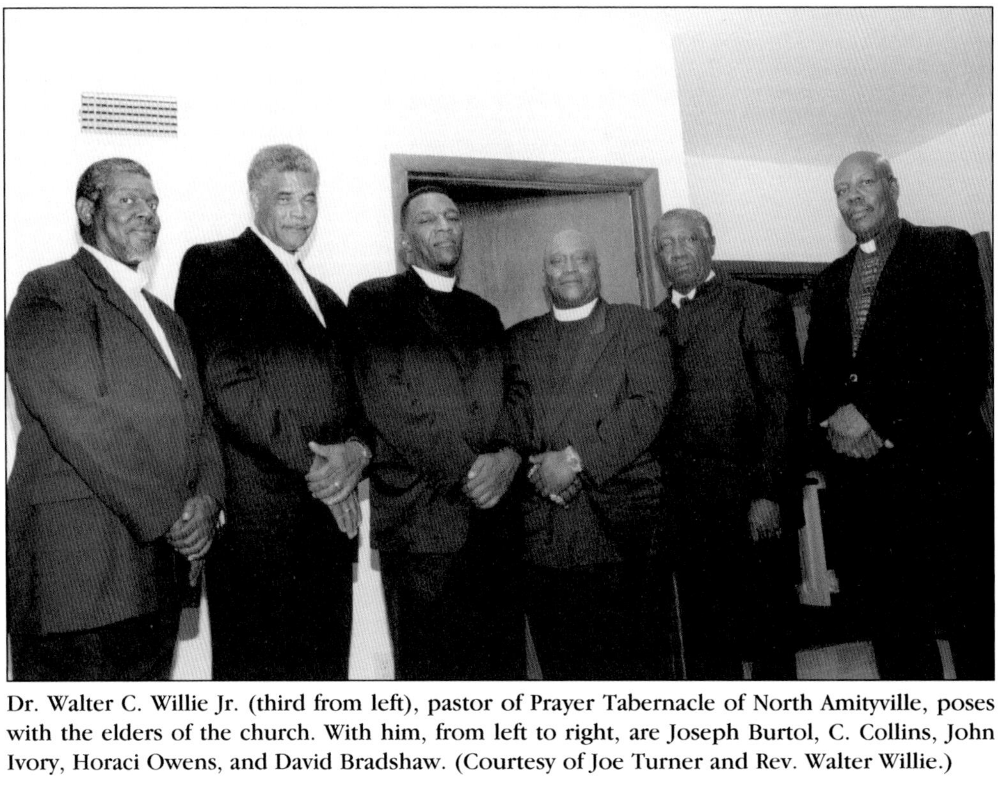

Dr. Walter C. Willie Jr. (third from left), pastor of Prayer Tabernacle of North Amityville, poses with the elders of the church. With him, from left to right, are Joseph Burtol, C. Collins, John Ivory, Horaci Owens, and David Bradshaw. (Courtesy of Joe Turner and Rev. Walter Willie.)

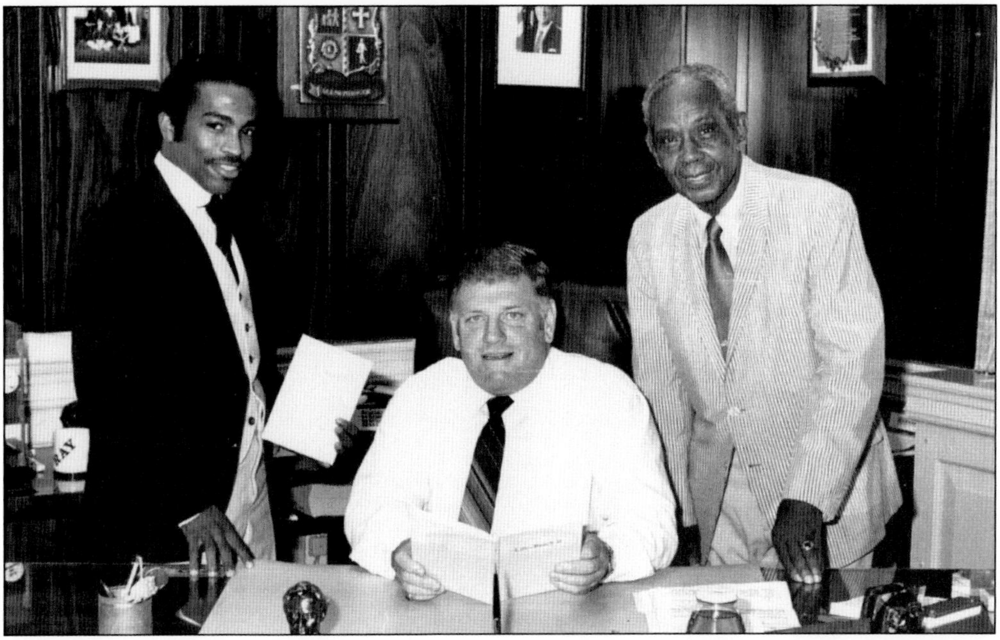

At the age of 70, musician Vernon Reid (right) started writing for the *Amityville Record* and proved to be an excellent journalist. He and his wife, Mabel Reid, a columnist for the *Record,* were consulted regularly on matters that affected the African American community. He is pictured with the editor and a staff member of the *Record.* (Courtesy of Mabel Reid and Joe Turner.)

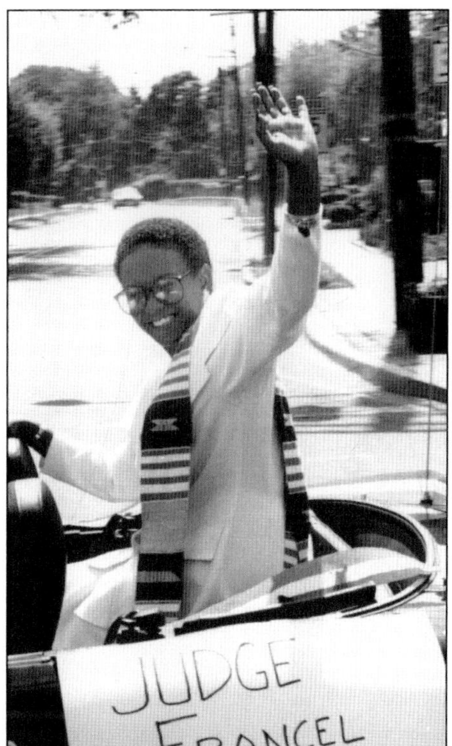

Francel Bellinger was one of the first African American women to serve as a judge on Long Island. Here, she participates at a parade in Babylon. (Courtesy of Joe Turner.)

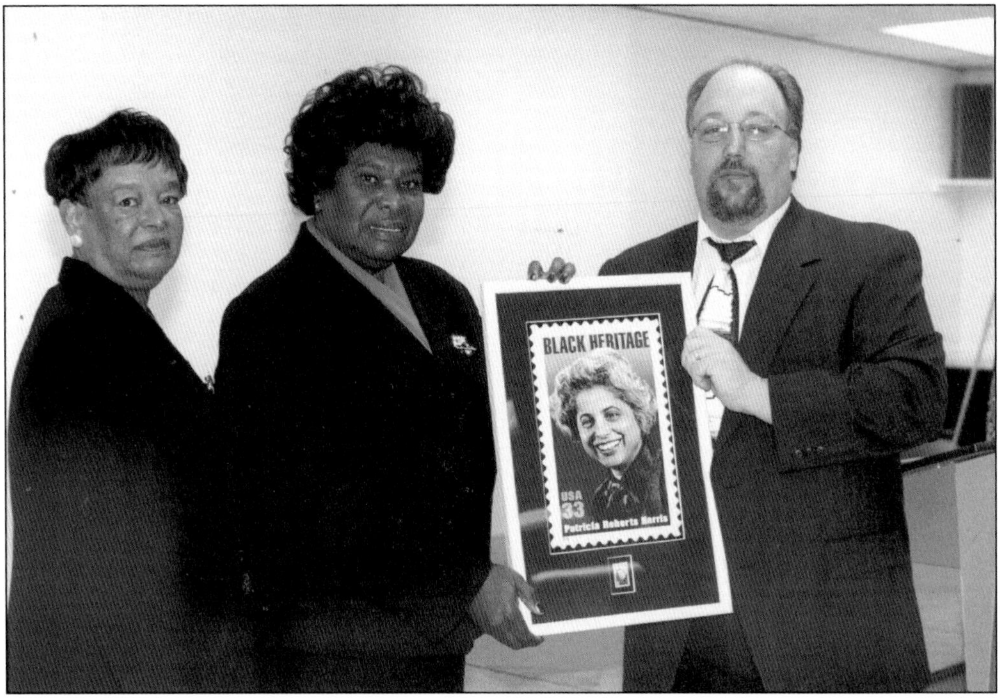

Myrna F. Taylor (left) and Rachel Davis are two prominent Babylon women and Links officials. They helped launch the postage stamp honoring Patricia Roberts Harris, the secretary of Housing and Urban Development appointed by Pres. Jimmy Carter in 1976. Pictured with them is the postmaster who supported the project. (Courtesy of Joe Turner.)

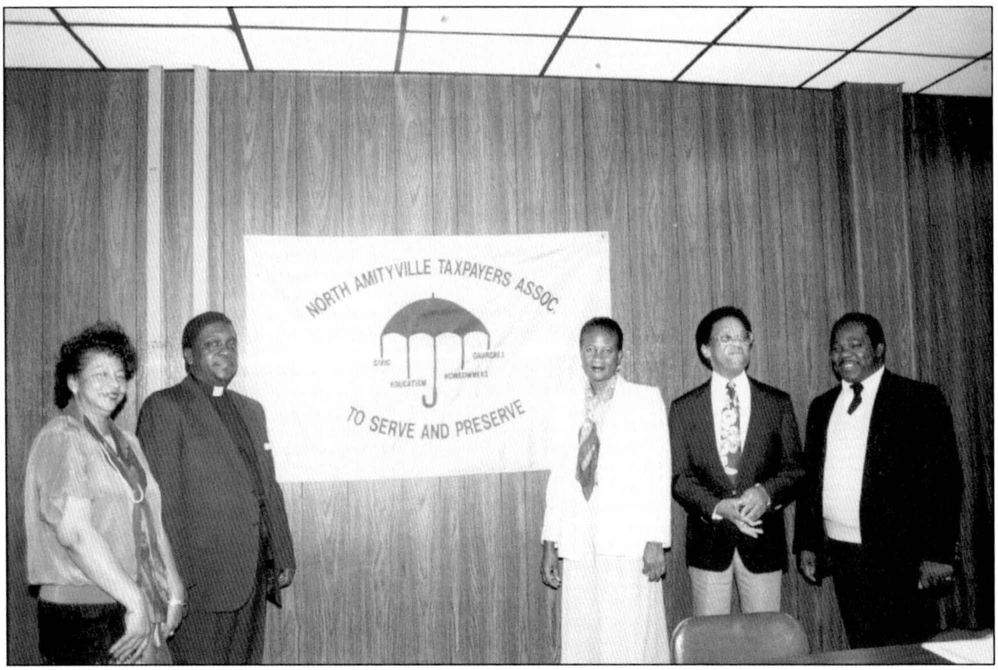

The North Amityville Taxpayers Association was a group that promoted worthy development projects. Some of its early members are shown this 1993 photograph. (Courtesy of Joe Turner.)

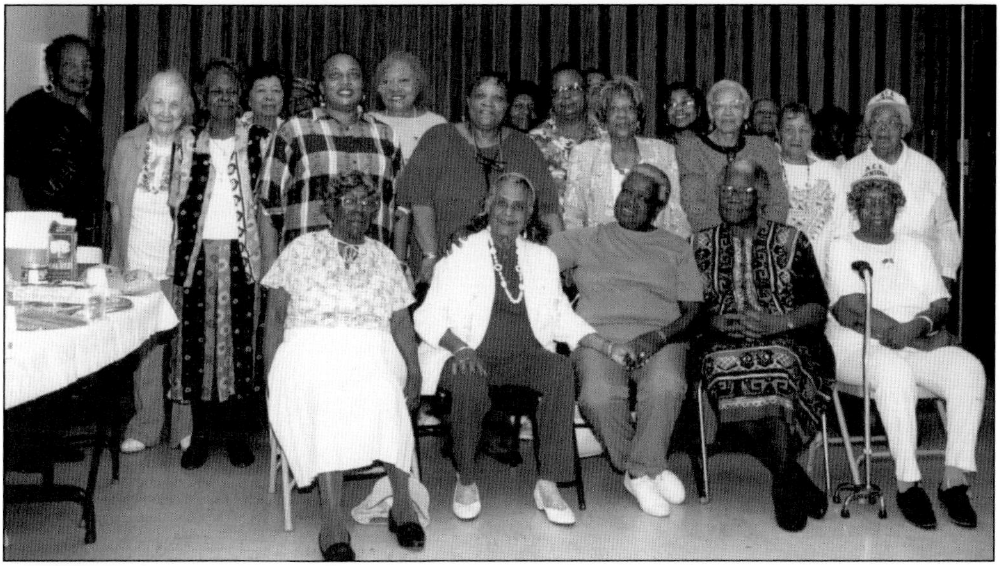

A group of North Amityville women and grandmothers meet on Wednesdays at 48 Cedar Road for games, discussions, and fellowship. They and their families have been part of Long Island for decades. The oldest member shown is E. Miller (front left), and the group's president is Dorothy Parker (standing, center). (Courtesy of Joe Turner.)

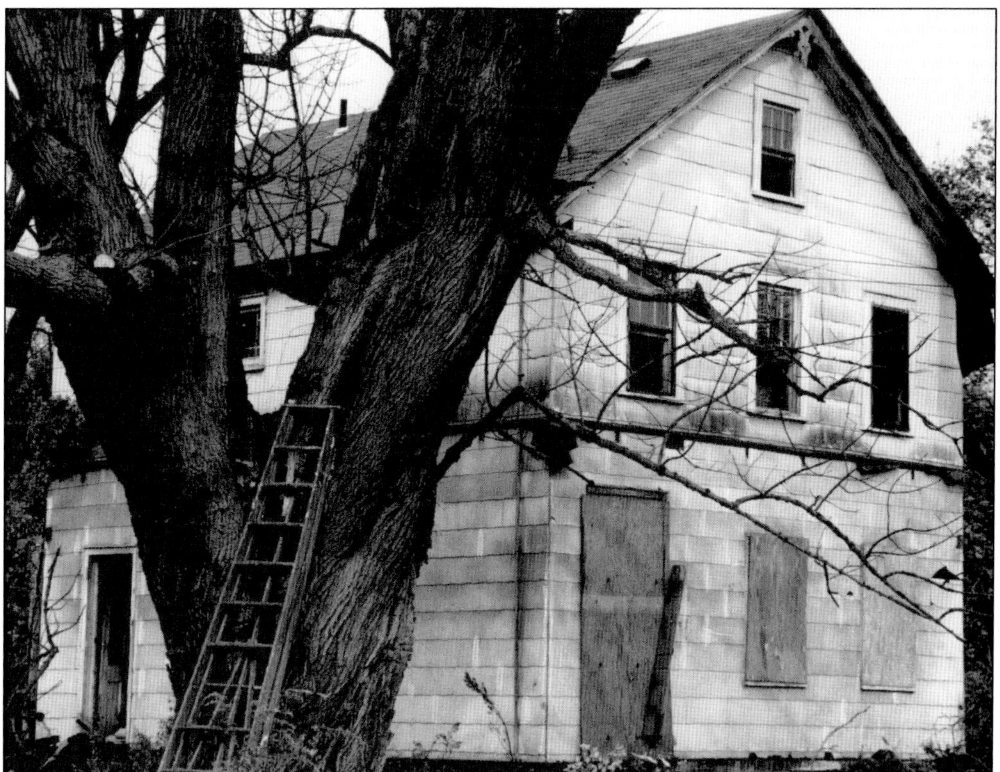

This photograph shows a building in North Amityville before it was renovated. (Courtesy of Joe Turner.)

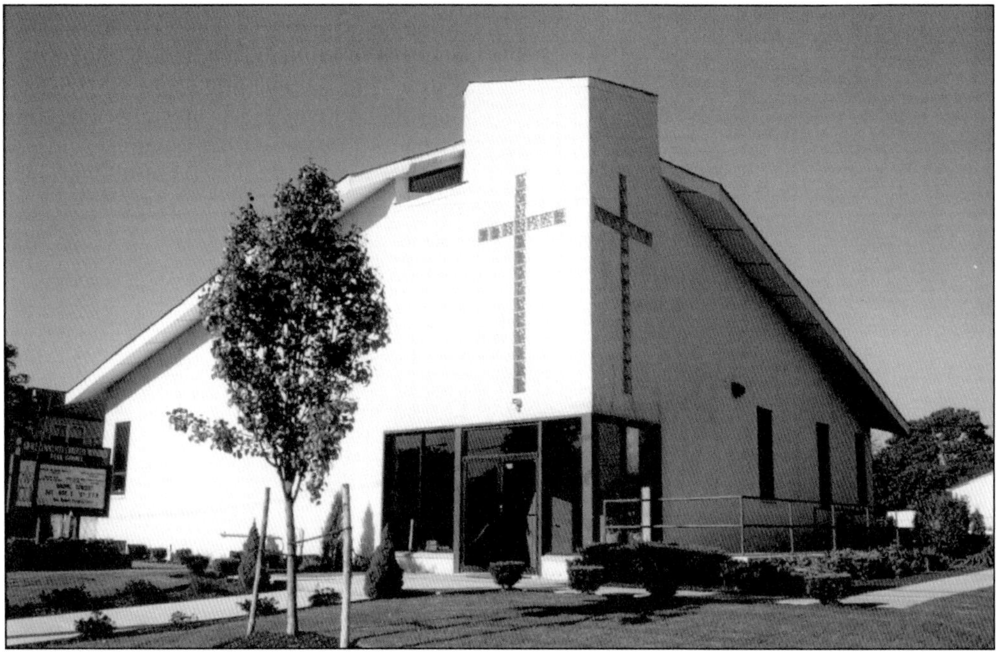

Grace Community Church is located in North Amityville. Rev. Robert L. Burgess is the pastor. (Courtesy of Joe Turner.)

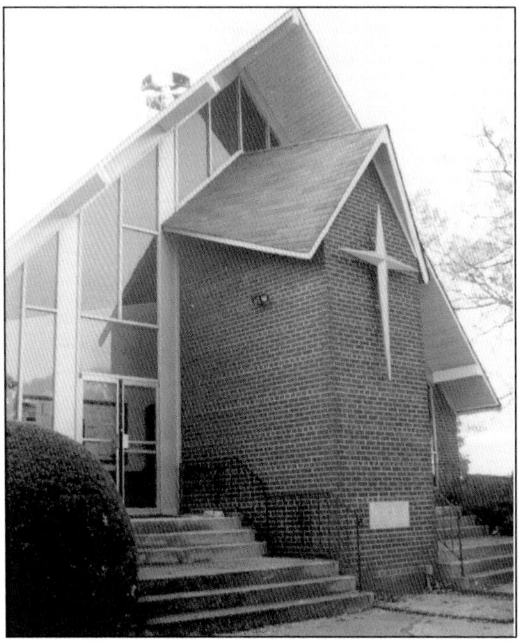

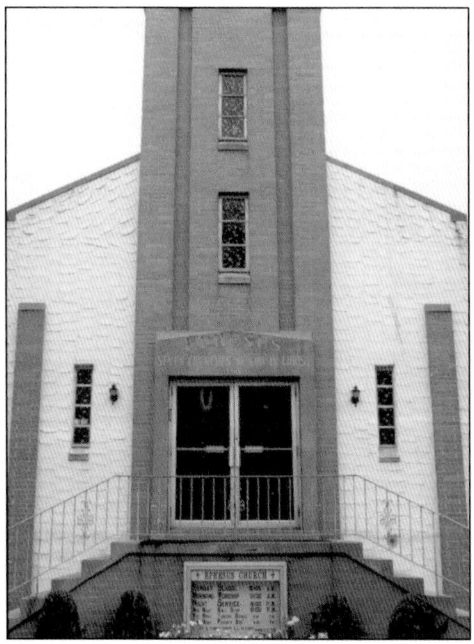

The Bethel African Methodist Episcopal Church in Copiague, led today by Rev. Dr. Eugene E. McAshan, was first formed in 1815 and is thought to be the oldest African American church on Long Island. The land for a church was acquired in 1874. The original building was destroyed by fire in 1901. The church was rebuilt in 1902. A campaign for a new building was launched in 1957, ground was broken in 1962, and the new church (left) was dedicated in 1967. The Ephesus Seven Churches of God in Christ (right) is located in North Amityville. (Courtesy of Joe Turner.)

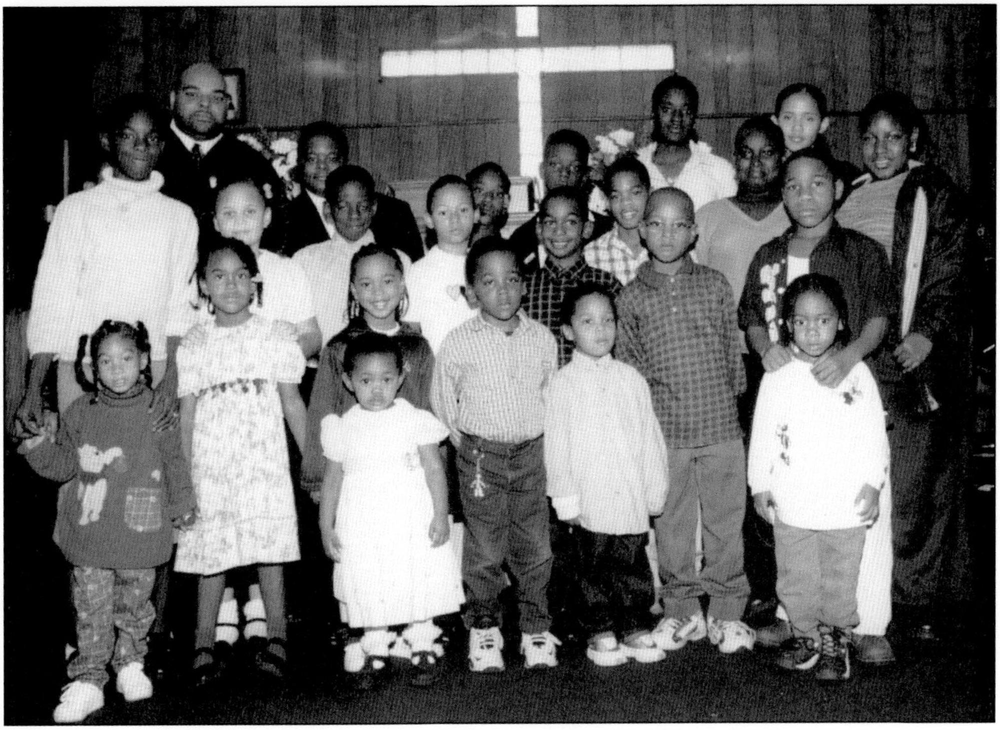

New Hope Institutional Baptist Church, at 30 Harrison Avenue in Amityville, has served the community for more than half a century. Rev. John A. Jackson (back left) is the pastor. He is pictured with children of the church. (Courtesy of Joe Turner and Rev. John Jackson.)

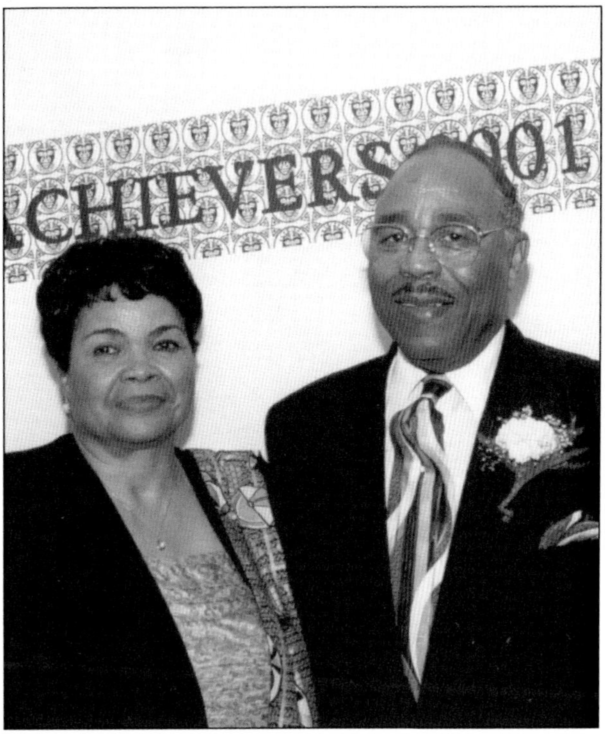

Rev. Dr. Eugene E. McAshan and Jewel D. McAshan of the historic Bethel African Methodist Episcopal Church in Copiague attend the awards ceremony of Black Achievers of Long Island. The ceremony was held during Black History Month at the Bethel Day Care Center. (Courtesy of Joe Turner, Rev. and Mrs. McAshan.)

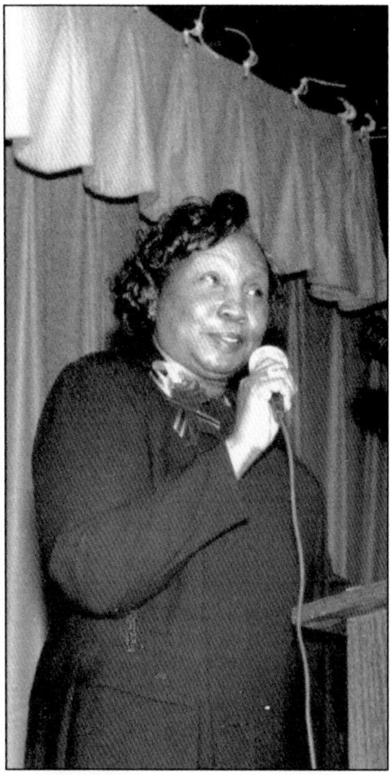

Connie Davis is one of the first African Americans to serve as the commissioner for human resources for the town of Babylon. (Courtesy of Joe Turner and Connie Davis.)

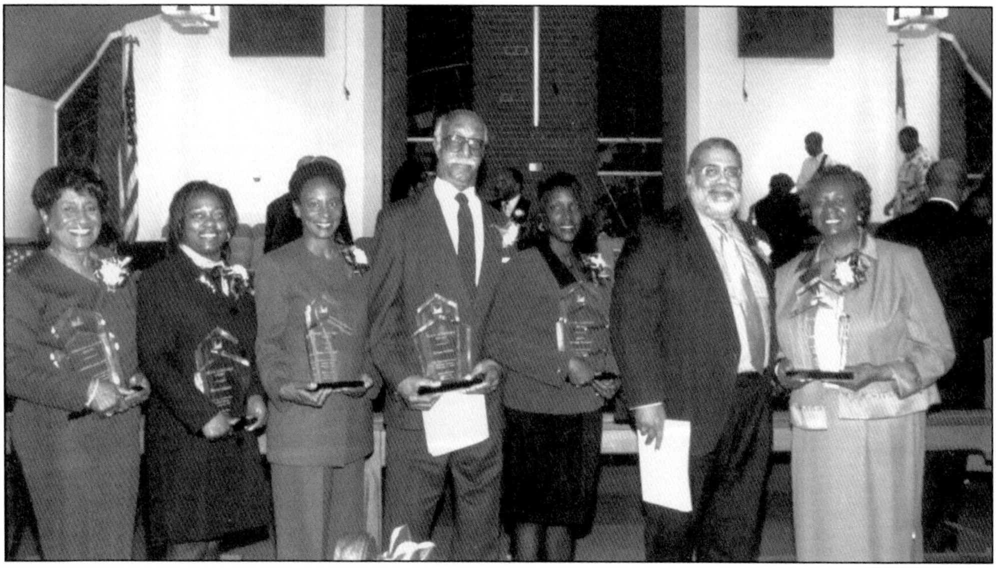

Attending a ceremony at the Bethel Church in Copiague are some of Long Island's African American "firsts." From left to right are Joan Johnson, the first elected to office in the town of Islip and the first female to run for Congress on a Republican ticket; Theresa Sanders, one of the first to serve as the chief executive of the Urban League of Long Island; Janice Tinsley-Colbert, the first elected as clerk of the town of Babylon; Veron Walter, Bethel member since 1947; Michelle Woodard, the first female lawyer elected as a judge of the state supreme court from Long Island; Rev. Charles A. Coverdale, pastor of the First Baptist Church of Riverhead; and Gwendolyn L. Brown, president of the Central Suffolk Branch of the National Association for the Advancement of Colored People (NAACP). (Courtesy of Joe Turner.)

As chairman of the Black Democrats of the town of Babylon, Eugene Burnett has he helped shape the course of political events in the area. The Burnett family has been on Long Island for many, many years. (Courtesy of Joe Turner and Eugene Burnett.)

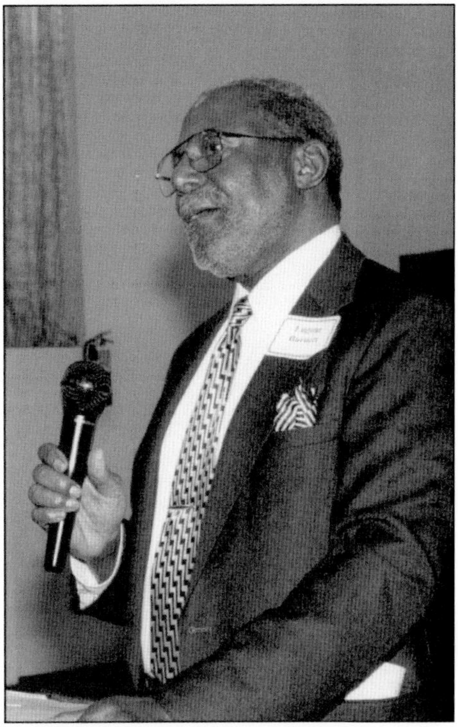

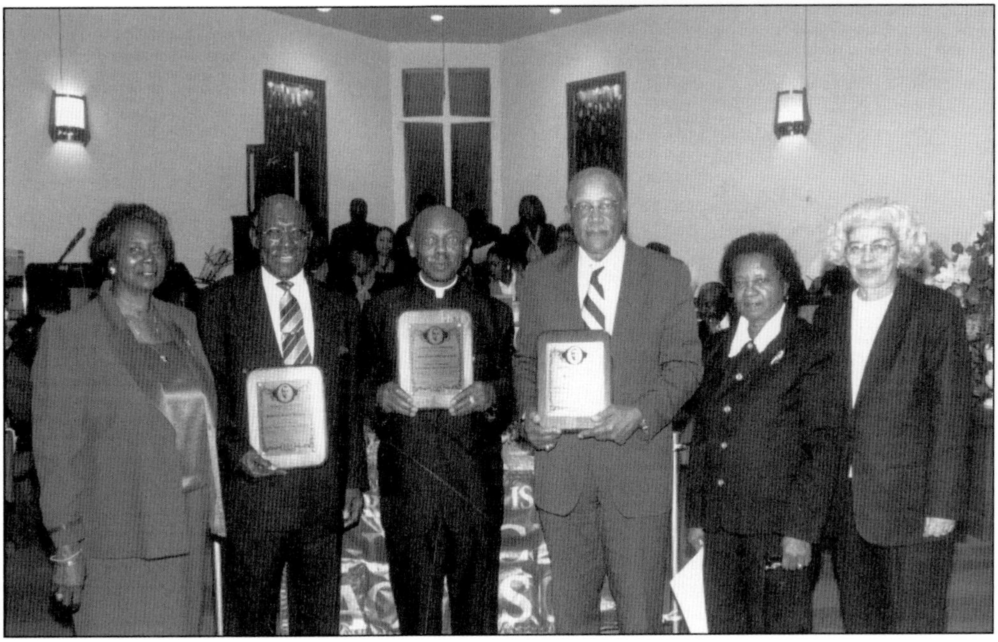

Participants celebrate the NAACP's 54th anniversary and Freedom Fund program at Grace Community Church. From left to right are Gwendolyn L. Brown; Rev. Robert L. Burgess, pastor of Grace Community Church; Rev. Dr. Eugene H. Purvis, pastor of Grace Community Church; Rev. Shaw Temple of the African Methodist Episcopal Zion Church; Judge Floyd, the first African American supreme court judge; and Louise Jones and Dolores Quintyne of the membership appeal and awards committee. (Courtesy of Joe Turner.)

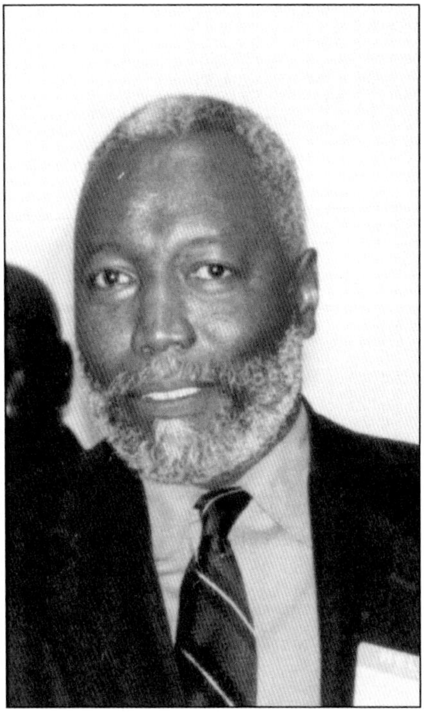

Wendell Cherry serves as the director of the Wyandanch Public Library. Selected to head the library, he started it in the basement of the Lutheran church until a new building was constructed in 1985 and his dream for Wyandanch came true. (Courtesy of Wendell Cherry.)

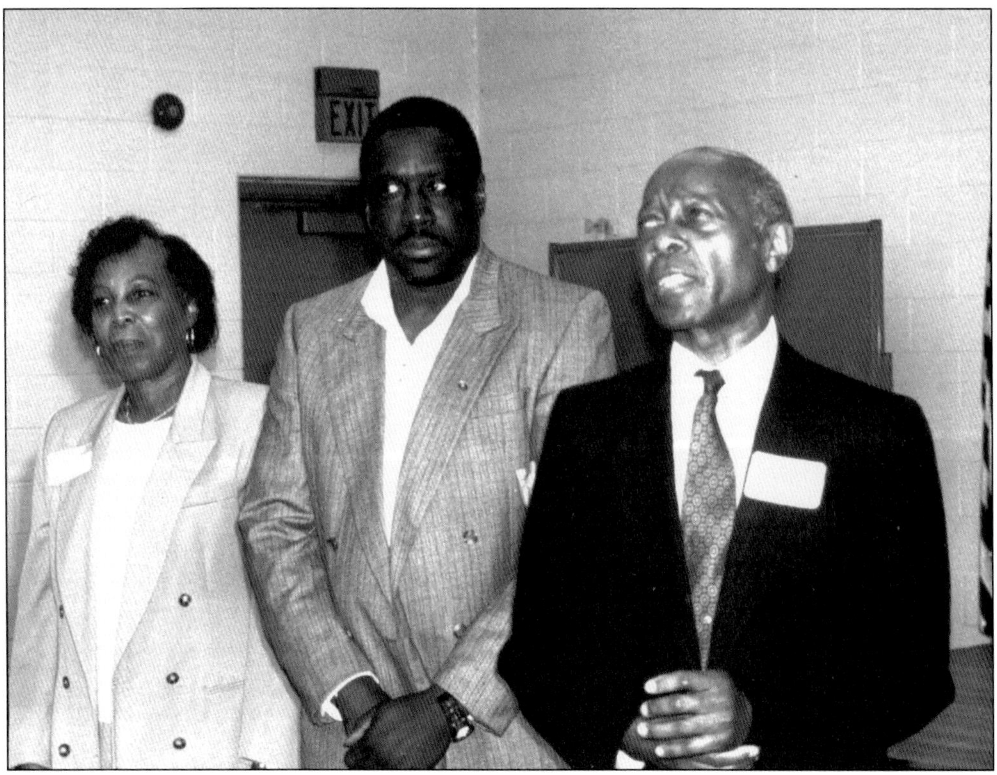

The three original trustees of the Wyandanch Public Library are Geraldine Diggs, Joseph P. Horton, and Kenneth Hobbs. (Courtesy of Wendell Cherry.)

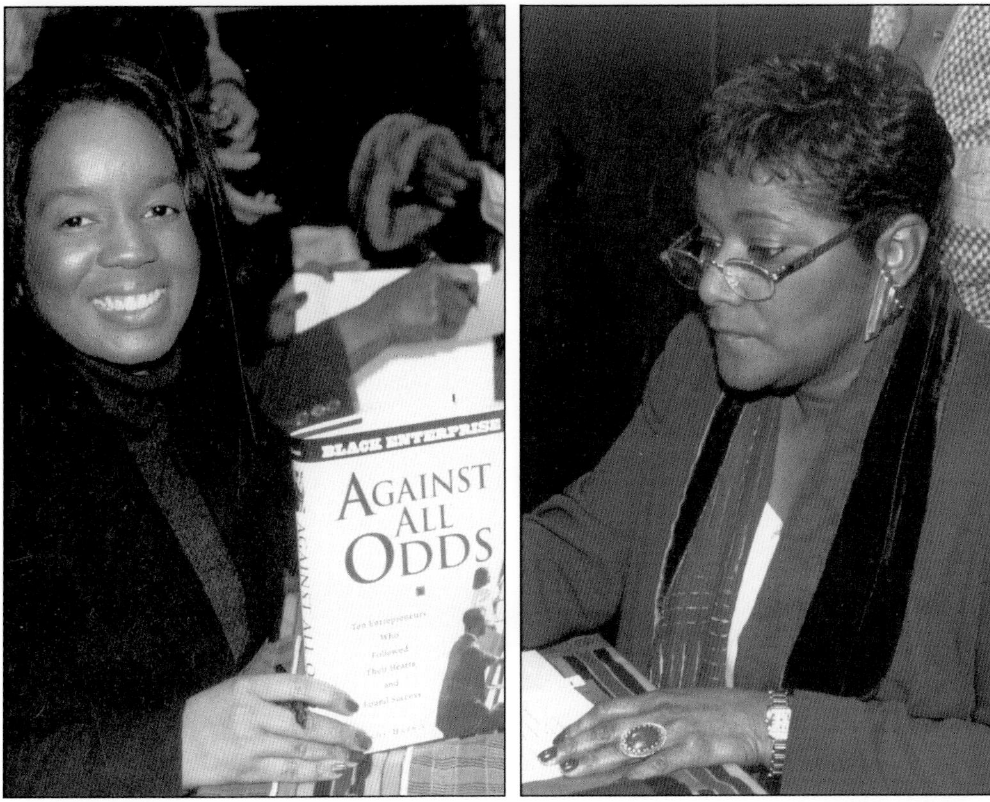

Attending a North Amityville Youth Organization event are Wendy Harris (left), author of *Against All Odds*, and Vera Moore (right) of Vera Moore Cosmetics, who was the keynote speaker. (Courtesy of Joe Turner.)

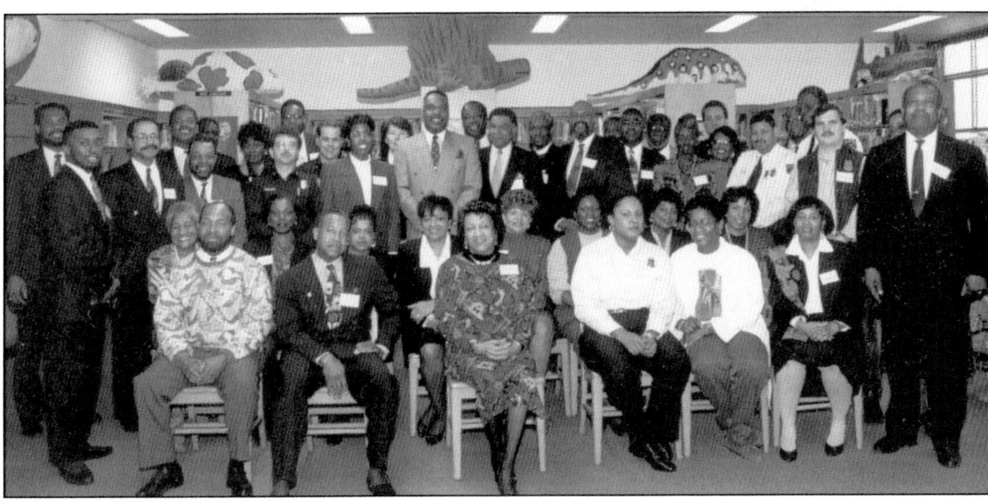

John Jackson (center), one of the first middle school principals in the area, shares Career Day with staff and students. (Courtesy of Joe Turner)

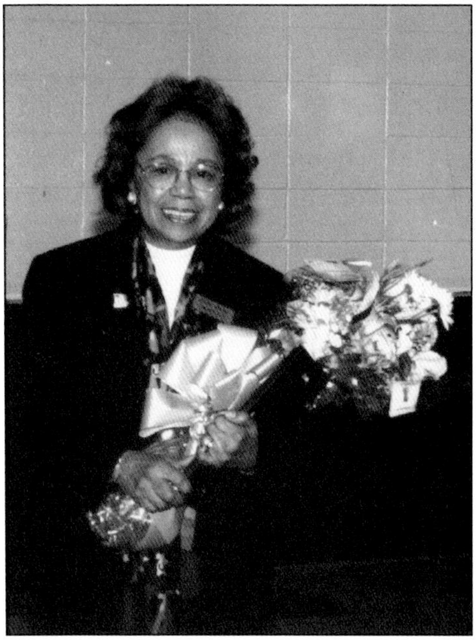

Mildred Browne is the current president of the Copiague Board of Education, on which she has served for more than 20 years. She is the recipient of the Council of Administrators and Supervisors (CAS) Award. She is also on the board of the Western Suffolk BOCES, of which she is a past president. She first became involved in serving on the board in 1958 and, since then, has become a very committed leader. The mother of one son and three daughters, she has seven grandchildren and one great-grandson. (Courtesy of Kathy Beatty, Syntax Communication.)

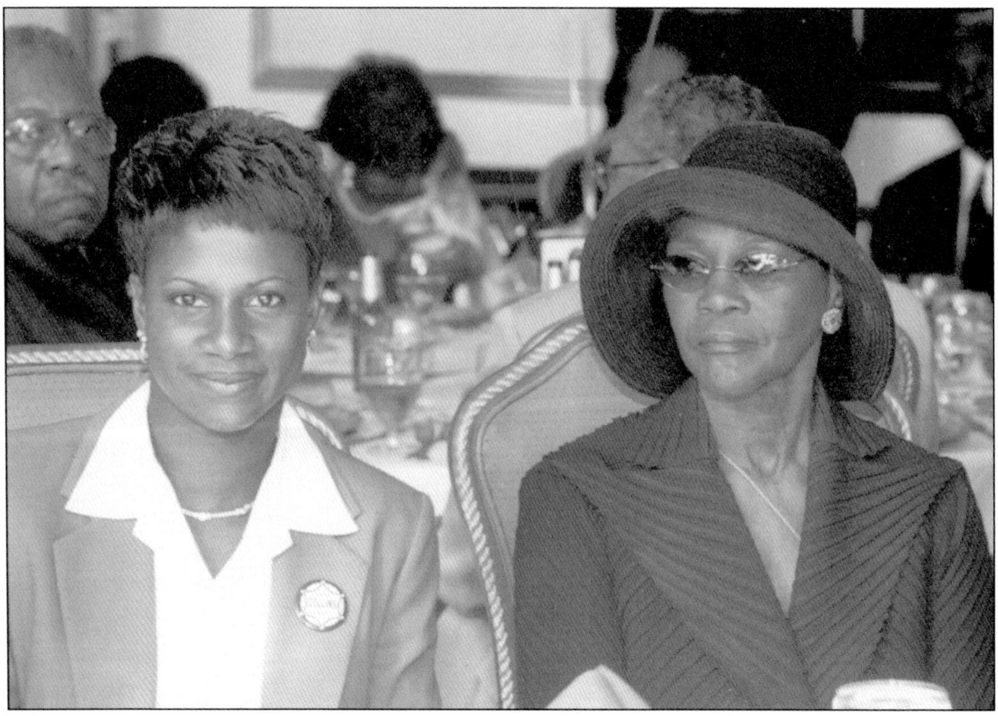

Attending a Links Inc. dinner and recognition ceremony are Felicia Collins (left), a police officer who ran for Suffolk County sheriff, and actress and celebrity Cicely Tyson. Each was first in her respective pursuit. (Courtesy of Joe Turner.)

Six

Islip to Bay Shore
Expectation and Endeavor

African Americans have lived in Islip for centuries. Although the exact figure remains unknown, some historical accounts indicate that some were in Islip by the 1700s. Most were slaves who served masters, working on farms or in factories. By the mid-1800s, however, many arrived in the Islip area in quest of greener pastures, first as migrant workers and later as settlers. The perception that segregation and discrimination were much less of a problem in the North partly spurred that movement. Additionally, Islip's proximity to New York City and the relative peace and calm that characterized the town provided incentives for migrants.

Between the 1900s and the 1950s, the migration peaked. Some of the newcomers settled in Bay Shore, Brentwood, Central Islip, and East Islip. A few built houses in the neighboring towns of Sayville, Ronkonkoma, and Oyster Bay. By the end of World War II, they had established a foothold and integrated themselves into all sectors of the community. This was evident in the growth and development of churches in the area.

Today, African Americans have made modest strides in all social, cultural, and economic sectors. Lawyers, doctors, engineers, accountants, educators, politicians, and pastors participate in the decision-making processes in their respective communities. Indeed, Joan Johnson made history when she emerged as Central Islip's first African American town clerk in the 1990s. Yet, the numbers of successful professionals are still few and far between, as people continue to face housing, employment, health, and other socioeconomic challenges.

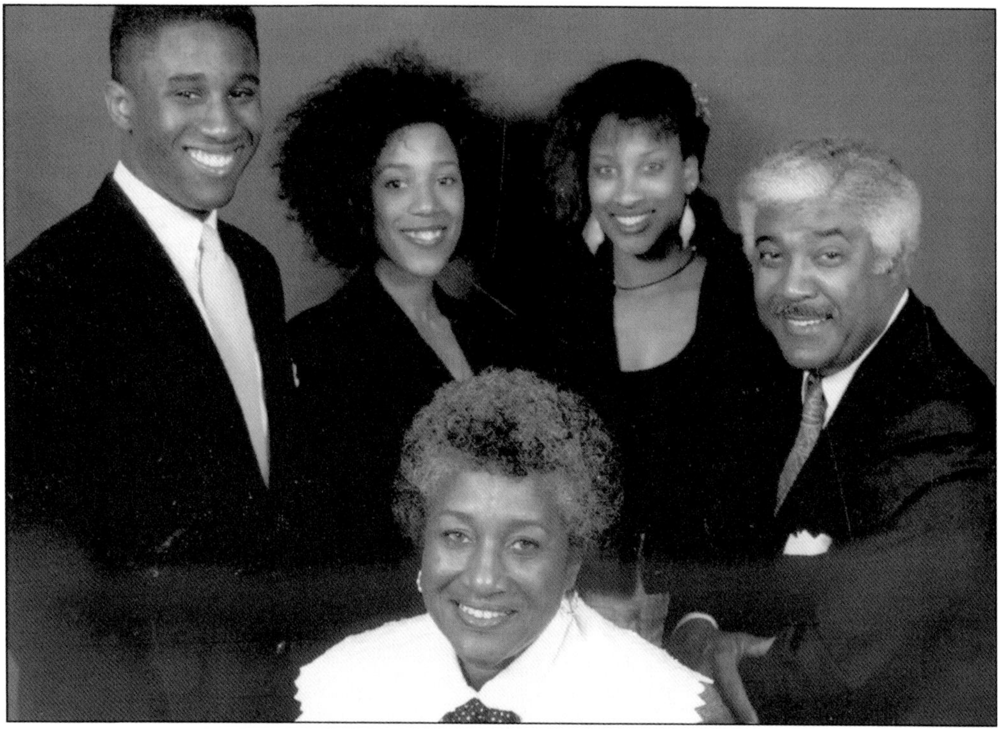

The honorable Joan B. Johnson (front) was the first African American appointed town clerk in Islip in the 1990s. In 1993 and 1995, she ran and won reelection, emerging as the first African American ever elected to office in Islip's 311-year history. More recently, she became the first African American female to run for Congress on a Republican ticket in the nation's history. She earned a master's degree in social work from Stony Brook University in 1977. She is married to Cleveland Johnson Jr. (right), who was the first African American deputy county executive on Long Island. Pictured with their parents are the Johnson children, from left to right, Cleveland II, Genevieve, and Kelly. (Courtesy of Joan and Cleveland Johnson.)

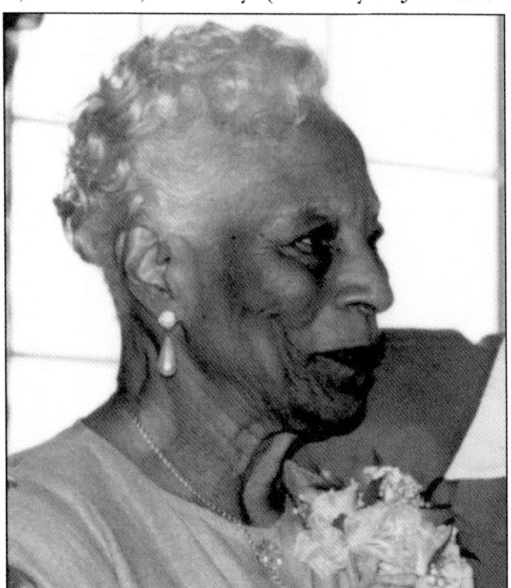

Mother Omega Pope is a well-respected educator and leader at the Bay Shore African Methodist Episcopal Church. She made a name for herself as the founder of one of the first African American nursery schools on the Long Island. (Author's collection.)

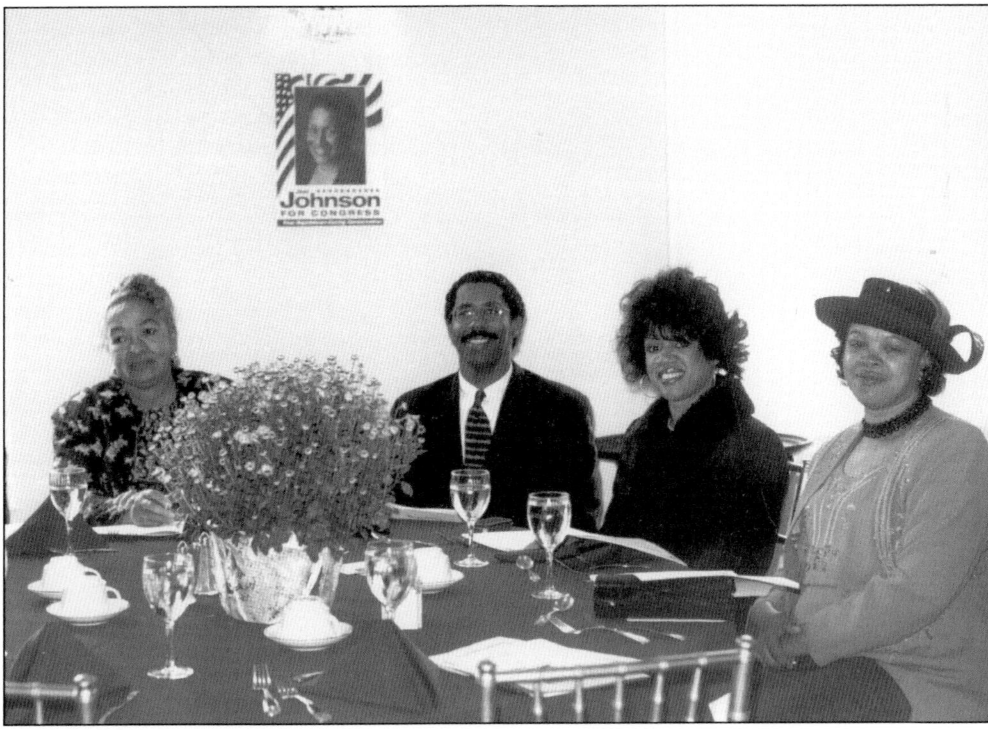

Seated together are some longtime area residents. From left to right are Beverly Thomas, Rodney Smith, Evelyn Smith, and Leona Johns. (Author's collection.)

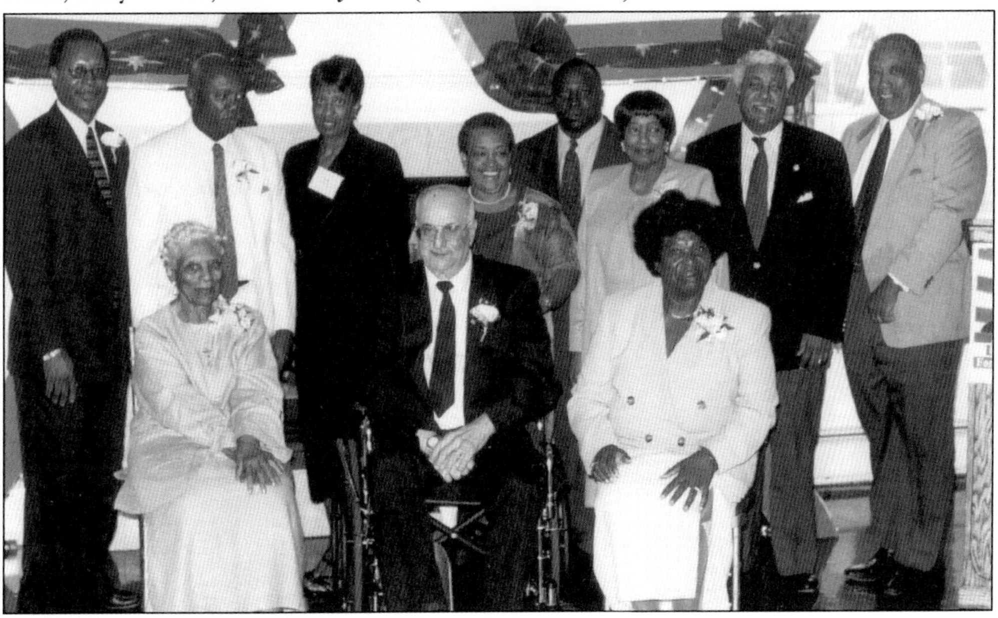

This awards ceremony was organized by the Frederick Douglass Club and the Central Long Island Republicans in Bay Shore. From left to right are the following: (front row) Omega Pope, Francis Duck, and Rachel Davis; (back row) James Buie, Rev. Radford, Gail Alleyne, Genevieve Durant, Michael Williams, Jean Payne, Cleveland Johnson, and unidentified. (Author's collection.)

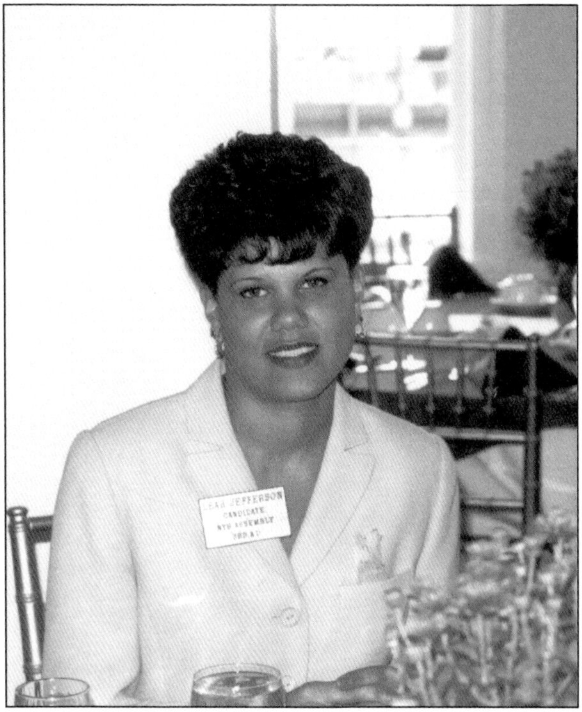

Lea Jefferson worked with former Congressman Michael Forbes of Long Island. She also ran for the Suffolk County legislature. She is a member of the Jefferson family of Long Island. (Author's collection.)

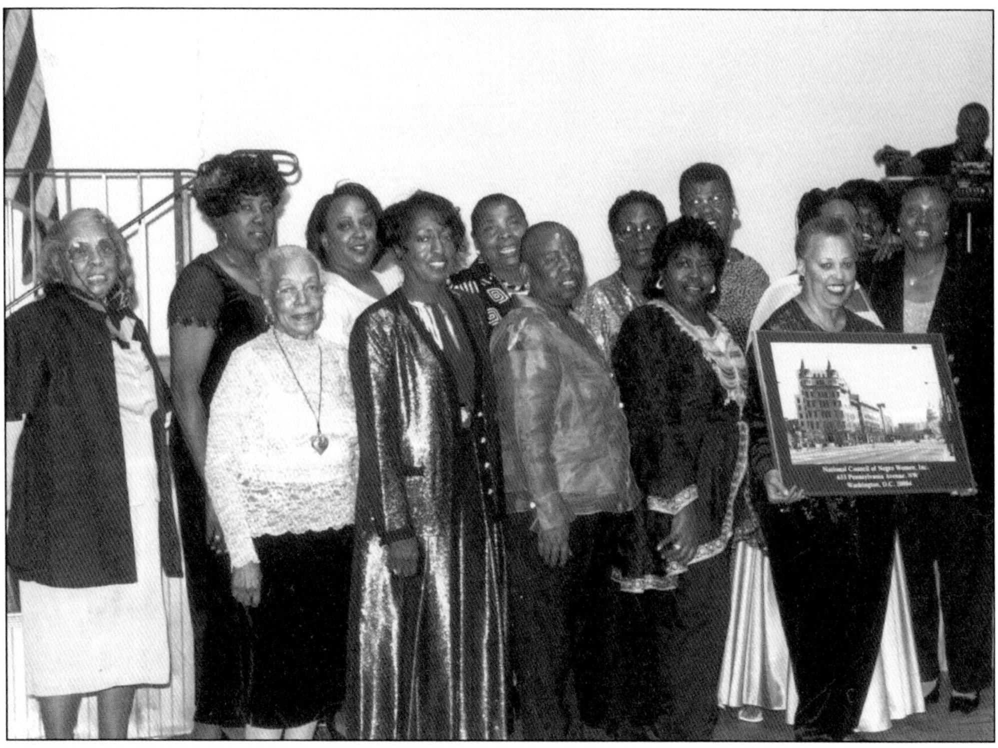

Members of the National Council of Negro Women of Suffolk County pose for a picture. Their organization holds special events and assists in voter registration. These women are from the neighboring areas of Bay Shore, Brentwood, Bellport, and Amityville. (Author's collection.)

Myrtle Bradshaw was one of the first African American school principals on Long Island. She taught for several years before becoming a principal. Active in the church and the community, she serves as president of the National Council of Negro Women of Central Long Island. (Author's collection.)

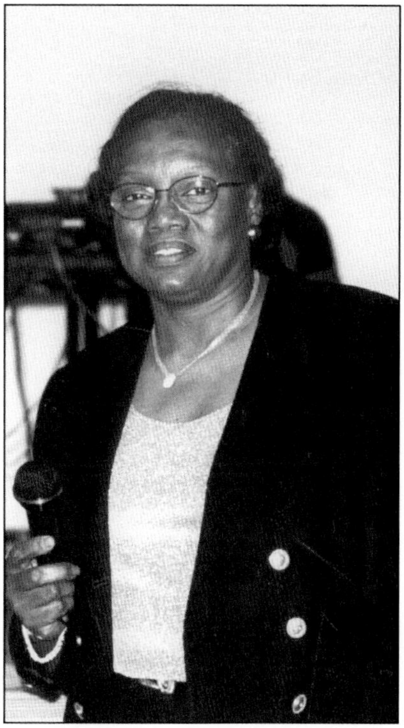

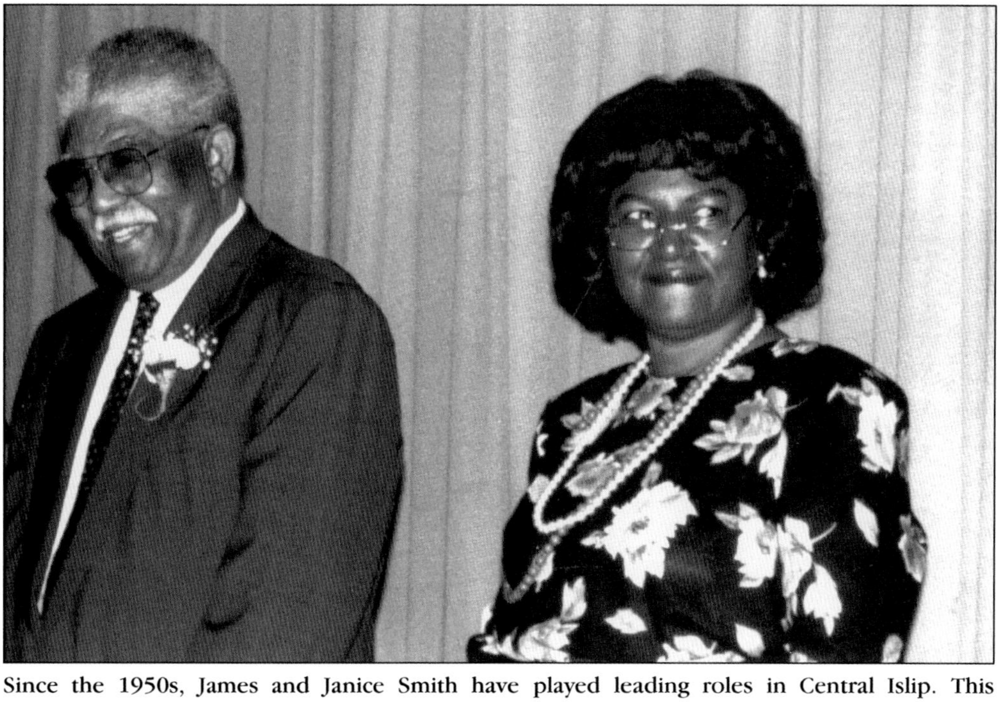

Since the 1950s, James and Janice Smith have played leading roles in Central Islip. This photograph was taken during a ceremony to honor James Smith upon his retirement from the construction industry. Smith played a leading role in mobilizing African Americans for self-help projects. Janice Smith worked with the library and was active in the community. (Courtesy of James and Janice Smith.)

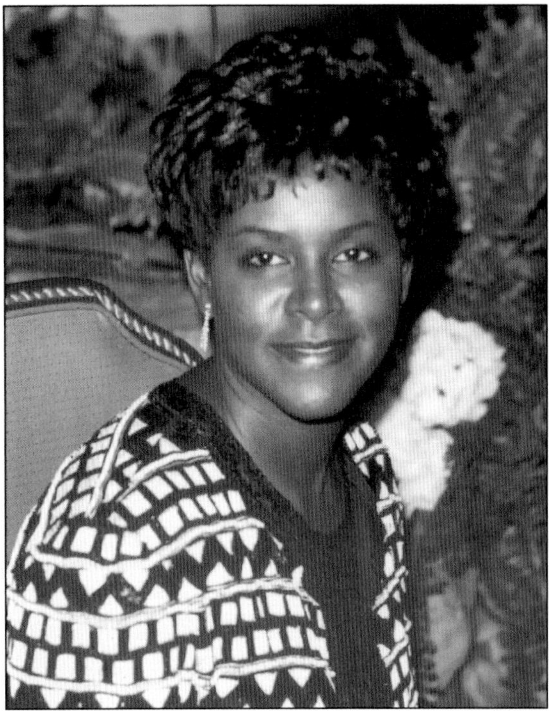

Bridget Wilson is one of the first African American school principals on Long Island who was born and raised in the area. After teaching and rising to the rank of vice principal in Mattituck, she was appointed a principal in the Central Islip School District. She holds bachelor's and master's degrees. (Author's collection.)

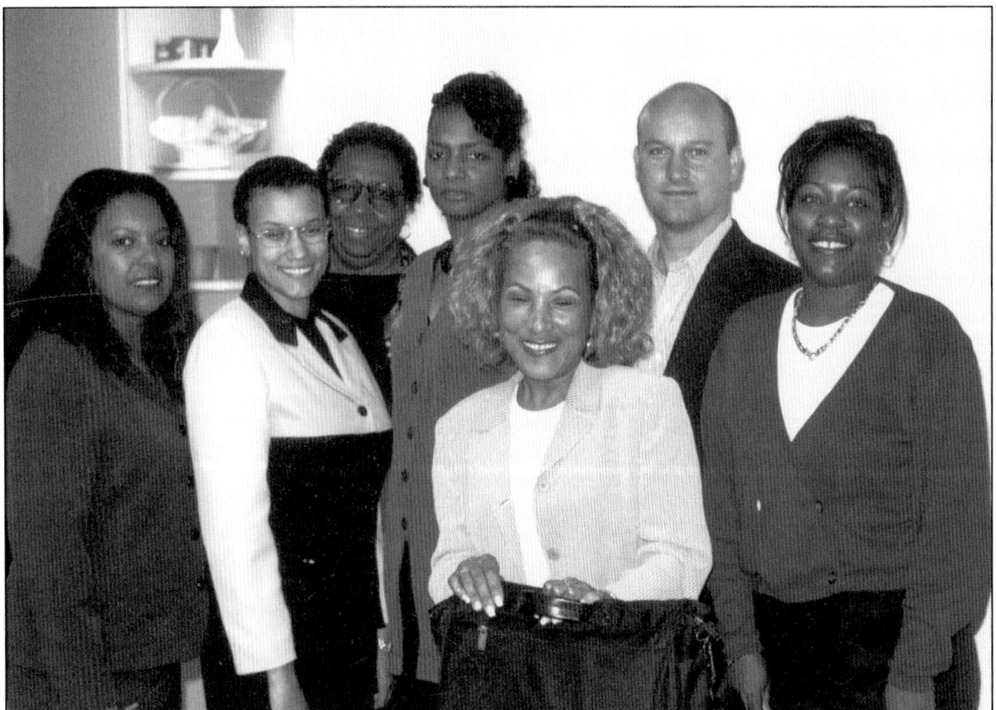

East and Central Long Island educators and community leaders discuss the prospects and challenges of a charter school for Long Island. At the far right is Teresa Sanders, director of the Urban League of Long Island, headquartered in Central Islip. (Author's collection.)

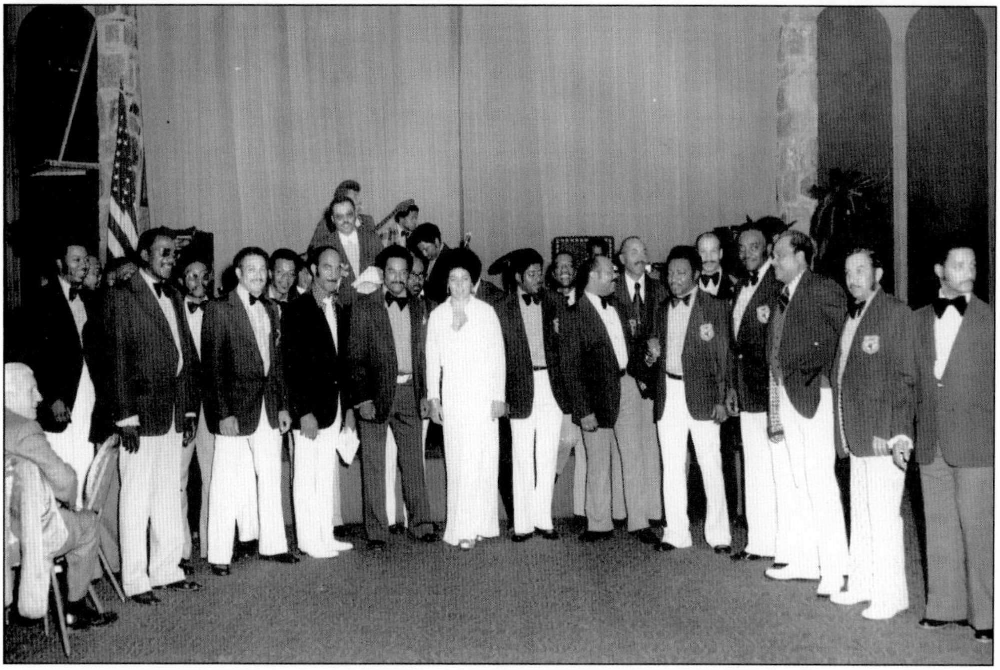

The Long Island Guardian's Association is shown in 1970. Founded in 1960, this group of Suffolk County police officers promoted good relationships with colleagues, organized social functions, and awarded scholarships. The first president was officer Wes Delay. (Courtesy of the Thomas family.)

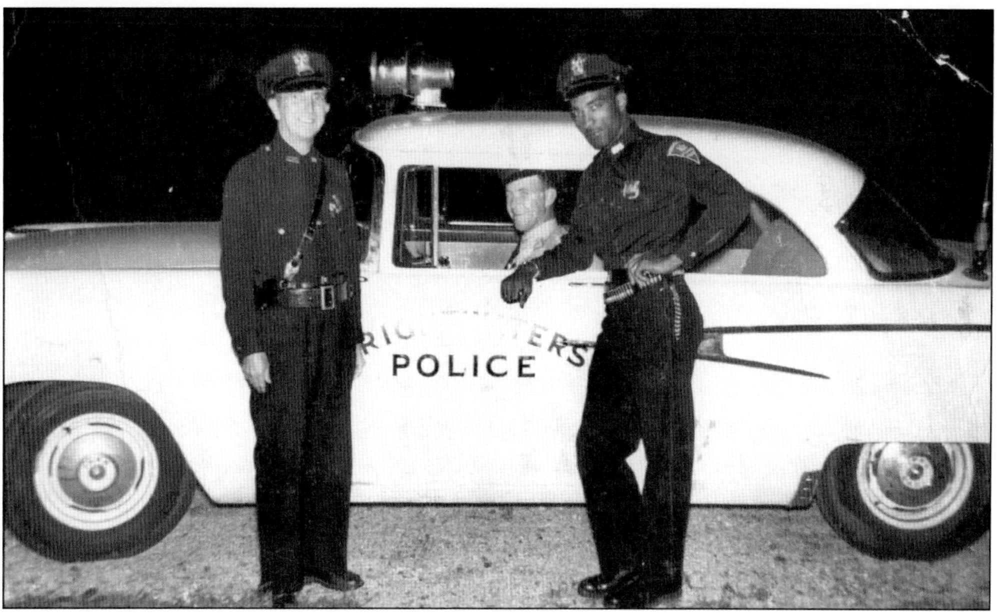

John Thomas (right) of Bay Shore was the first African American police officer in the town of Islip. Pictured in uniform with two fellow officers *c.* 1960, he was the son of Edna and George Thomas. He was born and raised in Bay Shore and attended Bay Shore High School. He and his wife, Beverly Daniels Thomas, lived on Harrison Avenue and raised four children. (Courtesy of the Thomas family.)

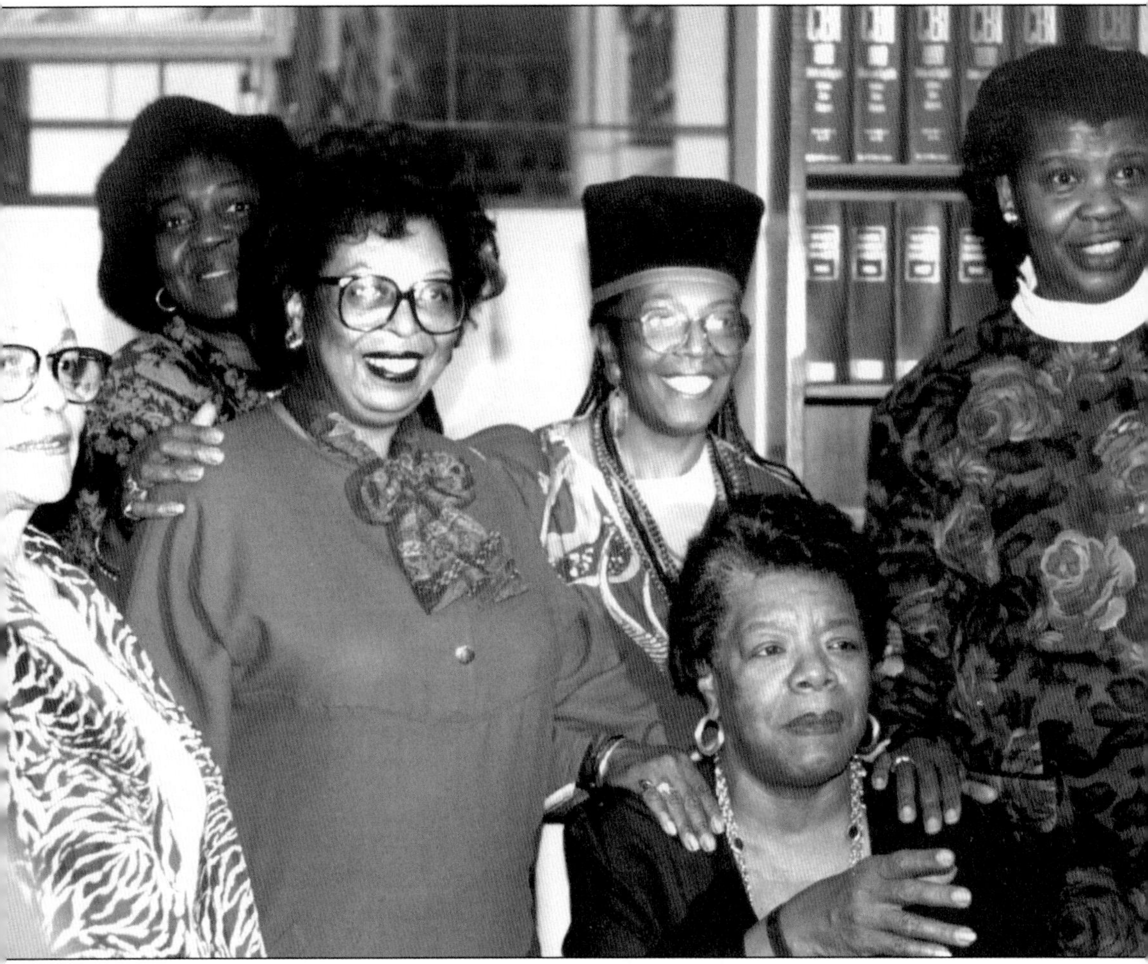

Poet Maya Angelou (second from right) visits with a group of Bay Shore women. From left to right are Helen Hamilton, Minell Wilson, Lillie P. Bowles, Frances Bell, and Jessie Ladsen. (Author's collection.)

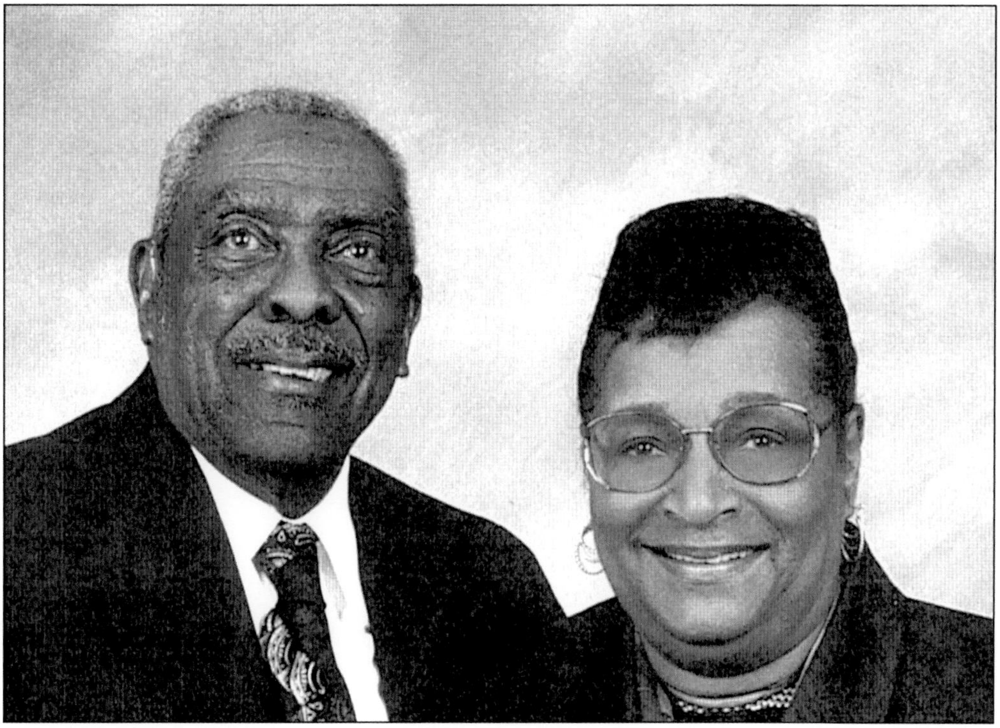

Louis and Eva Townsend are from families who settled in Central Islip *c.* 1932. The Townsends have contributed much to the educational, economic, and cultural life of the community. (Courtesy of the Townsends.)

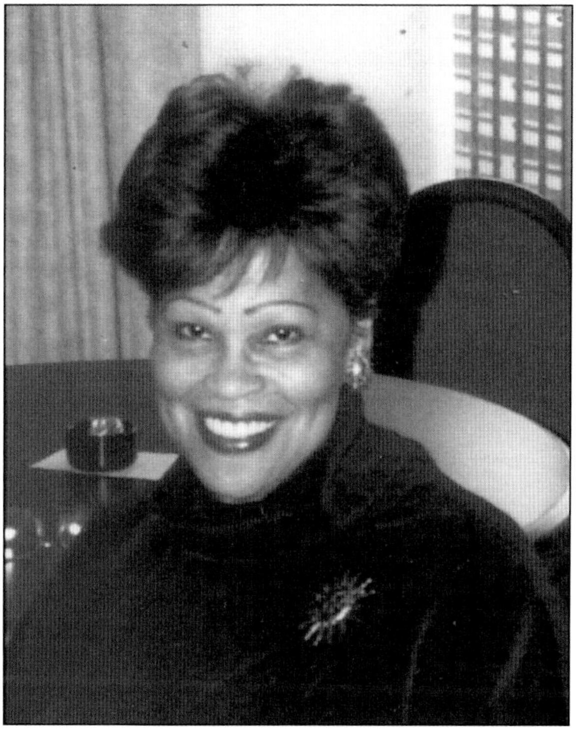

Miriam D. Couch was one of the first African American teachers in the town of Islip. She is a respected educator, mentor, and community leader. Her daughters are Jamir R. Couch, a Yale graduate, and Sasha D. Couch, a University of Renna political science graduate.

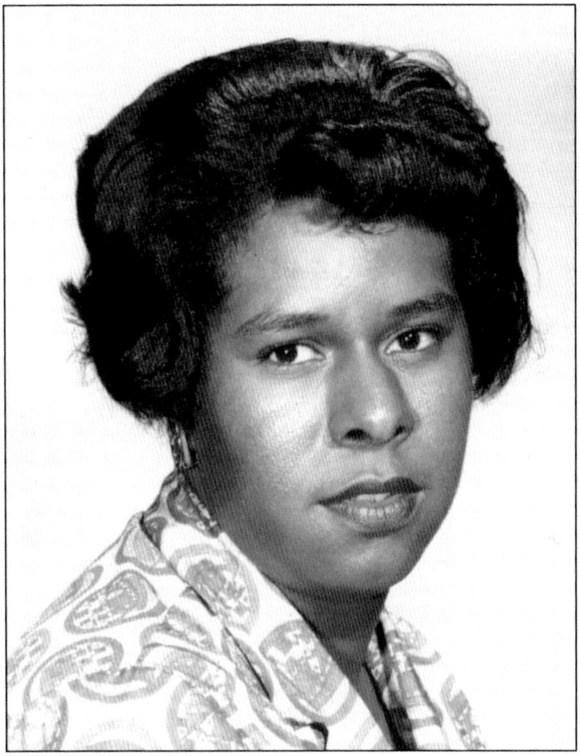

M. Maclin was one of the first African American teachers in Central Islip. After earning her bachelor's degree, she got a job with the school system and served for over three decades. She lives in Central Islip and is an active member of New Hope Baptist Church. (Courtesy of M. Maclin.)

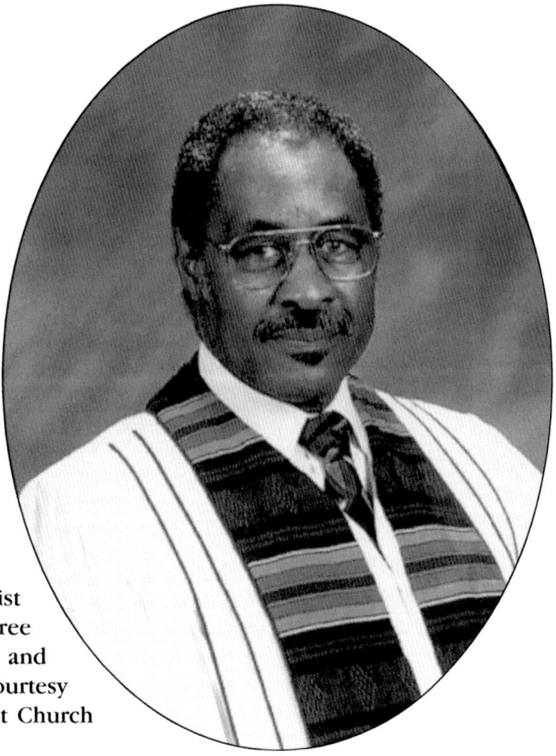

Rev. Albert Brown has served the First Baptist Church of Bay Shore for more than three decades. As pastor, he heads the church and participates in community activities. (Courtesy of Rev. Albert Brown and the First Baptist Church of Bay Shore.)

In 1997, John Smith became the first African American principal of Central Islip High School. He worked his way up, having served as a guidance counselor from 1978 to 1997 and as assistant principal from 1993 to 1997. Previously he served as a New York corrections officer from 1973 to 1976 and in the U.S. Air Force from 1965 to 1969, achieving the rank of sergeant. He holds bachelor's and master's degrees and certification in counseling and administration. (Courtesy of John Smith.)

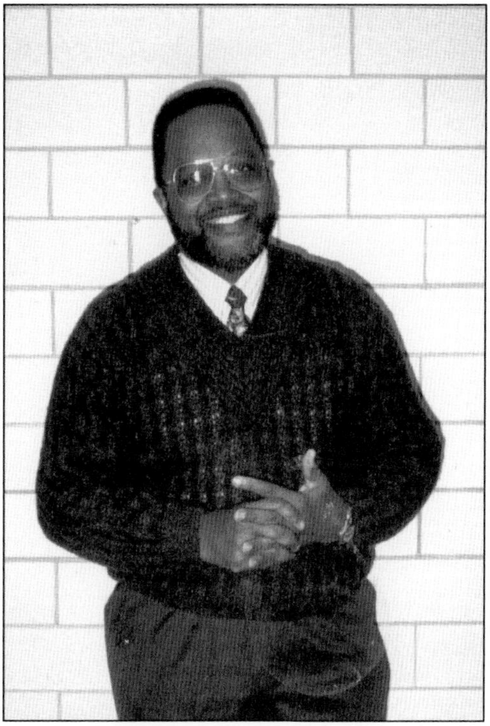

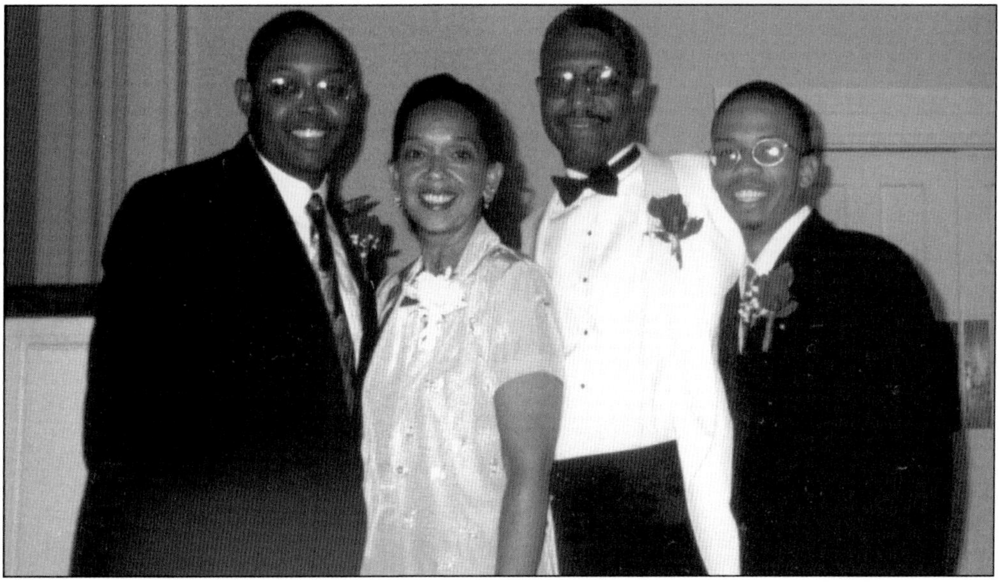

Jerry Watkins (third from left) was born in Hopkinsville, Kentucky, in 1950, the second child of 13. His family moved to Central Islip in 1965. After graduating from Central Islip High in 1968, he attended Ottawa University on a music and athletic scholarship, graduating in 1973 with a bachelor's degree in biology and education. In 1995, he was one of 24 educators chosen to study DNA and molecular genetics. Today, he works with city schools in developing DNA science curriculums in their mentor schools in New York City. He is married to Shinita E. Watkins (second from left) and is the father of two sons, Jermel, a research specialist, and Justin, a university student. (Courtesy of the Watkins family.)

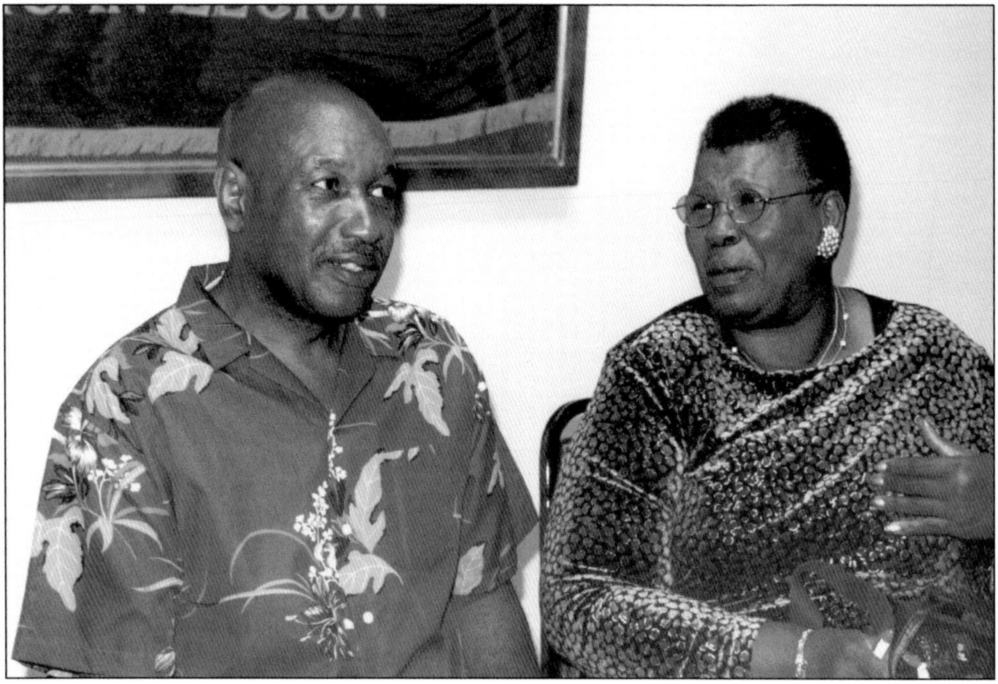

Moses Green (left) discusses issues in Bay Shore with Jessie Ladsen. A prominent educator, Green has served in the Bay Shore school system for several years and is known throughout the region for his commitment to youth development. (Author's collection.)

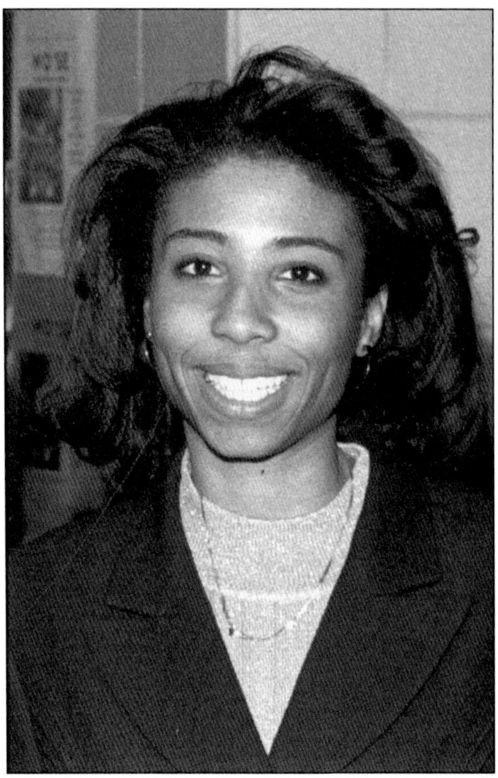

Christie Thomas is one of the first African American women to serve as the director of Suffolk County Department of Women's Affairs. She holds bachelor's and master's degrees and previously served as special adviser to the county supervisor on minority affairs. She is a strong advocate for women's issues on Long Island. (Courtesy of Christie Thomas.)

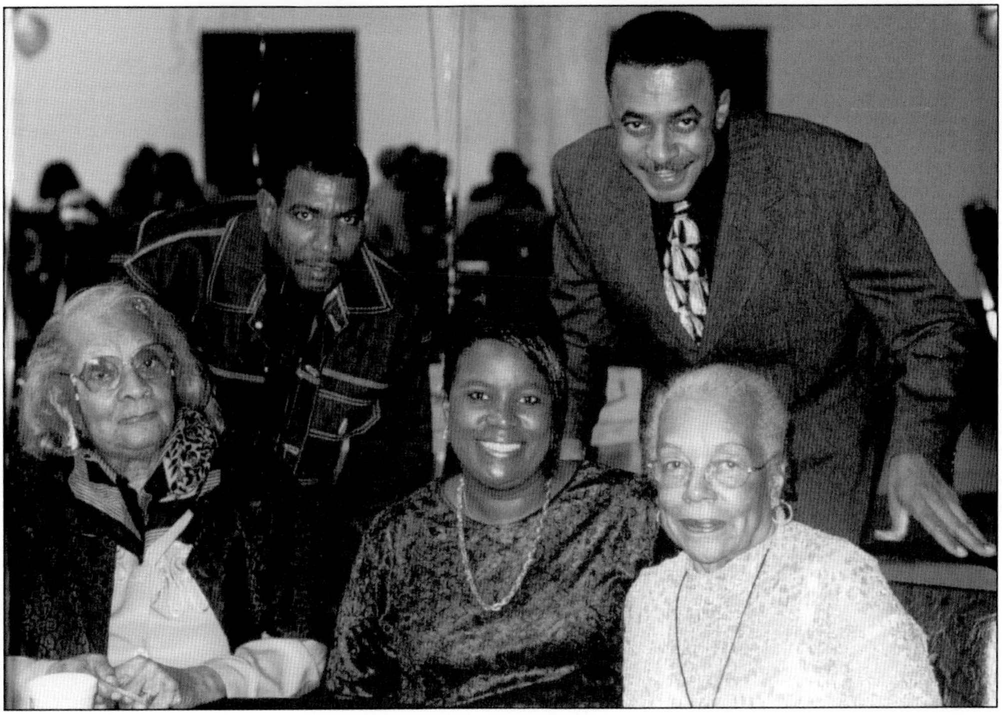

Helen Hamilton (right) resides in Bay Shore, attends First Baptist Church, and participates in club and community activities. Her career includes social work with senior citizens in New York City. Among those pictured with her is Alice Smith (left). (Courtesy of Helen Hamilton.)

Helen D. Taylor-Brannon was one of the first African American educators and school administrators on Long Island. She served the Islip School Board for 16 years. Her undergraduate degree is in business administration and education, and her graduate degrees are in special education and elementary education. She also has postgraduate certification in school administration. She is pictured with her grandchildren Trent and Taylor Stewart. (Courtesy of Helen D. Taylor-Brannon.)

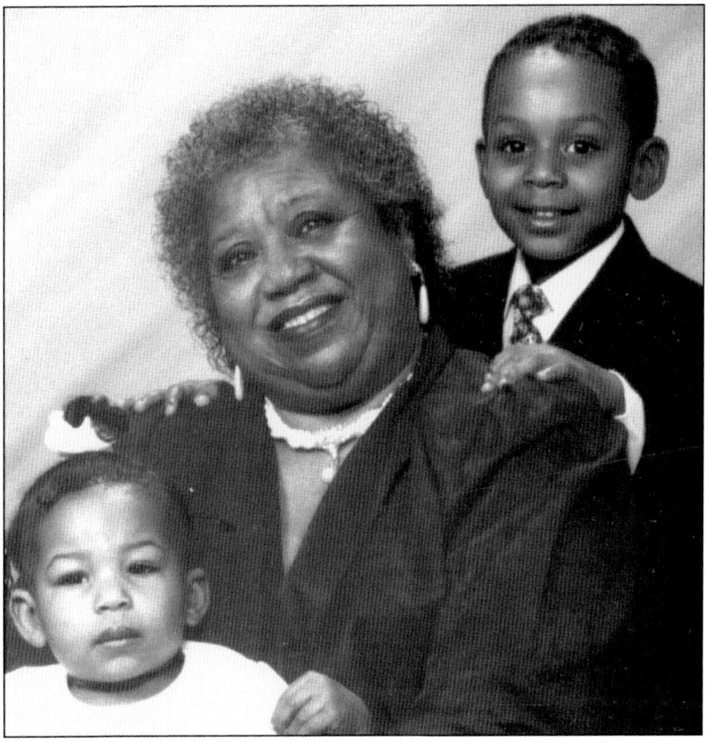

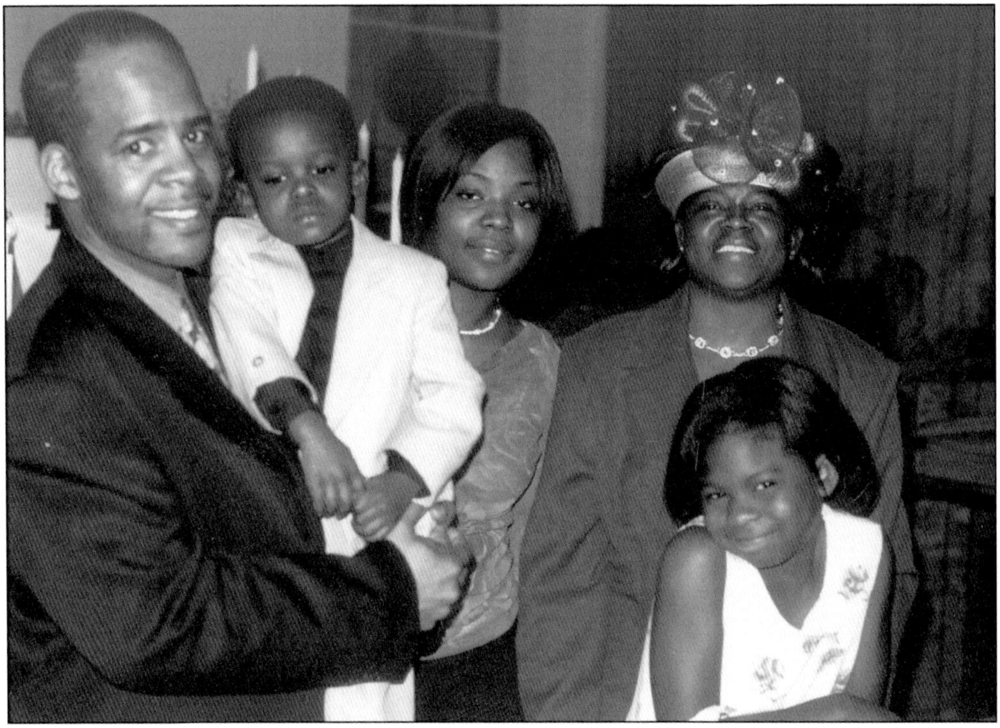

Rev. Leonard A. Edwards stands with his wife, Rev. Kathey N. Edwards, and children. The pastor of the Brentwood African Durham Methodist Episcopal Zion Church, he is active in the community and throughout Long Island.

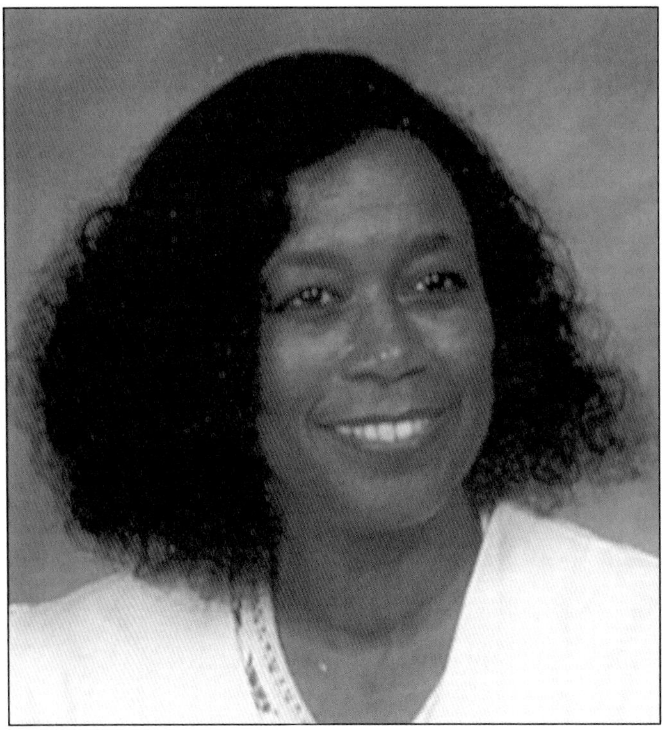

Leila Holmes is an educator in Brentwood and the pianist at the First Baptist Church of Bay Shore. Her family has been part of the area for many years. (Courtesy of Rev. Albert Brown and the First Baptist Church of Bay Shore.)

Seven

Stony Brook to Setauket
Charm and Choice

Toward the middle of Long Island are cities such as Stony Brook, Smithtown, Center Reach, Center Moriches, Brookhaven, and Setauket. Each of these settlements has a unique history and its own historical buildings, churches, museums, libraries, and landmarks. A common feature is the existence of excellent schools. The State University of New York at Stony Brook, with its Science and Medical Schools and School of Social Work, attracts students from all parts of the world. Similarly, Suffolk County Community College is fast becoming an important professional training center.

In this region, African Americans live in clusters. Some reside in Stony Brook, Smithtown, Center Reach, and Bellport. Like elsewhere on the island, migration occurred in phases, with the third phase encompassing professionals and well-to-do people searching for a better place to make a home and raise a family. These communities are benefiting from the contributions of African American educators, lawyers, nurses, doctors, engineers, accountants, pastors, musicians, and business executives.

This is a tranquil area of parks, shops, churches, and woodlands. Yet, MacArthur Airport, in Central Islip, and the ferry in Port Jefferson facilitate mobility. For those who can afford the amenities, the region provides relief from urban congestion and noise, although other challenges still remain.

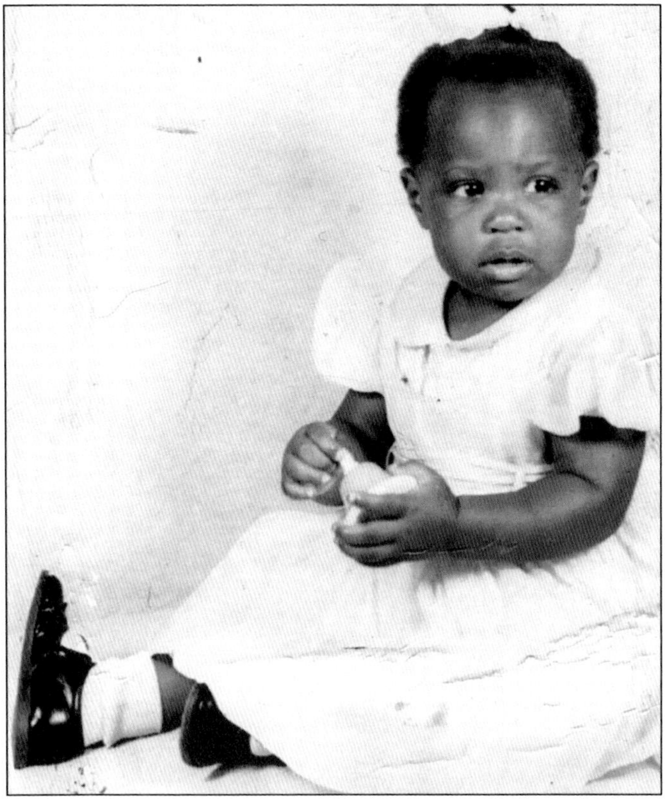

Joanne E. Braxton is currently the executive dean at Suffolk County Community College, Brentwood campus. A seasoned educator and administrator with bachelor's and master's degrees, she has also held the post of provost and has served the college for more than two decades.

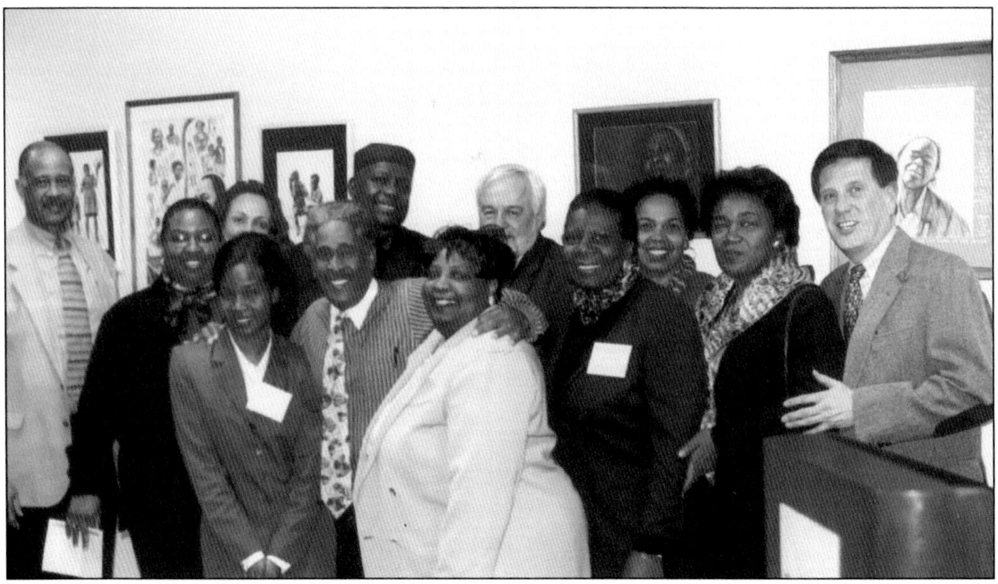

African American deans, senior administrators, professors and college authorities of Suffolk County Community College gather for photograph. Among those pictured are Dean Randy Manning (left) and the executive dean of the Brentwood campus, Joanne Braxton (front, center).

Darlene H. Shervington is one of the leading African American opera singers on Long Island. After earning undergraduate degrees in music and social work, she studied for a master's degree in social work. She has given concert tours throughout Europe, Korea, and the United States, performing at places such as Lincoln Center and the Academie de Musique in Paris, France. (Courtesy of Darlene Shervington.)

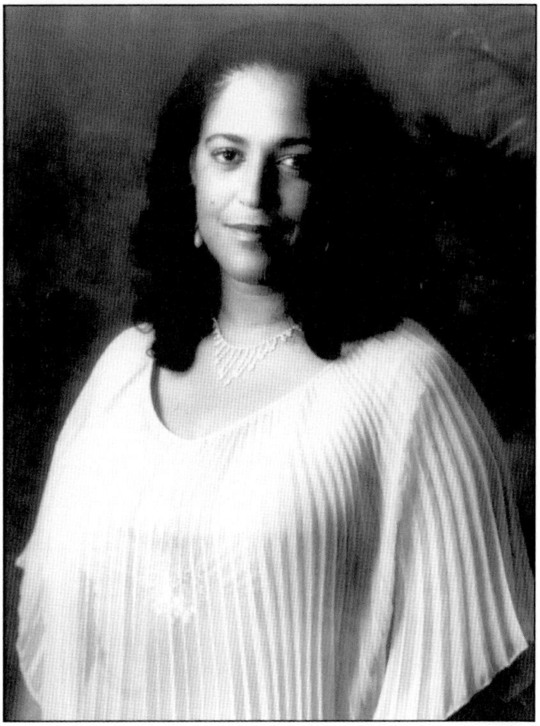

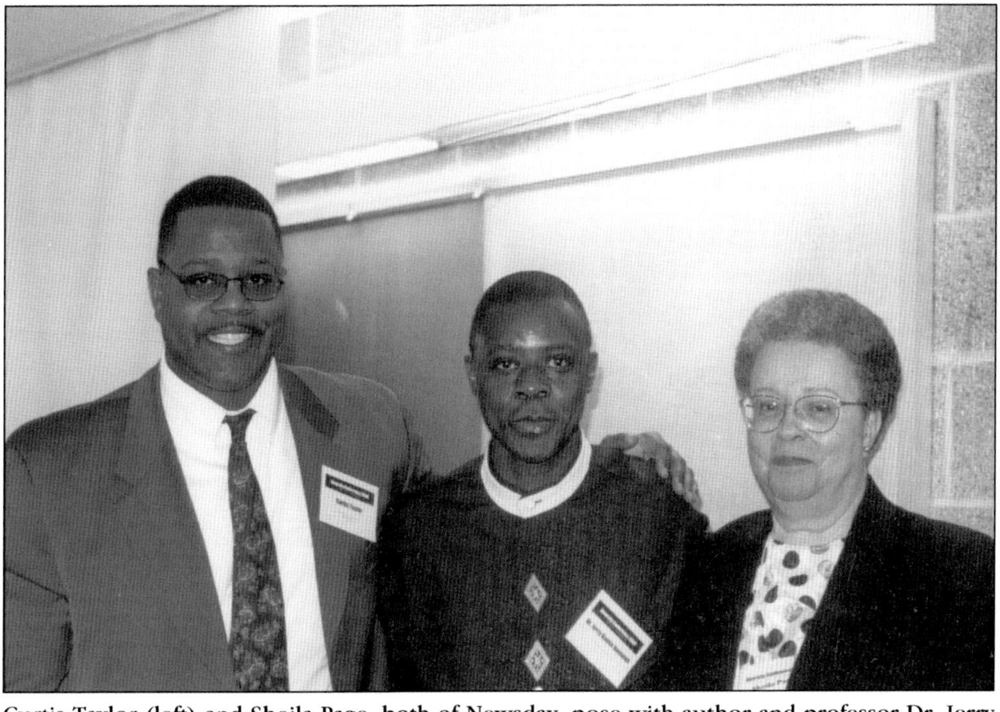

Curtis Taylor (left) and Sheila Page, both of Newsday, pose with author and professor Dr. Jerry Komia Domatob for a photograph at Stony Brook University during Diversity Week Celebrations. Sheila Page is the community affairs officer for Newsday. She was the founder of the group 100 Black Women. Taylor is a reporter with Newsday. (Author's collection.)

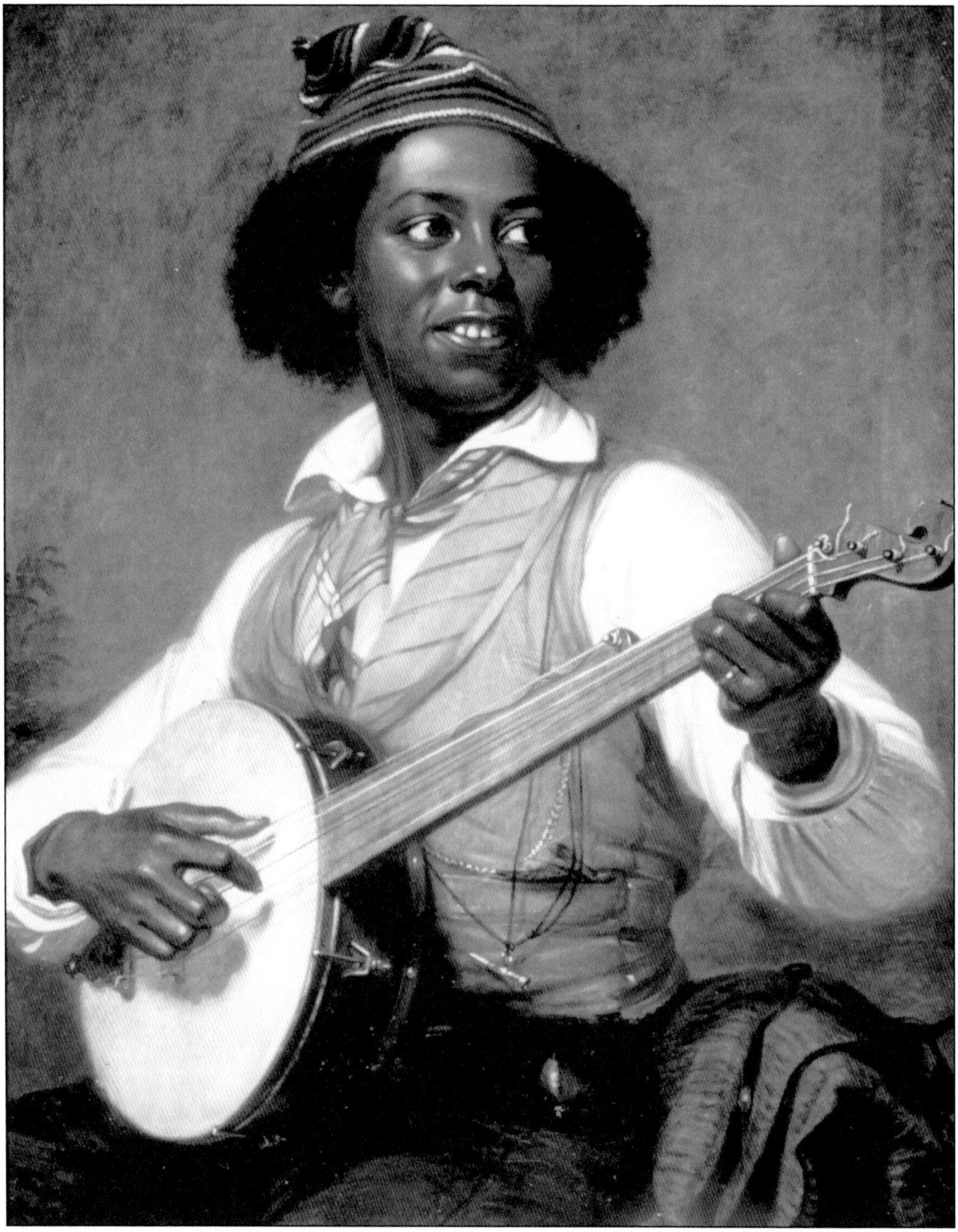

Stony Brook Museum introduces observers to one of the great artists who painted African American portraits. William Sidney Mount (1807–1868), who lived in the area, did this classic painting of a banjo player in 1856. (Courtesy of the Stony Brook Museums.)

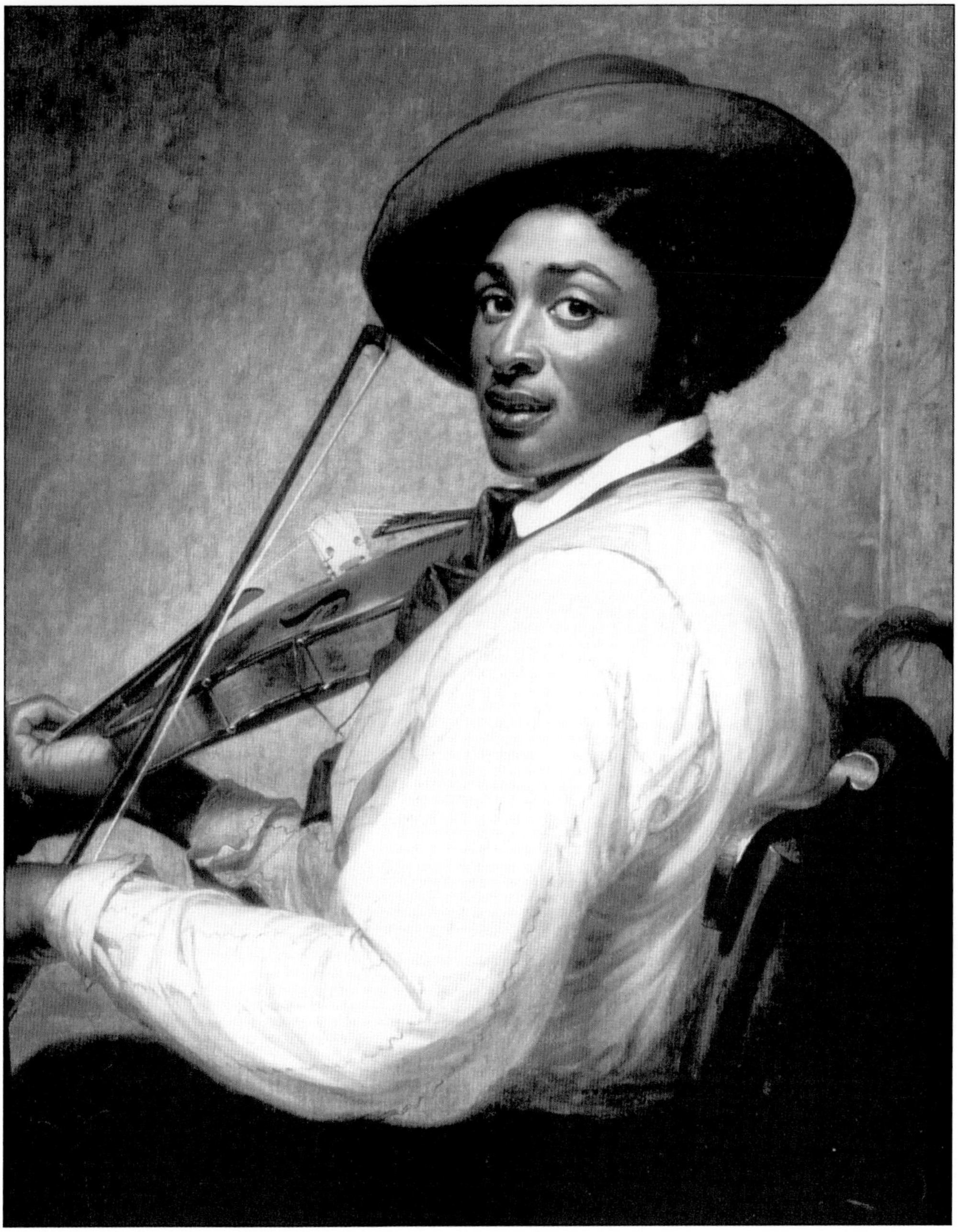

William Sidney Mount also painted the left-handed fiddle player. Some historians contend that this painting and the previous one were sent to Paris for lithographic reproduction. The two works are described as "Right and Left 1856." (Courtesy of the Stony Brook Museums.)

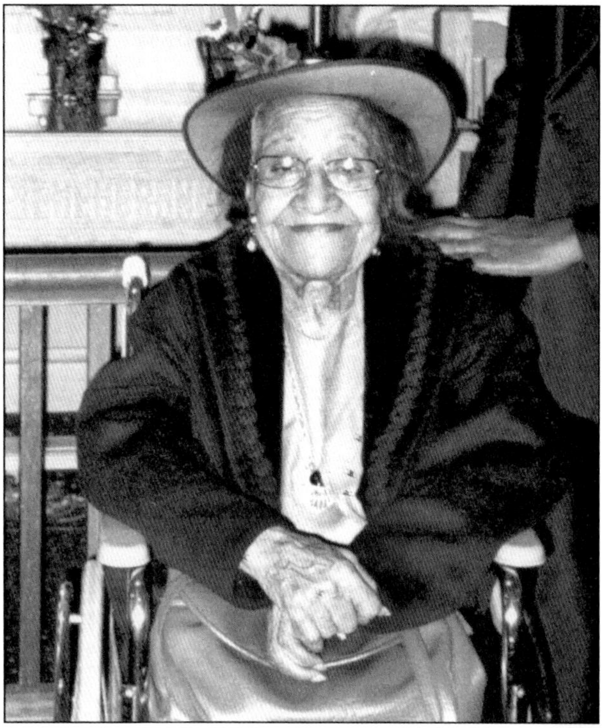

Caroline Moore is the church mother of the Bethel African Methodist Episcopal Church in Setauket. The church, established in the early 1800s, is said to have been one of the first African American churches on Long Island. (Courtesy of Rev. Leonard of Setauket AME Church.)

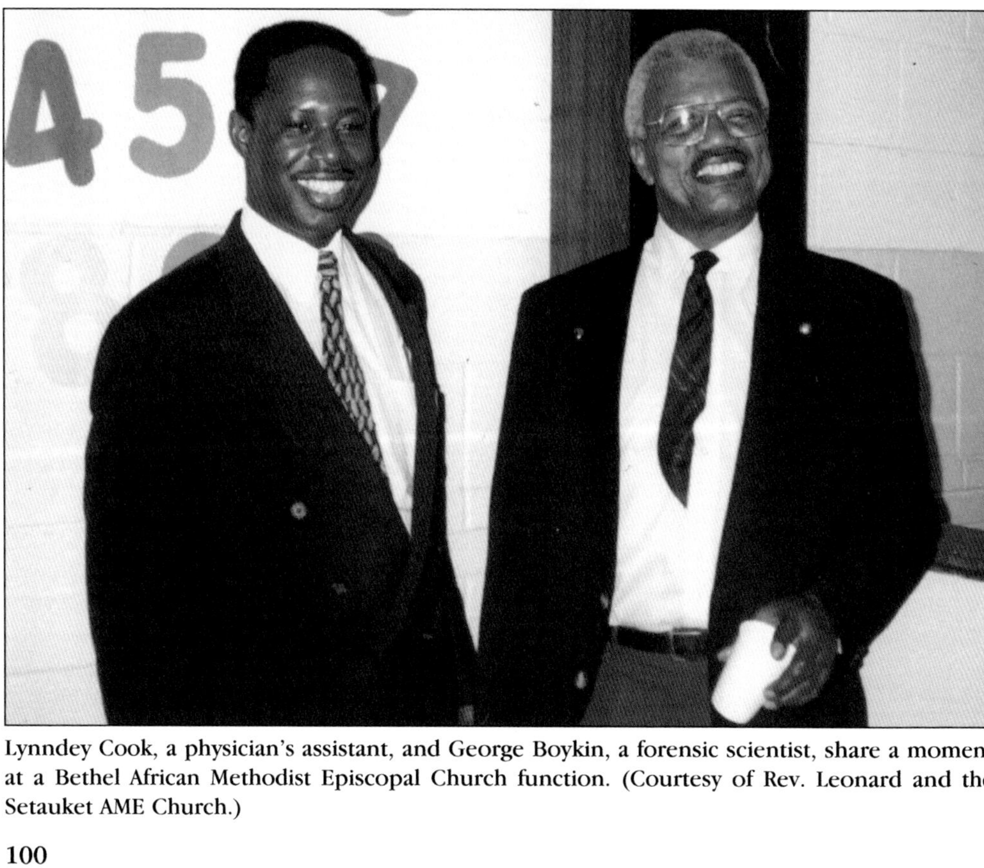

Lynndey Cook, a physician's assistant, and George Boykin, a forensic scientist, share a moment at a Bethel African Methodist Episcopal Church function. (Courtesy of Rev. Leonard and the Setauket AME Church.)

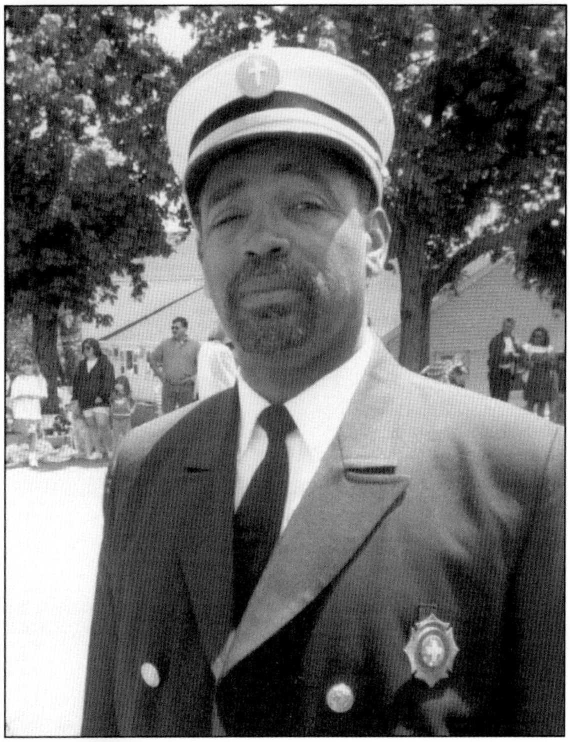

Rev. Gregory Leonard serves not only as pastor of the Bethel African Methodist Episcopal Church in Setauket but also with the local fire department. A community-oriented individual, he provides assistance wherever his services are needed. (Courtesy of Rev. Leonard and the Setauket AME Church.)

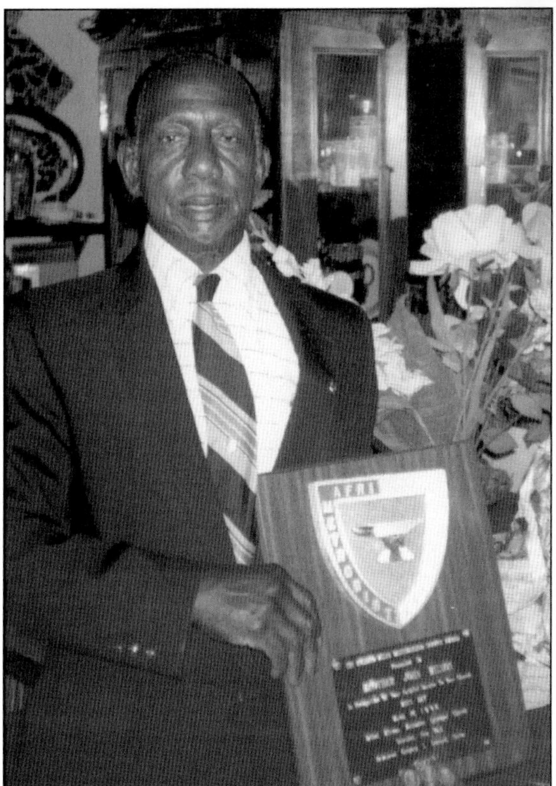

George Wilson is a church steward who has lived in the area for decades. (Courtesy of Rev. Leonard and the Setauket AME Church.)

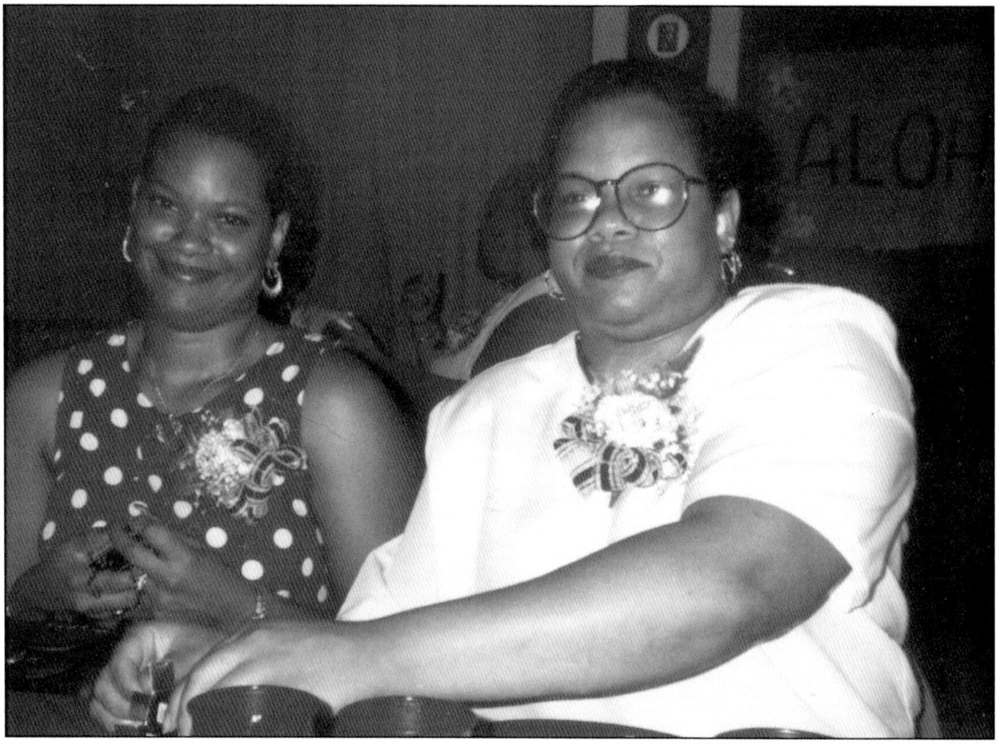

The Calvin twins are active in church and community affairs. Their family has lived in this area of Long Island for some time. (Courtesy of Rev. Leonard and the Setauket AME Church.)

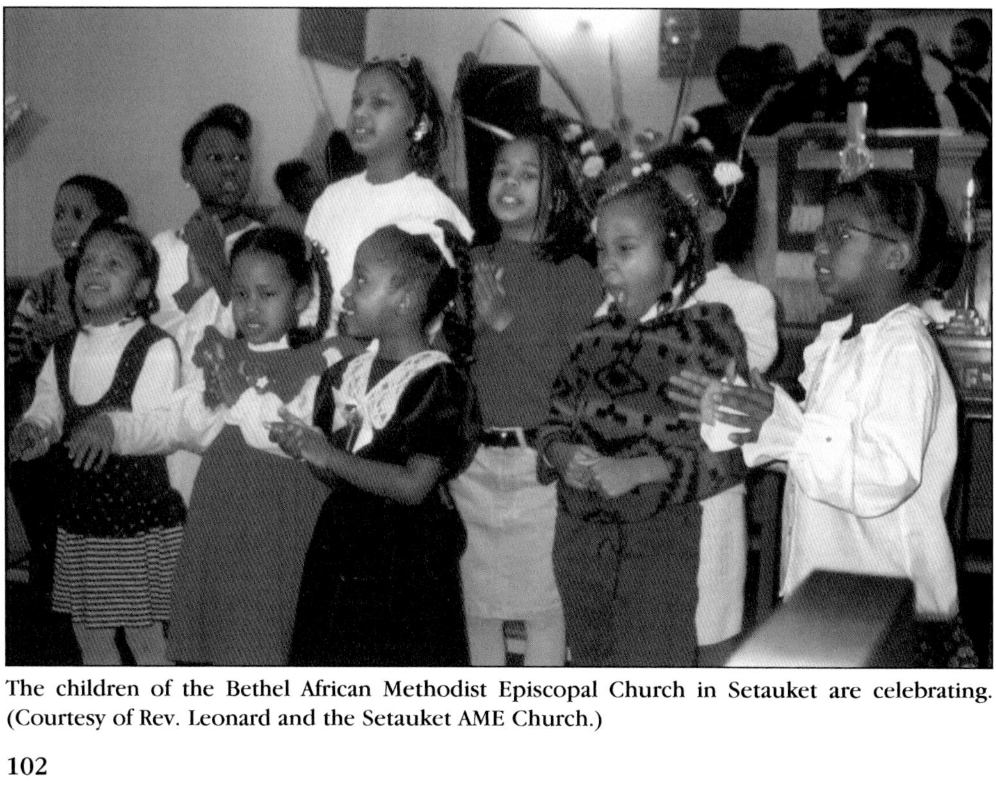

The children of the Bethel African Methodist Episcopal Church in Setauket are celebrating. (Courtesy of Rev. Leonard and the Setauket AME Church.)

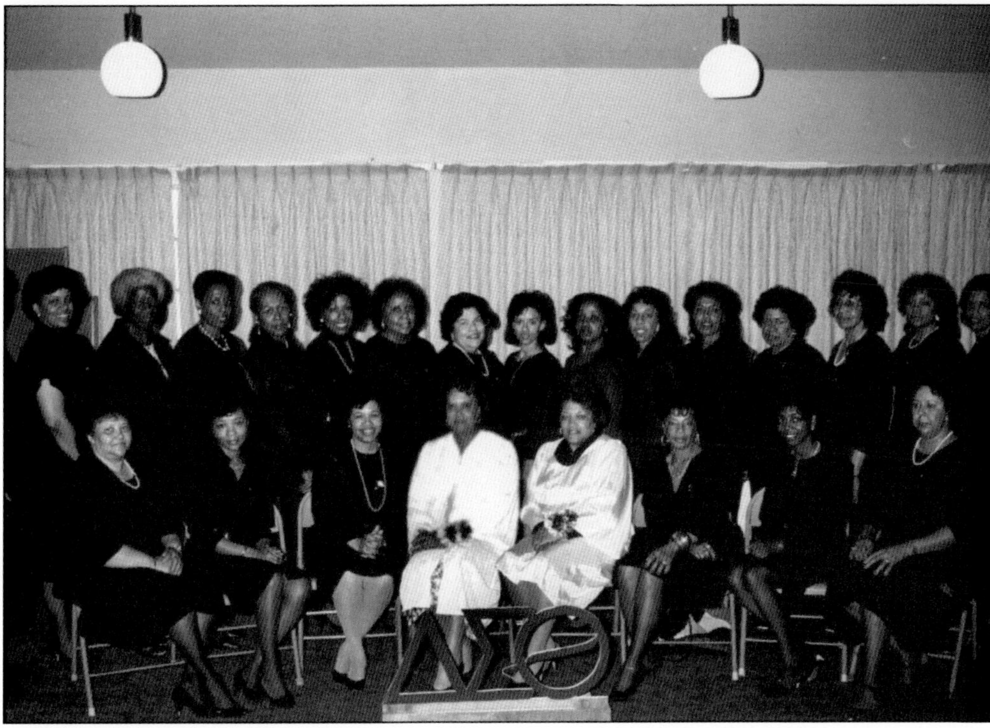

Shown are members of the Suffolk County Alumnae Chapter of the Delta Sigma Theta Sorority. They include women who have distinguished themselves in various spheres of human endeavor. (Courtesy of Claire Conquest and the Suffolk County Alumnae Chapter, Delta Sigma Theta Sorority Inc.)

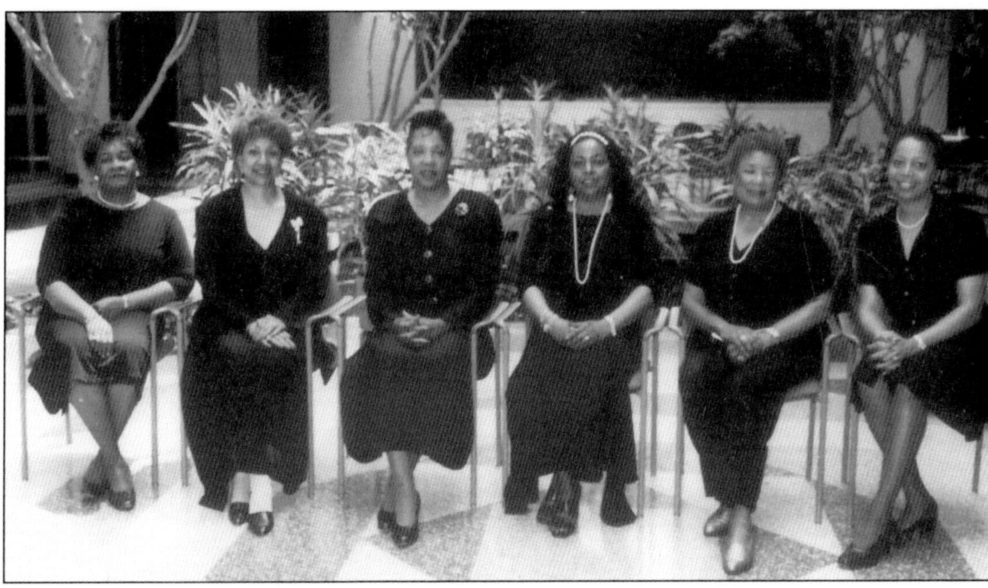

The leaders of the Suffolk County Alumnae Chapter of the Delta Sigma Theta Sorority pose for a picture. (Courtesy of Claire Conquest and the Suffolk County Alumnae chapter, Delta Sigma Theta Sorority Inc.)

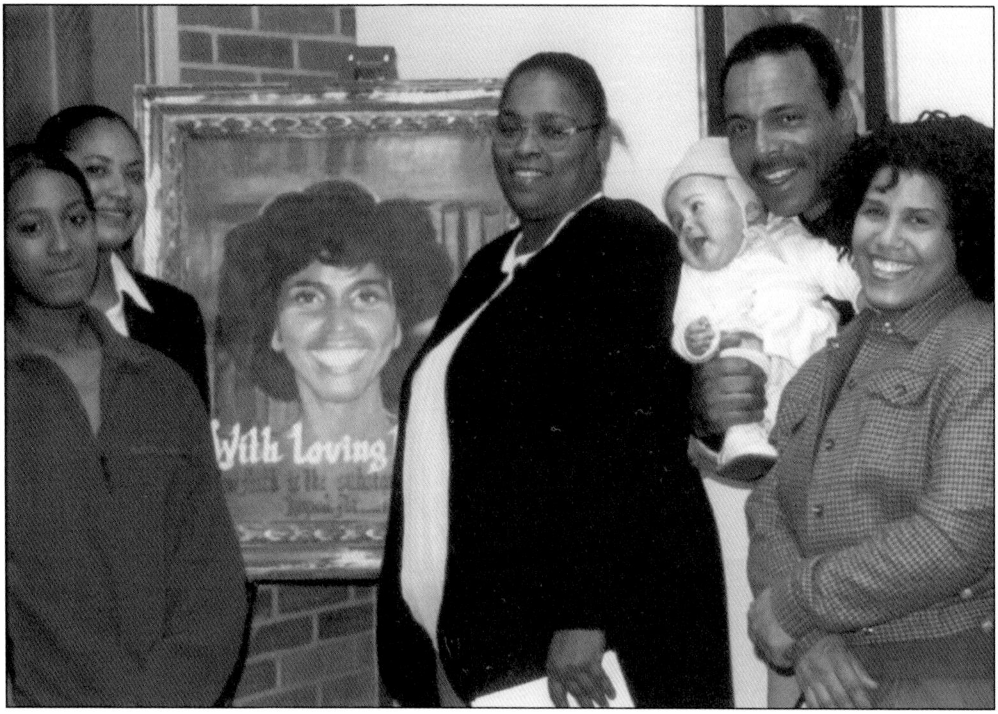

Mildred Green (in the framed portrait) was the first African American instructor at Suffolk County Community College. She taught mathematics and endeared herself to her students and colleagues. A room at the college was named after her posthumously. Shown at the naming ceremony are members of her family. (Author's collection.)

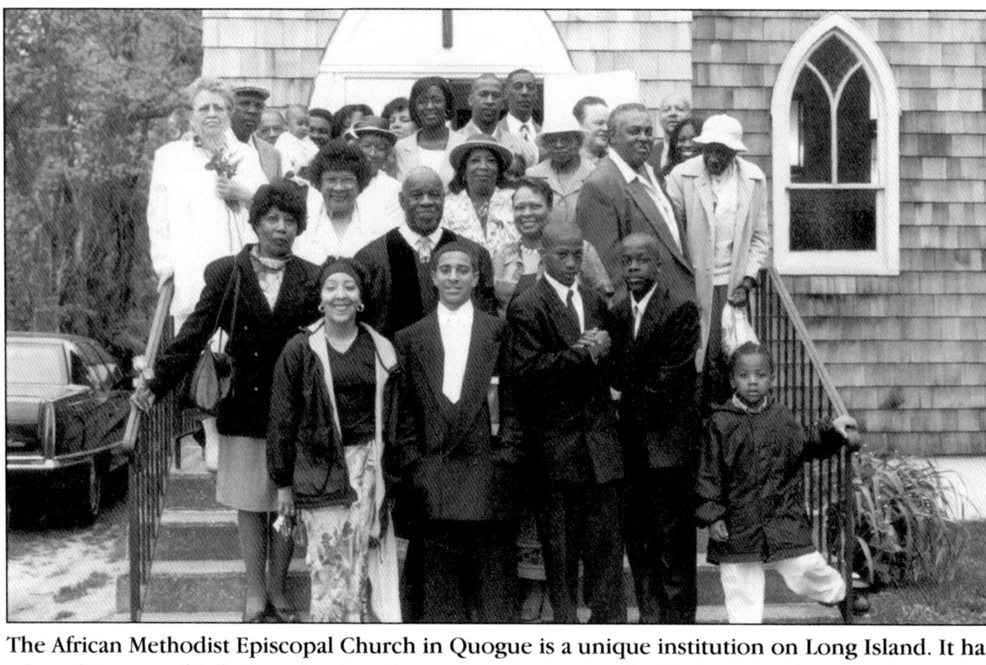

The African Methodist Episcopal Church in Quogue is a unique institution on Long Island. It has a long history and is believed to have been one of stops on the Underground Railroad. Pictured are current members of the congregation.

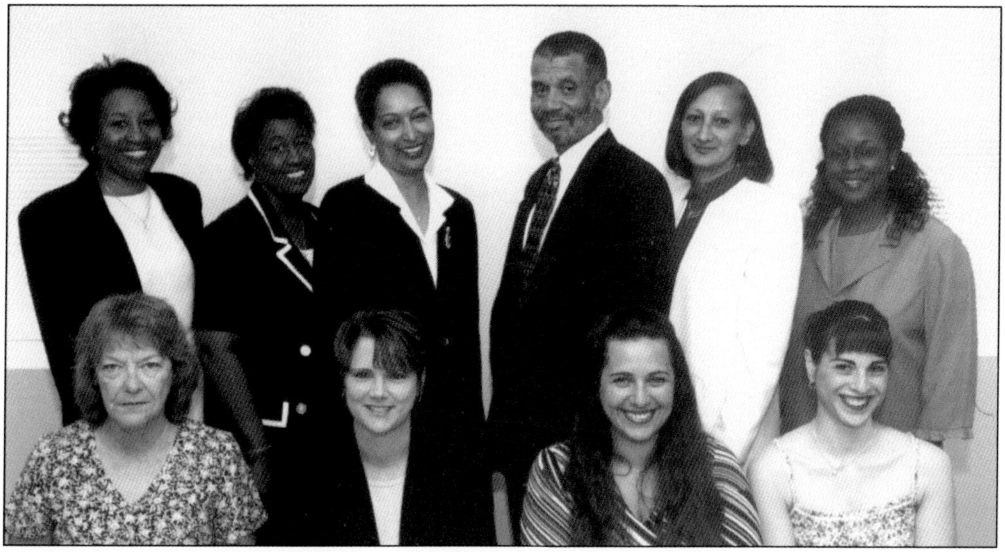

The Economic Opportunity Council of Suffolk County is one of the best nonprofit organizations on Long Island. Founded over three decades ago, it excels in human services, AIDS prevention, housing, economic empowerment, advocacy, and overall community development. Under the leadership of the chief executive, Adrian Fassett (back, fourth from left) the council has grown by leaps and bounds. Pictured with Fassett are current staff members, from left to right, as follows: (front row) Sharon Gangloff, junior accountant; Kelly Mahr, accountant; Nina Sampfli; and Stephanie Loehr, program assistant; (back row) Rabia Aziz, chief of operations; Anne Stewart, director of planning; Angela Harmon, director of housing; Adrian Fassett, chief executive officer; Maria Winston, executive assistant; and Songhi Scott, chief financial officer.

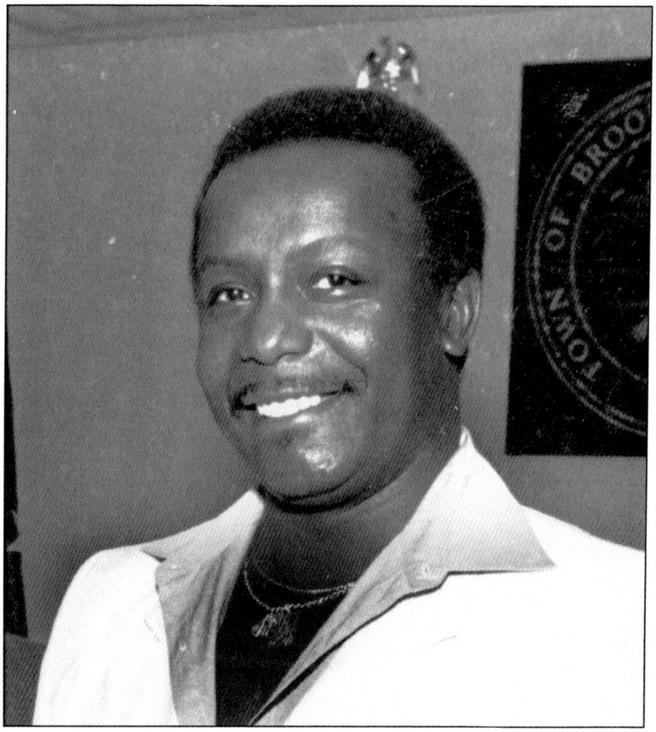

Multicultural affairs director Jim Banks also serves as an adviser and adjunct professor at Suffolk Community College. (Courtesy of Prof. Jim Banks.)

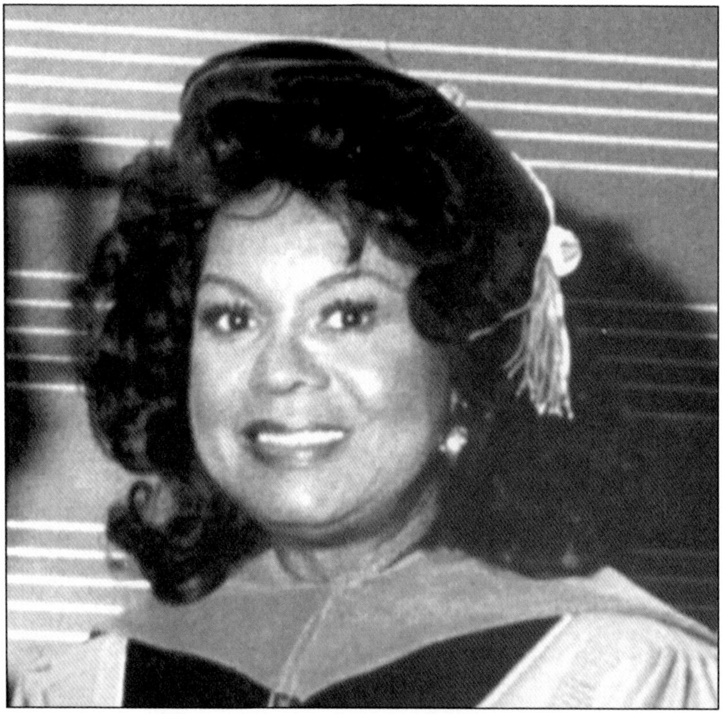

Dr. Vickie Wacksman serves as a board member of Suffolk County Community College. A business consultant, she holds a doctoral degree and serves in many capacities on Long Island. (Courtesy of Dr. Vickie Wacksman.)

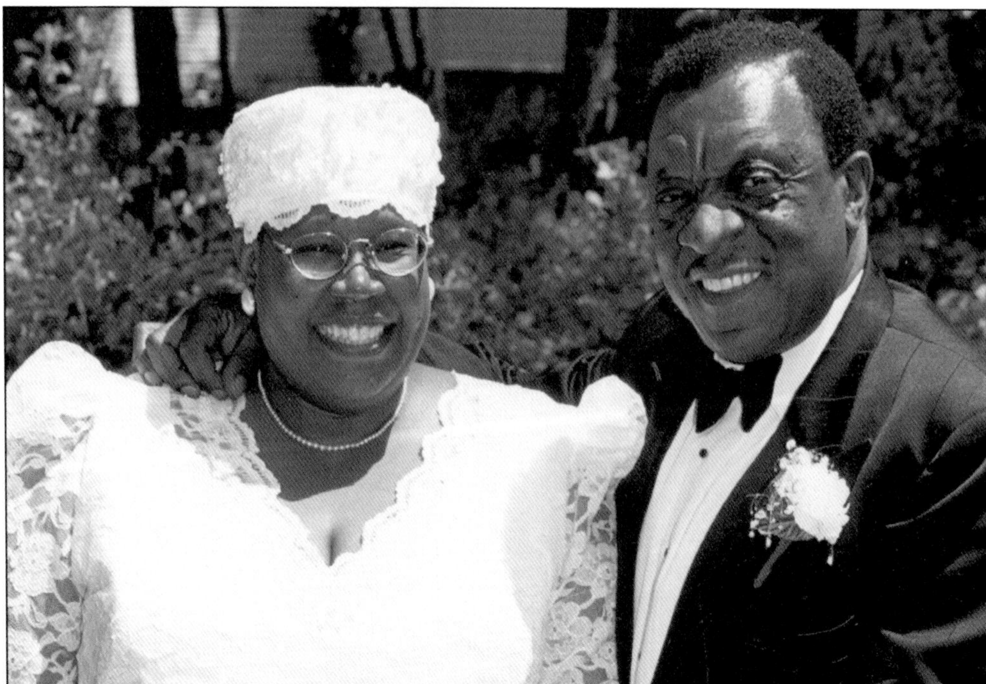

Diane and Bill Robinson renew their matrimonial vows. Diane Robinson is one of the first African American vice presidents of a financial services company. She helps families recover from debt and save money. She attended Empire State College and earned her financial license. Bill Robinson manages a soup kitchen at St. Paul's Episcopal Church in Patchogue.

Dr. Levai McIntyre and his wife live in Bay Shore. He is the principal of Longwood Junior High School. For nearly a decade, he has served that institution. Previously, he was an assistant principal. He graduated from Jamaica's Mico Teachers' College and taught science in secondary schools. He earned bachelor's and master's degrees from Indiana University, an Ed. D. from the University of South Florida, and a certificate of labor management studies from Stonybrook University. He is a member of the First United Methodist Church in Central Islip, where he serves as the organist and president of the board of trustees. (Courtesy of Dr. and Mrs. McIntyre.)

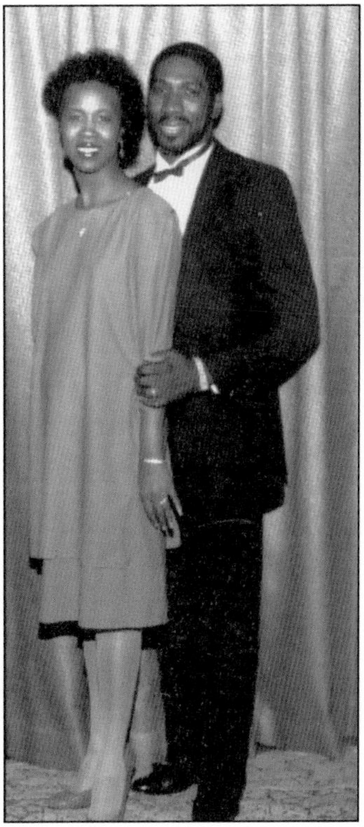

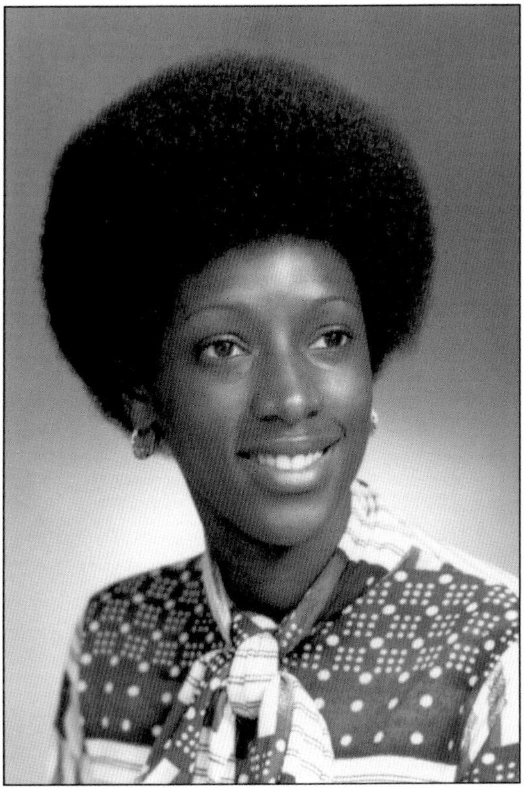

Michelle Woodard became the first African American elected as a state supreme court judge in Nassau and Suffolk Counties. (Courtesy of the Honorable Judge Michelle Woodard.)

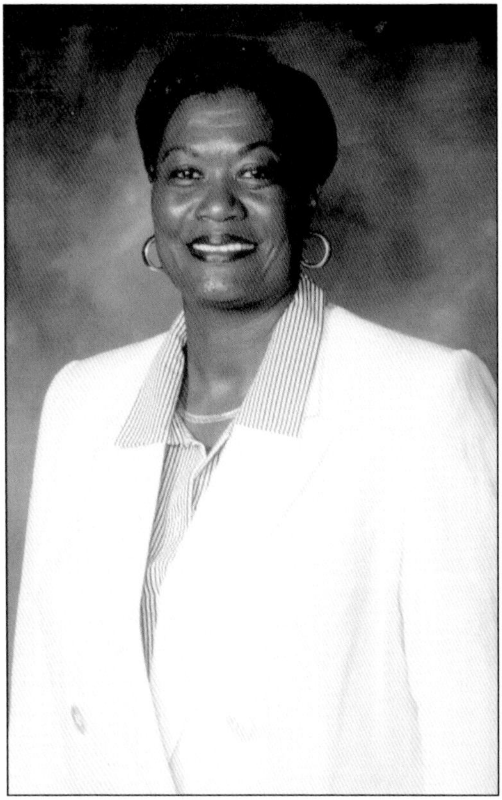

With one of the fastest starts in Stony Brook's basketball history, Trish Roberts has been head coach for three years. Born in 1945, the basketball legend still holds Tennessee single-season school records for points (929) scoring average (29.9) and field goals (428). She played on the U.S. Olympic team at Montreal in 1976 and won a Silver Medal. In 1979, she was named Tennessee Female Athlete of the Year, Kodak All-American, and Street & Smith All-American. From 1978 to 1982, she played in the Women's Basketball League with the Minnesota Fillies and the St. Louis Streak. Inducted into the Women in Sports Education Hall of Fame in 1996, she was selected for the Women's Basketball League All-Pro squad. She earned four winning seasons as coach at the University of Maine and went on to become head coach at the University of Michigan. During her inaugural season at Stony Brook University (1999–2000), she won 18 games, setting a school record. She was inducted into the Women's Basketball Hall of Fame in 2000. (Courtesy of Trish Roberts and the Stony Brook University Public Relations Office.)

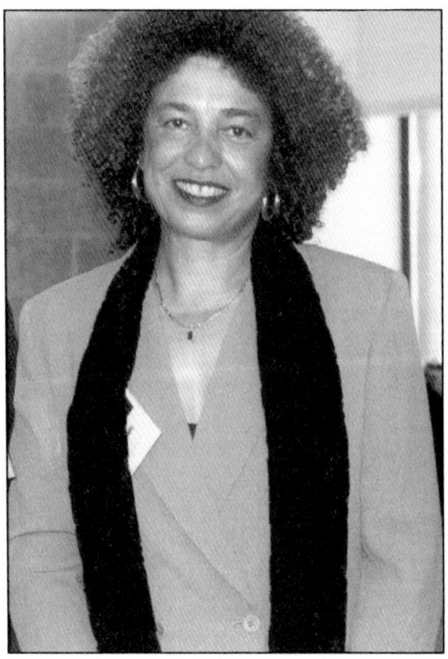

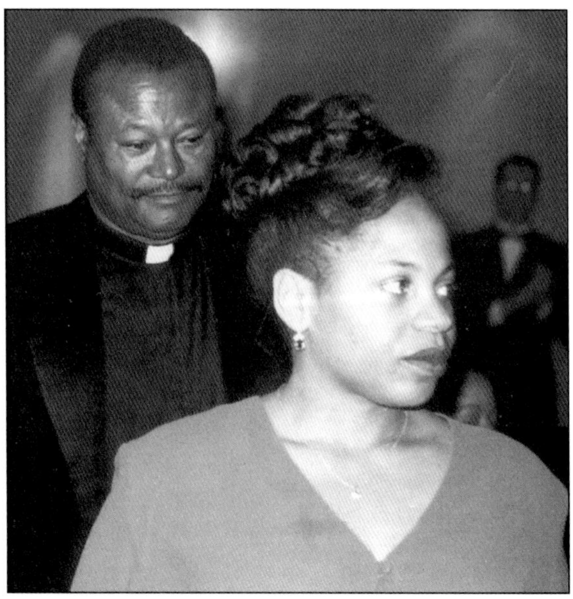

Author and professor Angela Davis (left) was the keynote speaker on Diversity Day 2000 at the State University of New York at Stony Brook, attracting a huge crowd. Based in Patchogue, Tarsha Smith (right) was one of the first African American town attorneys. Also pictured is Larry McCord, a member of the Amistad Black Bar Association in Babylon.

Eight

Gordon Heights
Tenacity and Teamwork

Covering an area of about 3,000 acres, Gordon Heights is situated south of Middle Island and east of Coram in Brookhaven. Named for "Pop" Gordon, one of the early settlers, it is a unique African American community, one in which residents have demonstrated initiative and leadership, cooperation and teamwork, and collective decision making.

It was begun by architect Louis Fife, the head of the Gordon Heights Development Corporation. Fife first offered this rather rugged and idyllic dreamland to African Americans in 1926. His advertisements for land in the heart of Long Island's pine forest, 60 miles east of the center, appeared in Harlem church bulletins. He initially sold five 100-by-100-acre plots to interested parties. The first settlers came in 1927 from New York, specifically from Harlem, Brooklyn, and the Bronx. More newcomers followed—factory workers, janitors, and a few professionals with West Indian and southern roots. Some paid as little as $10 a month for the land. The thick and lush woods, luxuriant meadows, and scattered ponds also attracted wealthy blacks, who made it a holiday mecca. However, the town quickly developed into a year-round community, and the children were enrolled in Yaphank School.

Early settlers included Evelyn Ellis and Louise Adams-Hall, a distinguished dancer featured in the Broadway show *Porgy and Bess*. Among others who contributed to the community's development were Gladys Mae Hylton Pinto, Tyrell Wilson, Ada Phillips, Thelma Hall, Margaret Spence, Benjamin Carpenter, Alberta Beach, James Beaton, Sidney Murray, and Tracy Hanes.

Recognized as one of the pioneer African American communities on Long Island, Gordon Heights started and managed its own civic association, clubs, and churches. When, in 1946, the small church burned and no firefighters rushed to extinguish the fire, residents decided to form their own fire department. They did so in 1947, and it became one of the few all–African American fire departments in the county.

Acting on behalf of the Gordon Heights Development and Building Corporation, Fife donated to the town of Brookhaven two acres of land as a playground in 1950. The tract is a full 200-by-400-foot block, surrounded by Central Parkway, Baldwin Lane, Pine Grove Avenue, and Shirley Lane. In 1959, the community started its own credit union since it was difficult if not impossible to secure loans from existing banks. In 1951, a new chapter of the National Council of Negro Women was organized at St. Michael and All Angels Church, with Elizabeth Flemming serving as the first president. Today, Gordon Heights waxes strong and continues to grow as newcomers choose it as their home.

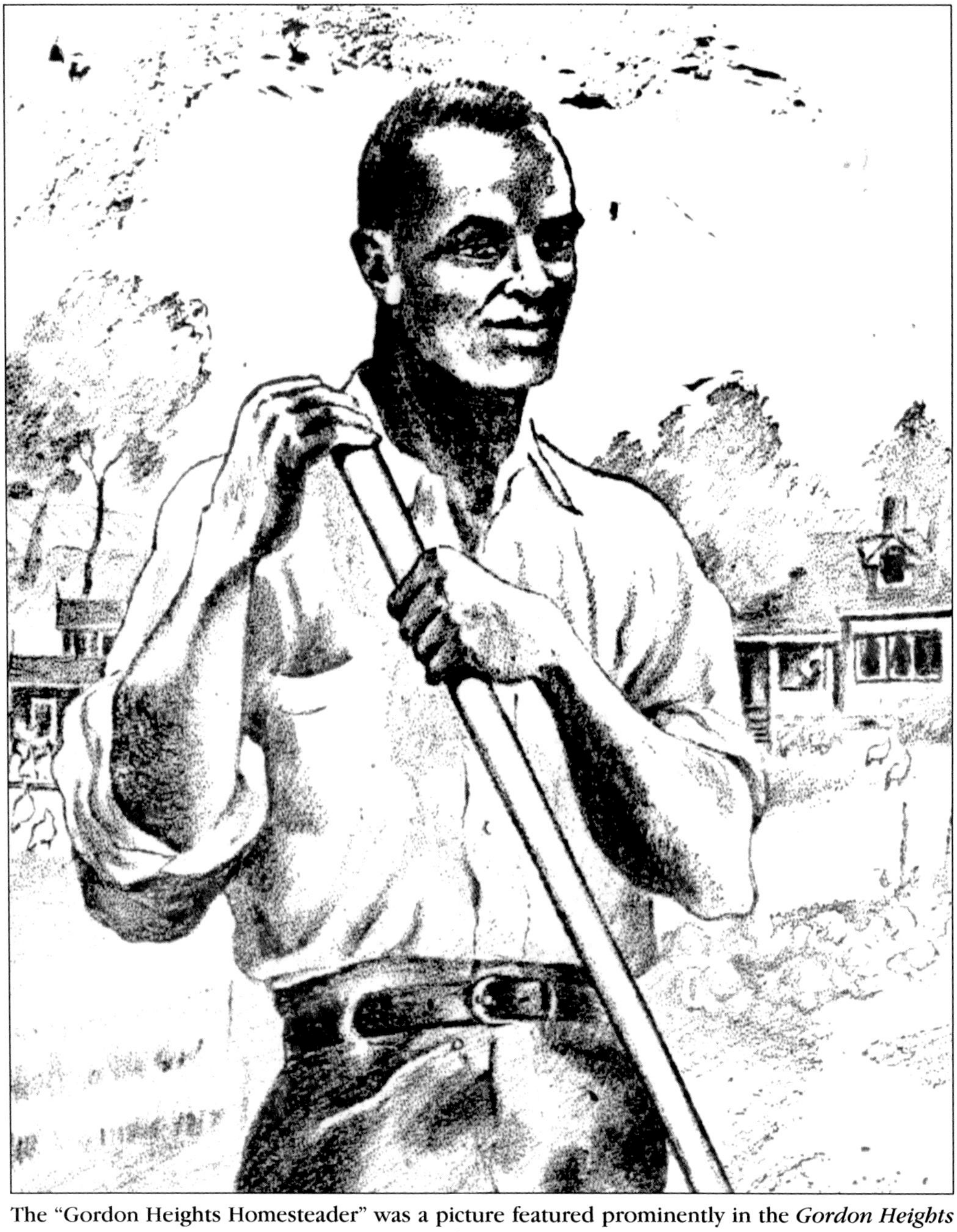

The "Gordon Heights Homesteader" was a picture featured prominently in the *Gordon Heights Bulletin,* published from the 1930s to the 1960s. (Courtesy of Robert Wilson.)

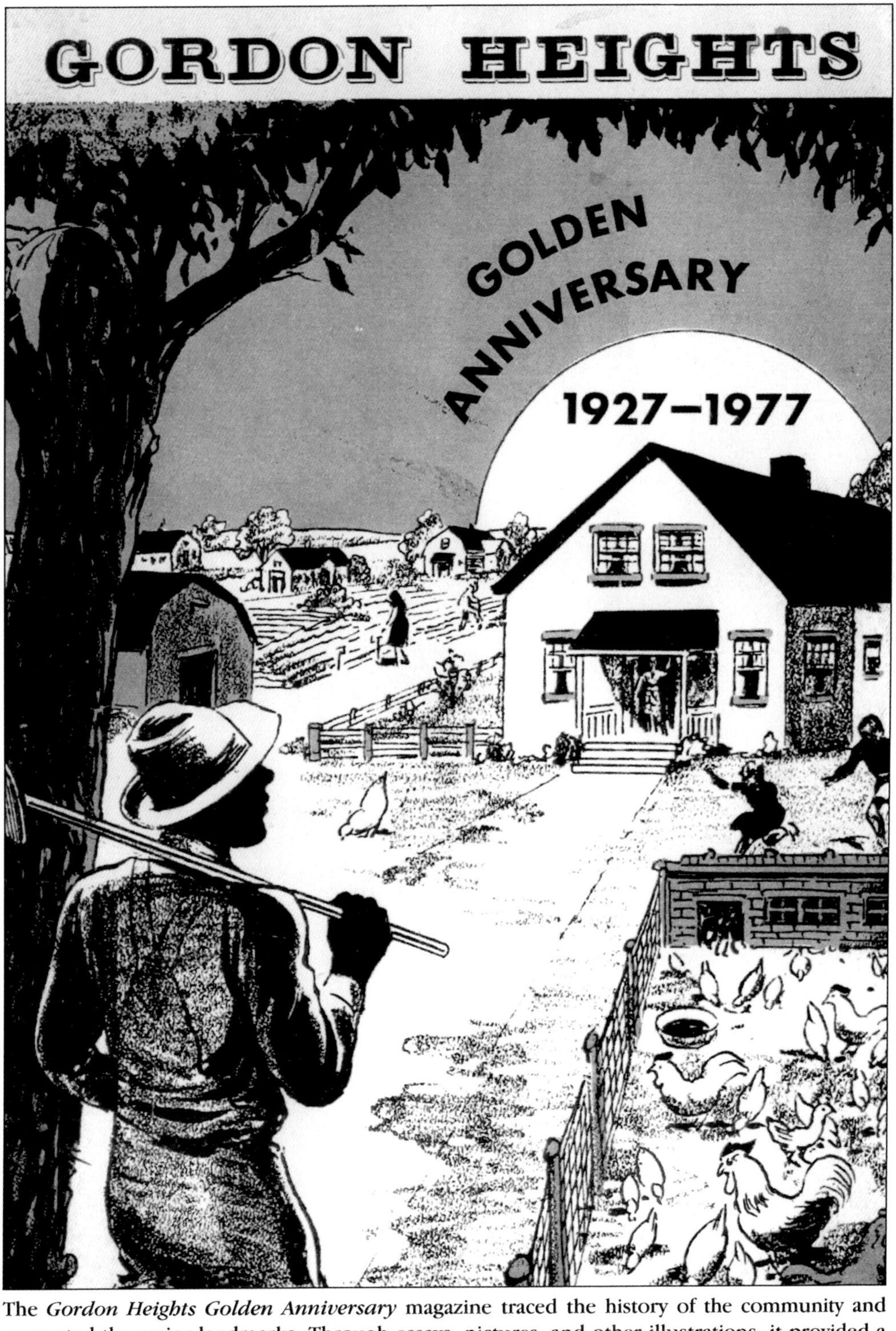

The *Gordon Heights Golden Anniversary* magazine traced the history of the community and presented the major landmarks. Through essays, pictures, and other illustrations, it provided a vivid description of the area and its evolution. (Courtesy of Gordon Heights Civic Association.)

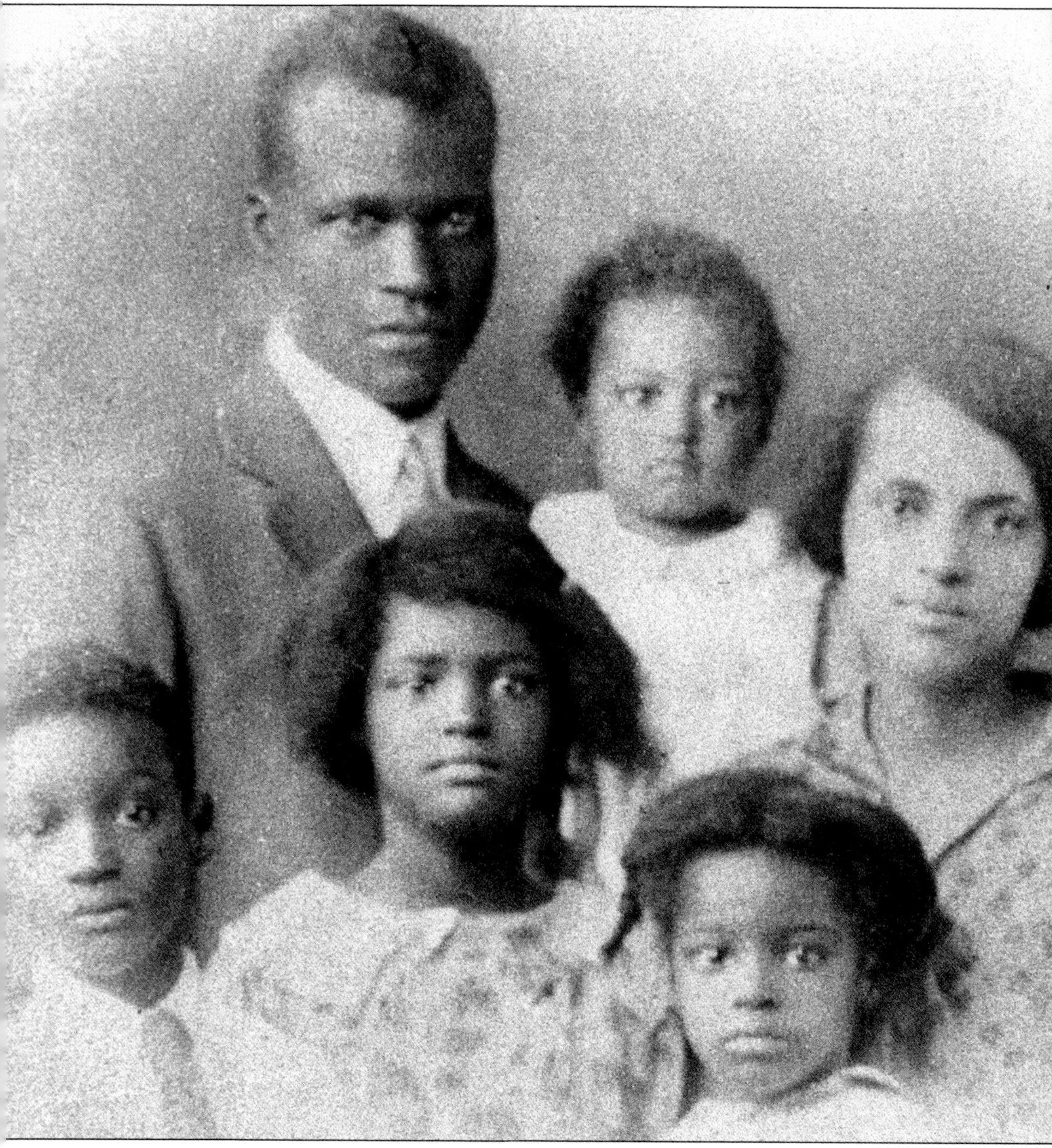

The Wilsons were among the pioneer settlers in Gordon Heights. Shown in a 1929 photograph, they include, from left to right, the following: (front row) Tyrell Wilson Jr., Esther Wilson (deceased 1929) and Ruth Lee; (back row) Tyrell Wilson Sr., Robert Wilson, and Iris Wilson. Tyrell Wilson Sr. was born in Jamaica, West Indies, in 1891. He came to New York in 1918 and opened a radio repair shop. He helped found the Gordon Heights Civic Association in the 1940s. His son Tyrell Jr. served in the U.S. Air Force during World War II, became commissioner of the Gordon Heights Fire Department, and had three sons. Son Robert Wilson was born in 1927, graduated from Long Island University with a degree in chemistry in 1951, served in the U.S. Army from 1953 to 1955, retired from Brookhaven National Laboratory after 32 years as an analytical chemist, and serves today as a community facilitator. (Courtesy of Robert Wilson.)

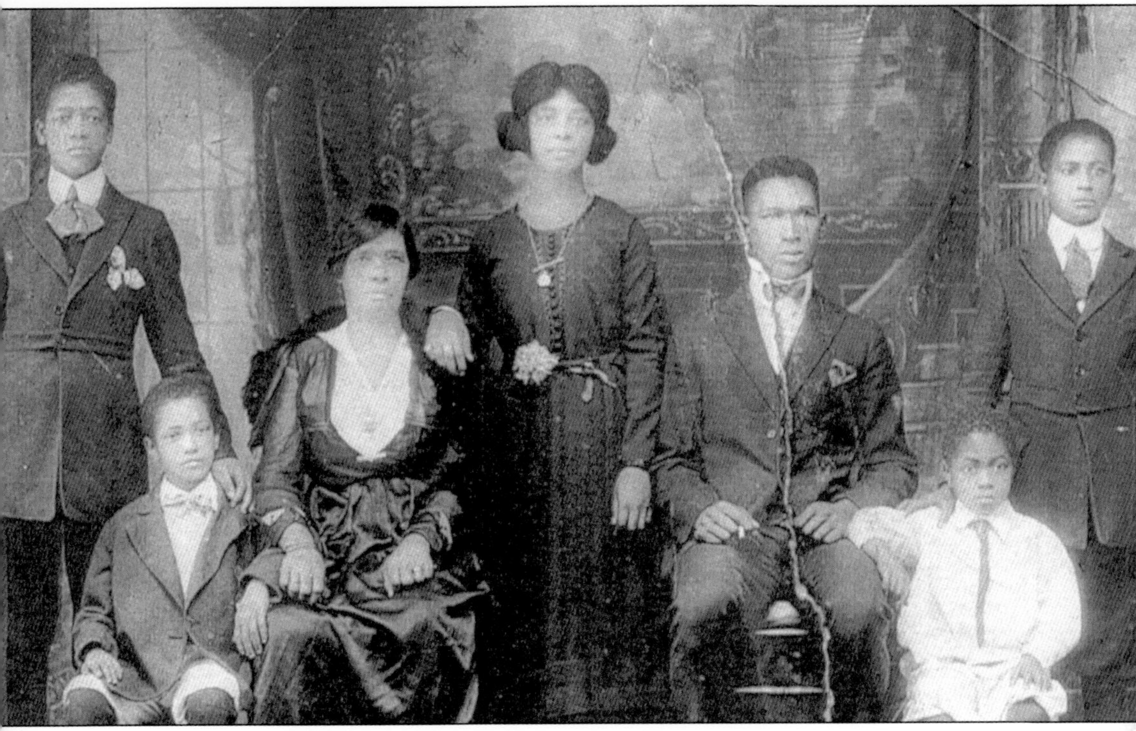

Lucretia Carpenter (third from left) came from St. Kitts Island to the United States in the 1800s. Pictured with her, from left to right, are family members Thomas Carpenter, Nevil Carpenter, Gustina Carpenter, Peter Burke (a cousin), William Carpenter, and Benjamin Charles Carpenter Sr. Benjamin Charles Carpenter Sr. bought property in Gordon Heights in 1938. He worked as a delivery man and did odd jobs. He built his house on Barbara Lane. (Courtesy of Joan Carpenter.)

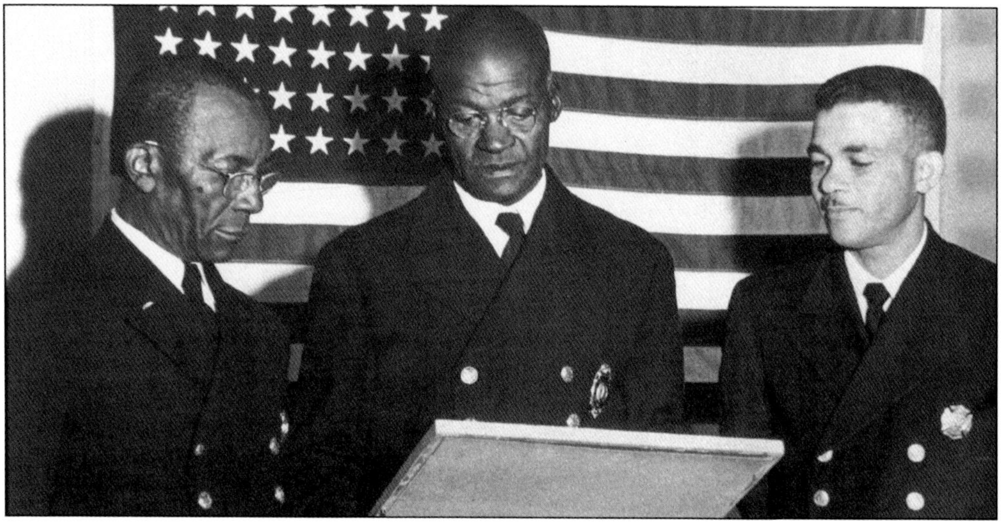

Tyrell Wilson (center) was one of the early settlers of Gordon Heights. Born in 1891 in Jamaica, West Indies, he moved to Manhattan in 1918. He met and married Iris and they moved to Long Island from the Bronx. A radio repair shop proprietor, he helped found the Gordon Heights Civic Association in the 1940s. He was one of the first members of the Suffolk County Human Rights Commission and a founder of the Brookhaven Chapter of the National Association for the Advancement of Colored People (NAACP). He also served 22 years as a board member of the Middle Island School Board. Additionally, he was a founder of the Gordon Heights Credit Union and was a Liberal party candidate for office twice in Suffolk County. He is flanked by Jacob Williams (left) and John Pryor of the Gordon Heights Fire Department in 1957. (Courtesy of Robert Wilson.)

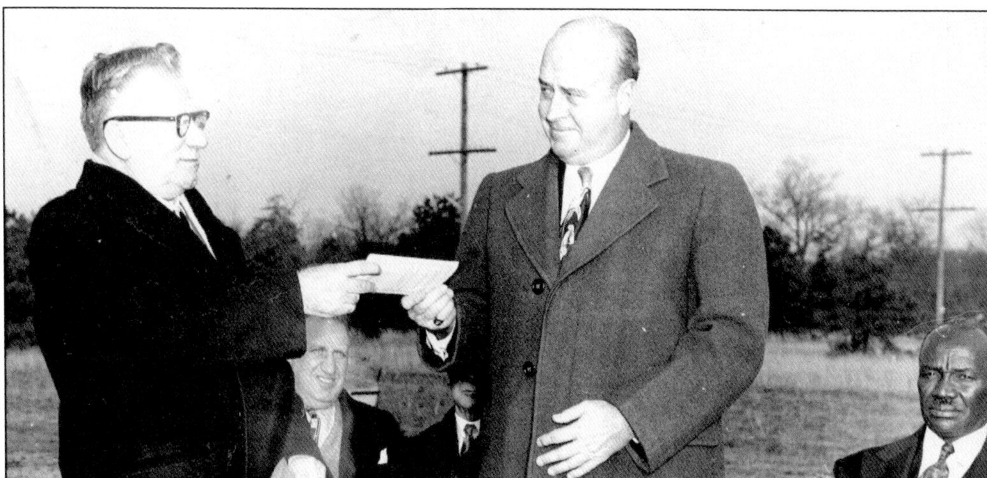

The Gordon Heights playground was dedicated in 1950. The two-acre field was turned over to the town of Brookhaven in a public ceremony. The tract covers 200 feet by 400 feet within a full square block. It is bordered by Central Parkway, Baldwin Lane, Pine Grove Avenue, and Shirley Lane. At the dedication ceremony, Louis Fife (left), president of the Gordon Heights Development and Building Corporation, presents the deed for the playground to Philip A. Hattemer, Brookhaven town supervisor. Seated, from left to right, are Albert Bayer, Gordon Heights Development & Building Corporation; Edward Pioneer, town assessor; and James Beaton of Ebenezer Church. (Courtesy of Robert Wilson.)

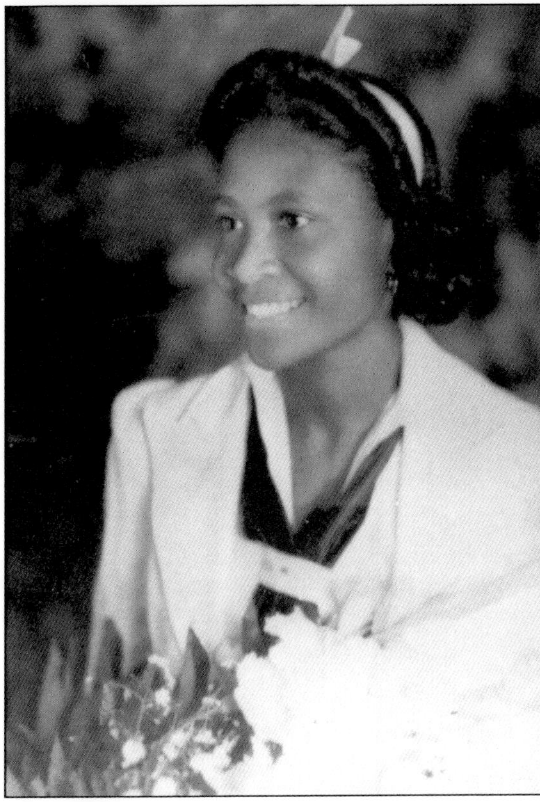

Bernice Flack (right) came to Long Island in the 1940s. Her daughter Renée Flack (below) is an adjunct professor and the multicultural affairs officer at St. Joseph's College. She is also a youth mentor at the Brookhaven National Laboratory, where she organizers workshops, seminars, and training for students. Associated with the island since the 1940s, she holds bachelor's and master's degrees. She is pictured with students at one of the training workshops in 1989. (Courtesy of Renée Flack.)

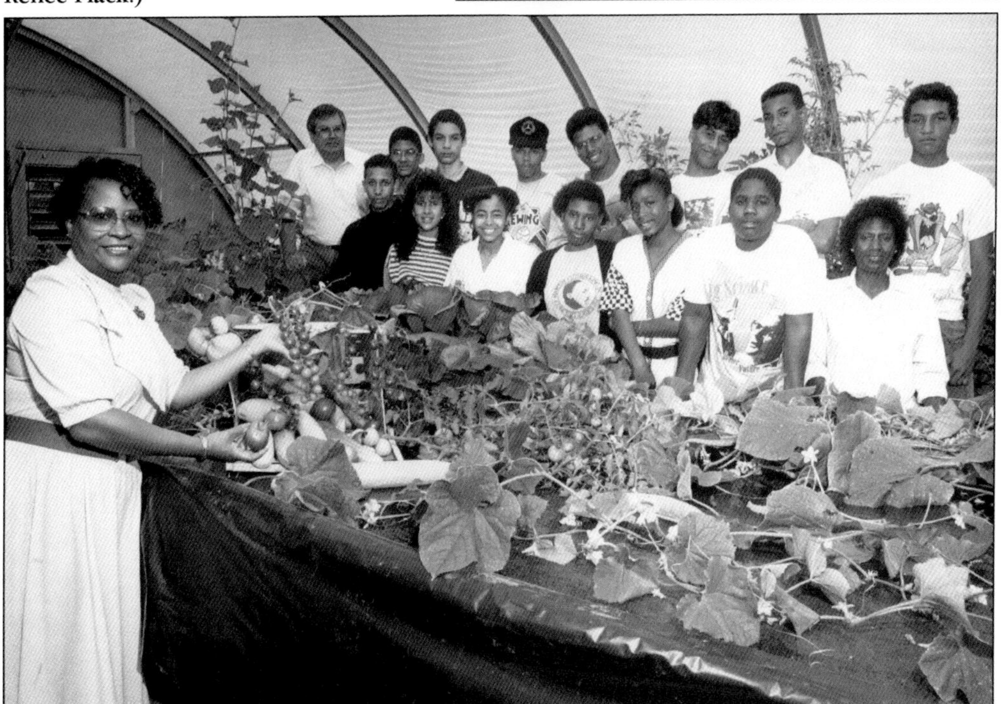

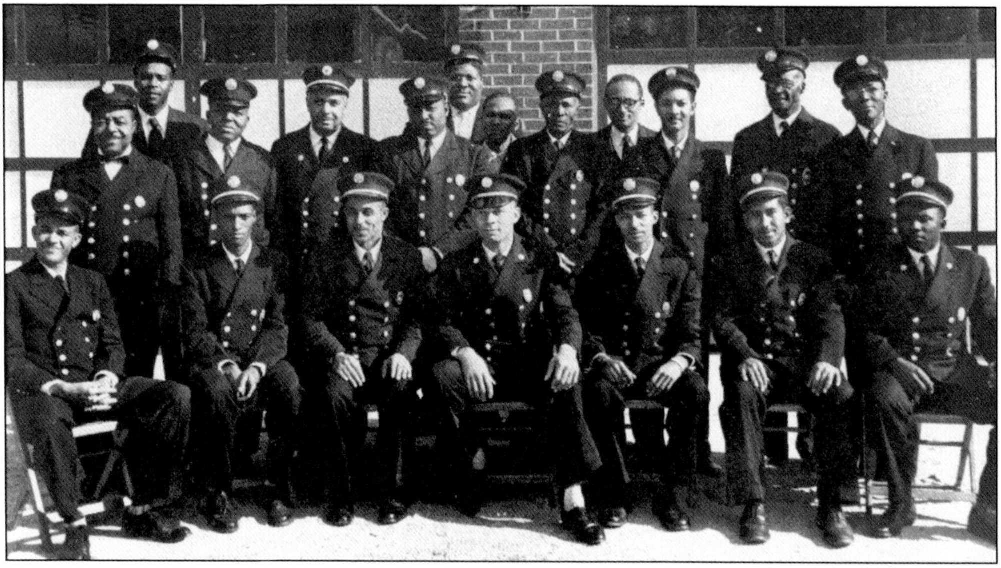

The Gordon Heights Fire Department was established in 1947 by the Gordon Heights Civic Association. Its first equipment, a chemical fire truck with two tanks, went into operation in 1948. The Gordon Heights Progressive Association purchased the property where the firehouse was built. Shown are some of the early members of the Fire Department, among them founders Jacob Williams (back right) Tyrell Wilson Sr. (back, second from right) and Christopher Henry (back center). At the time, this was the only all–African American Fire Department on the East Coast. The first fire commissioners appointed by the town included Charles Sander, Cyril Woodburn, Bertram Riddock, Christopher Henry, and Benjamin Carpenter. (Courtesy of Robert Wilson.)

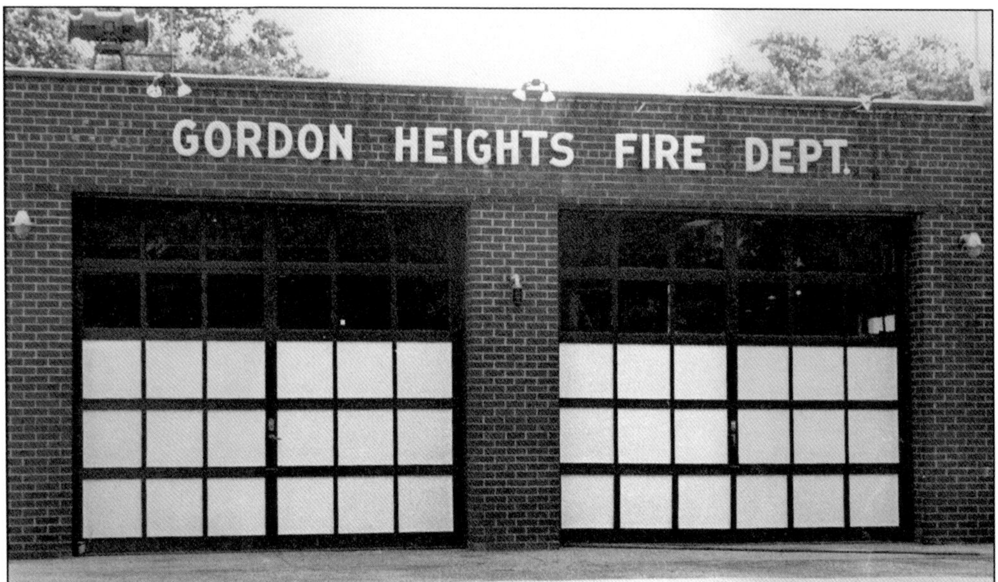

The Gordon Heights Fire Department building was built on Hawkins Avenue. The first addition was put on in 1954. The firehouse had two bays, where trucks could be parked. (Courtesy of Robert Wilson.)

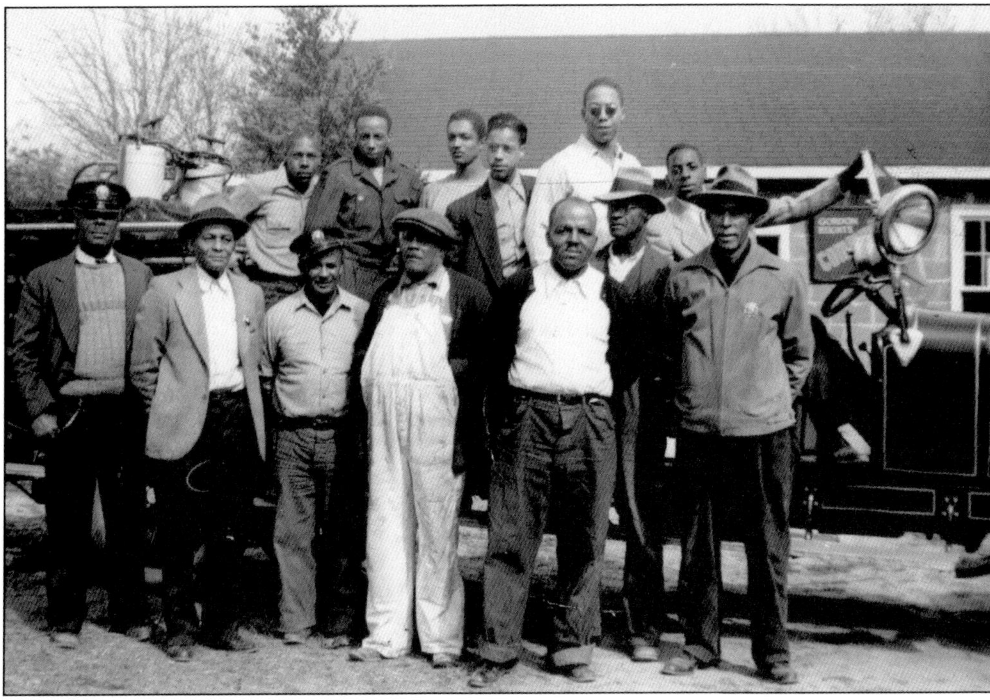

Some of the original members of the Gordon Heights Fire Department are pictured in 1949. From left to right are the following: (front row) Joel Fredricks, Charles Sanders, Benjamin Carpenter (chief), Tracy Haynes, Paul Hall, Tyrell Wilson Sr., and Allen Wilcox; (back row) Ronald Armstrong, Benjamin Lee, Otis Freeland, Earl Tatum, and Lawrence Clark. (Courtesy of Robert Wilson.)

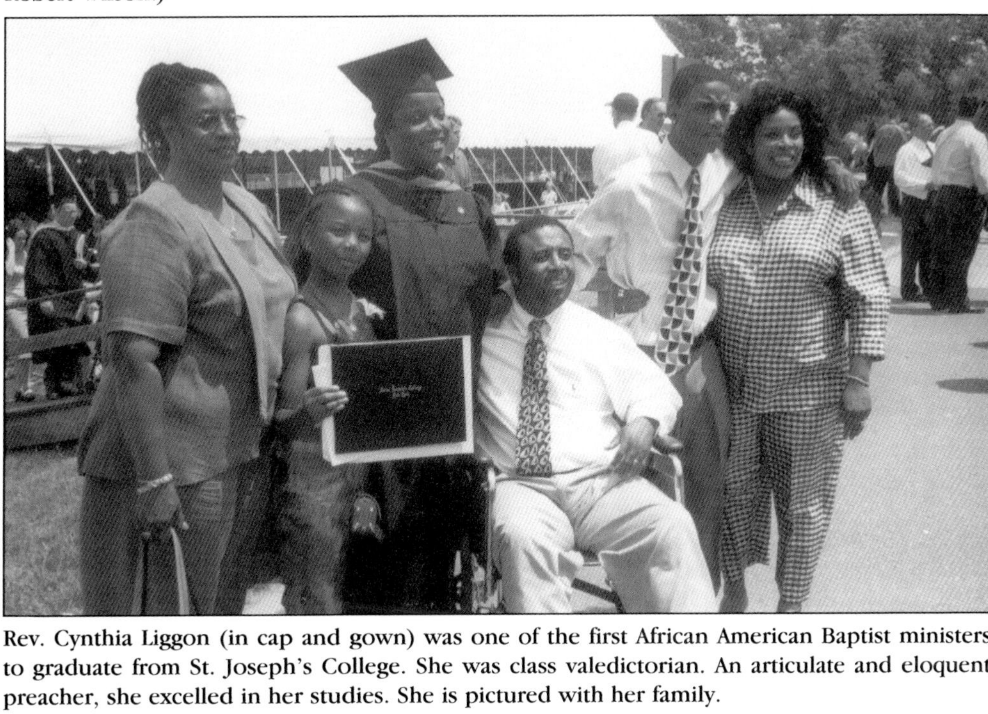

Rev. Cynthia Liggon (in cap and gown) was one of the first African American Baptist ministers to graduate from St. Joseph's College. She was class valedictorian. An articulate and eloquent preacher, she excelled in her studies. She is pictured with her family.

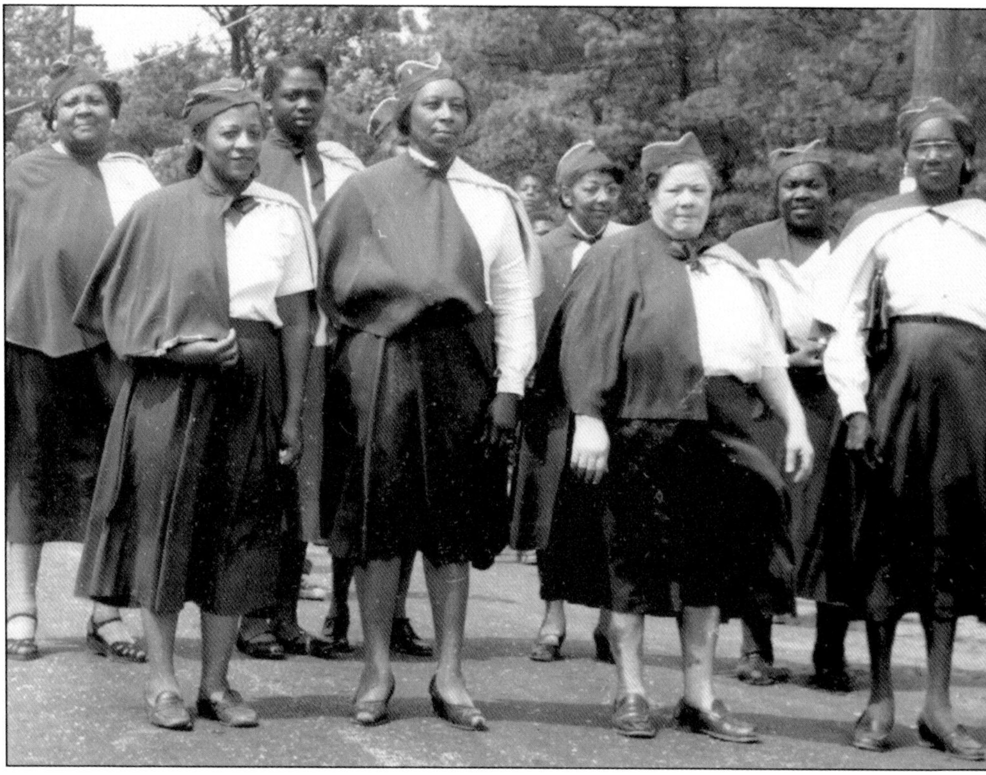

The Gordon Heights Fire Department Ladies Auxiliary is shown in 1940. From left to right are the following: (front row) M.R. Woodburn, M. Saunders, L. Miller, and G. Hilton; (back row) ? Haynes, D. Robinson, L. Smith, and A. Beach. (Courtesy of the Armstrongs.)

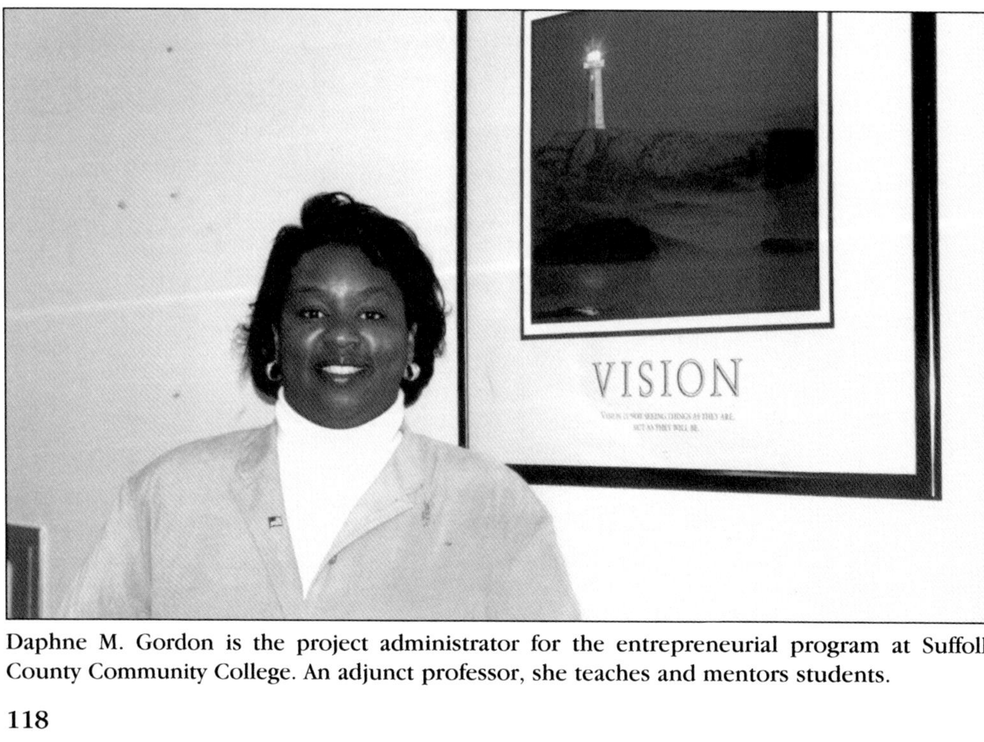

Daphne M. Gordon is the project administrator for the entrepreneurial program at Suffolk County Community College. An adjunct professor, she teaches and mentors students.

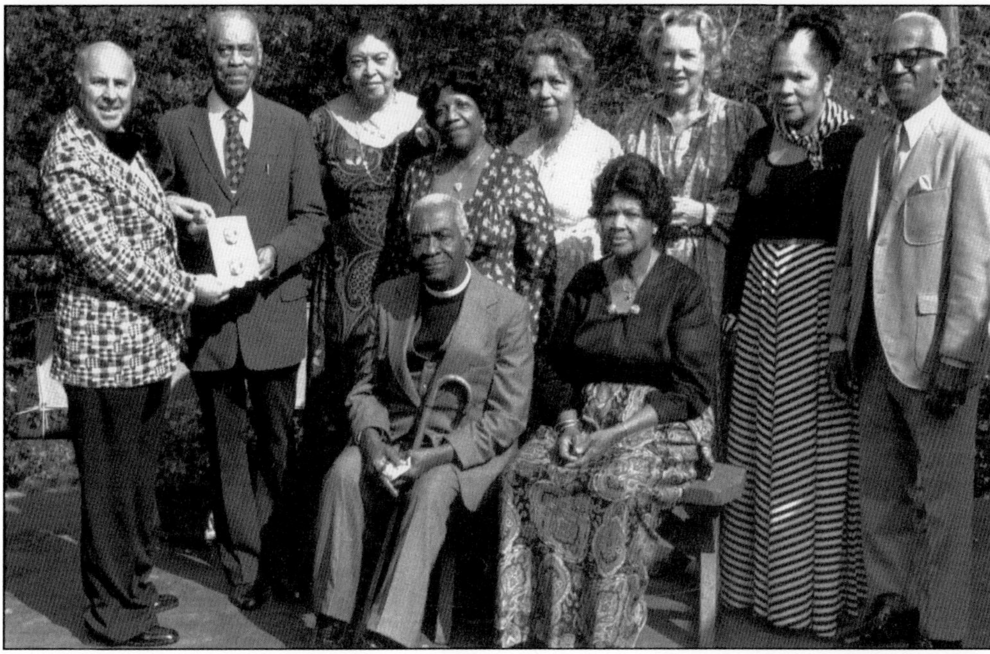

The Gordon Heights Senior Citizen Club was inaugurated in 1968. From left to right are Peter Pulos, Albert Tinnie, Jo-Anna Tinnie, Elizabeth Davis, Purina Dayton, Adliede Silkworth, Innez Solomon, and Alfred Kirton. Many of the members are early settlers in the area. (Courtesy of Robert Wilson.)

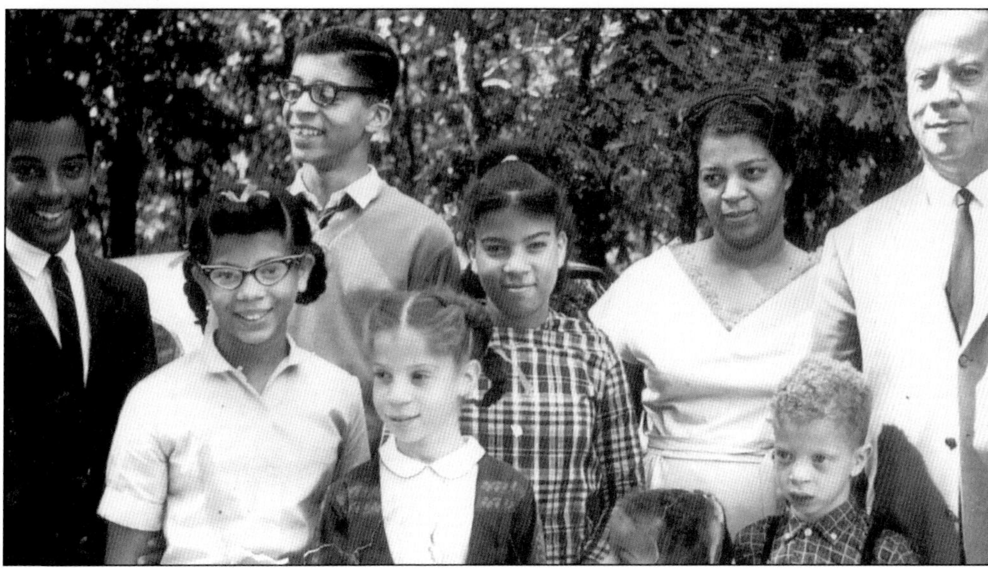

The Mitchells came from Jamaica, West Indies. The parents emigrated to the United States in their twenties, met in New York City, got married, and raised seven children in Gordon Heights: Carlton, an employee of the New York City mayor's office); Frederick, a dentist; Patsy, an assistant director of public housing for the city of Danbury, Connecticut; Ruthy; Danny; Jeannine, a nurse at Stony Brook Hospital; and Lois Tinsley, a teacher and board of education member in the Longwood School District and former president of the Eastern Long Island Black Educators Association. This photograph was taken in 1966.

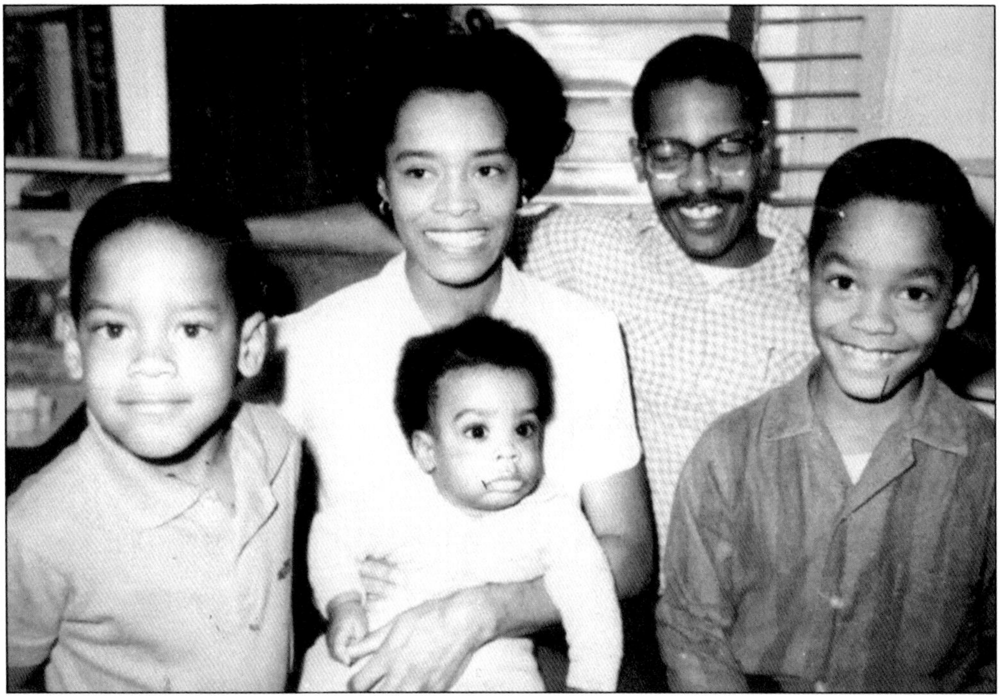

The Armstrongs arrived in Gordon Heights in the 1940s. Ronald Amstrong (back row), a social worker, has served as moderator at workshops. From left to right are Timothy, Barbara (who became one of the first principals from Gordon Heights), Philip, and David Armstrong.

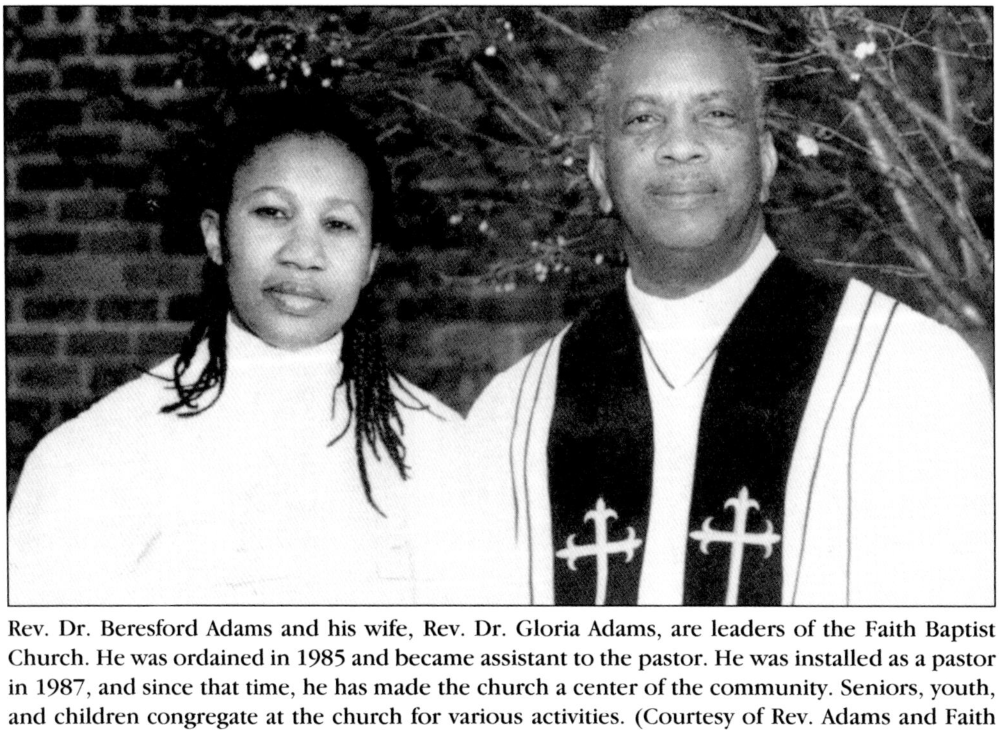

Rev. Dr. Beresford Adams and his wife, Rev. Dr. Gloria Adams, are leaders of the Faith Baptist Church. He was ordained in 1985 and became assistant to the pastor. He was installed as a pastor in 1987, and since that time, he has made the church a center of the community. Seniors, youth, and children congregate at the church for various activities. (Courtesy of Rev. Adams and Faith Baptist Church.)

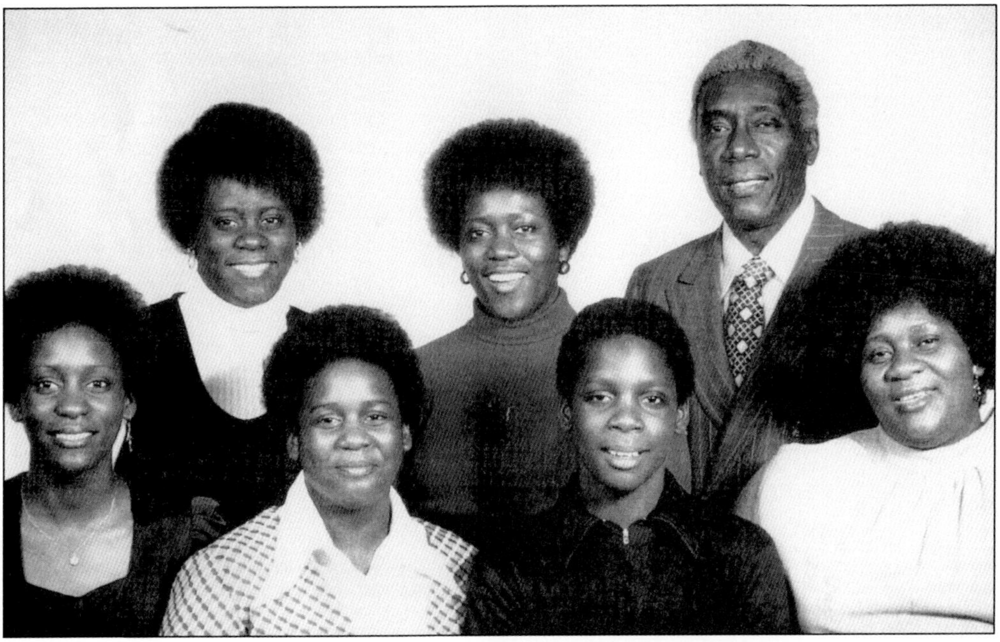

The Owens family is well respected on the Island. Elsie Owens came to Gordon Heights in the 1950s. She worked as a custodian at the State University of New York at Stony Brook and later returned to school and earned her master's in social work from the same university. She has distinguished herself as a community leader serving on several boards and committees. She was the president of the local National Association for the Advancement of Colored People (NAACP) for four consecutive terms. (Courtesy of Elsie Owens and family.)

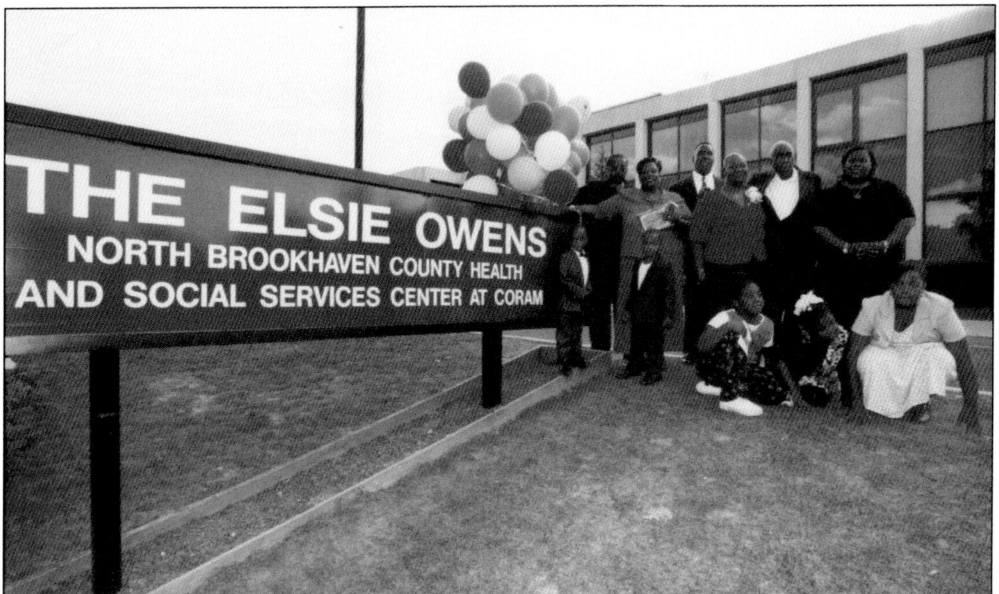

The Elsie Owens North Brookhaven County Health Center and Social Services Center was established in 1987 with the support and encouragement of Elsie Owens and other community leaders who lobbied for it for more than a decade. Run by the county and the state, the center provides all primary health care services. (Courtesy of Elsie Owens and family.)

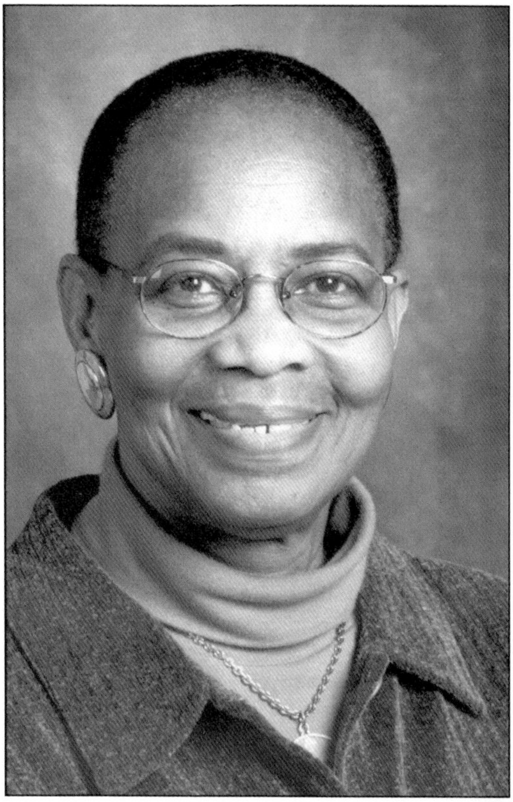

Dr. Frances L. Brisbane is the dean of social work at Stony Brook University. A respected writer, professor, and author, she enjoys national and international respect for her work at home and abroad. A seasoned teacher, she is admired as an administrator and an international scholar. (Courtesy of Dr. Frances L.Brisbane.)

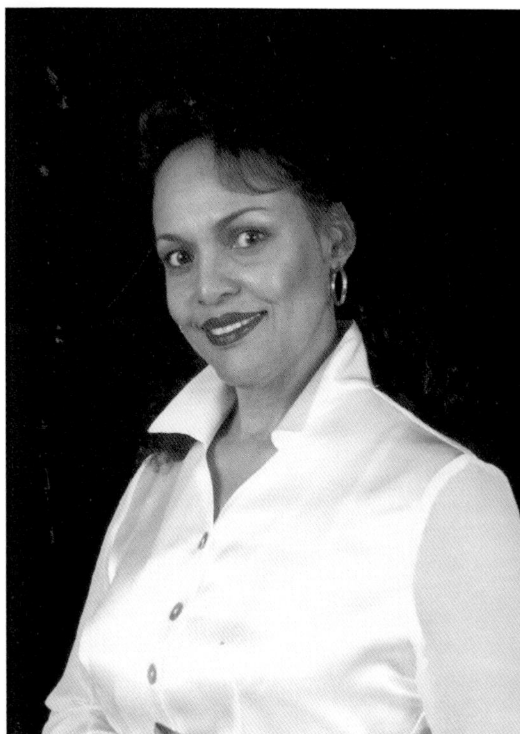

Dr. Cecile Forte of Brookhaven is a distinguished author, scholar, and educator on Long Island. She earned her doctorate from Hofstra University in 1975 and has served as a teacher, administrator, and consultant in public schools. She was an academic dean at Suffolk Community College, has served on numerous national and regional committees, and has won several awards. Her association with Long Island dates back to her childhood school days. (Courtesy of Dr. Cecile Forte.)

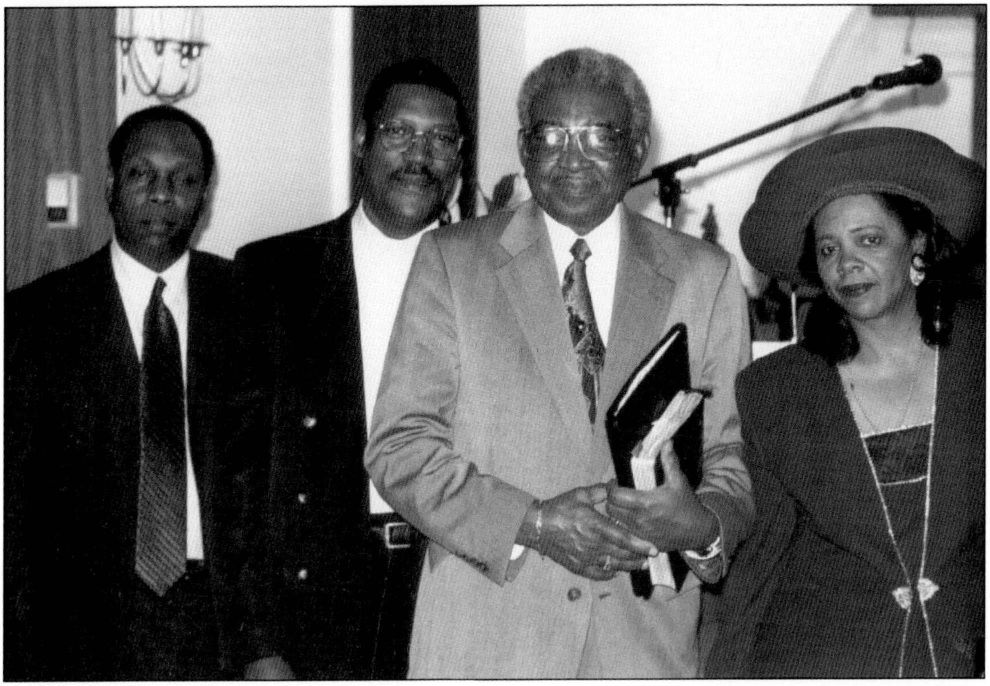

Pastor Willie Jones (second from right) poses with his ministerial associates. He is one of the founders of Christ Baptist Church in Coram. He supports the promotion of women in the ministry and plays an active role in the community. (Author's collection.)

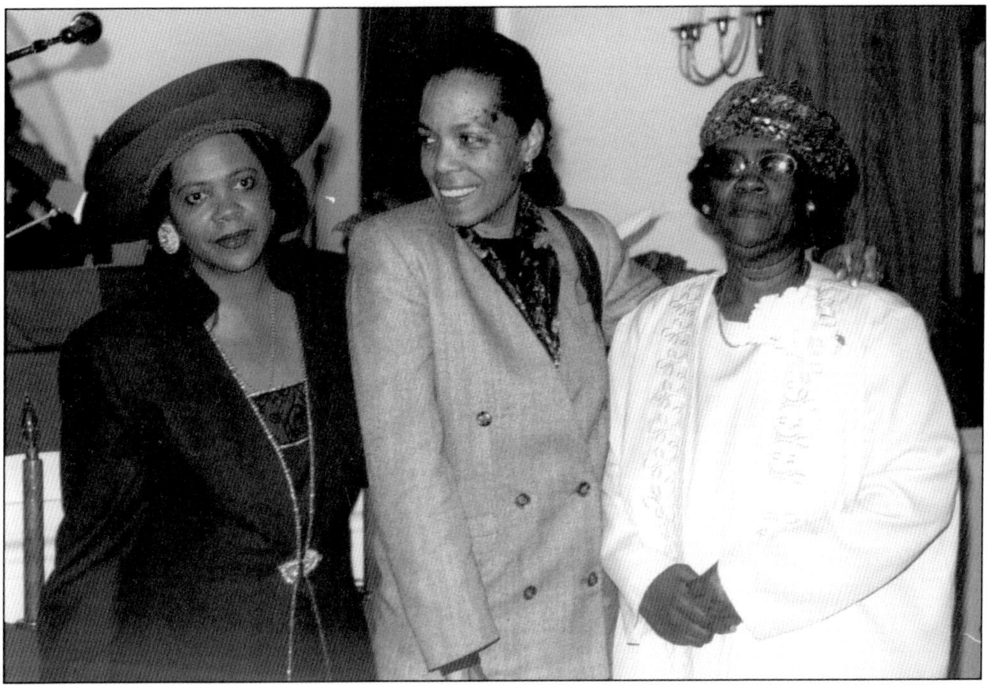

Shown are three women pastors on Long Island. Agnes Dozier (right) heads the Triune Baptist Church in Sag Harbor. She is a musician and an accomplished organist. The other two ministers are associates at Christ Baptist Church in Coram. (Author's collection.)

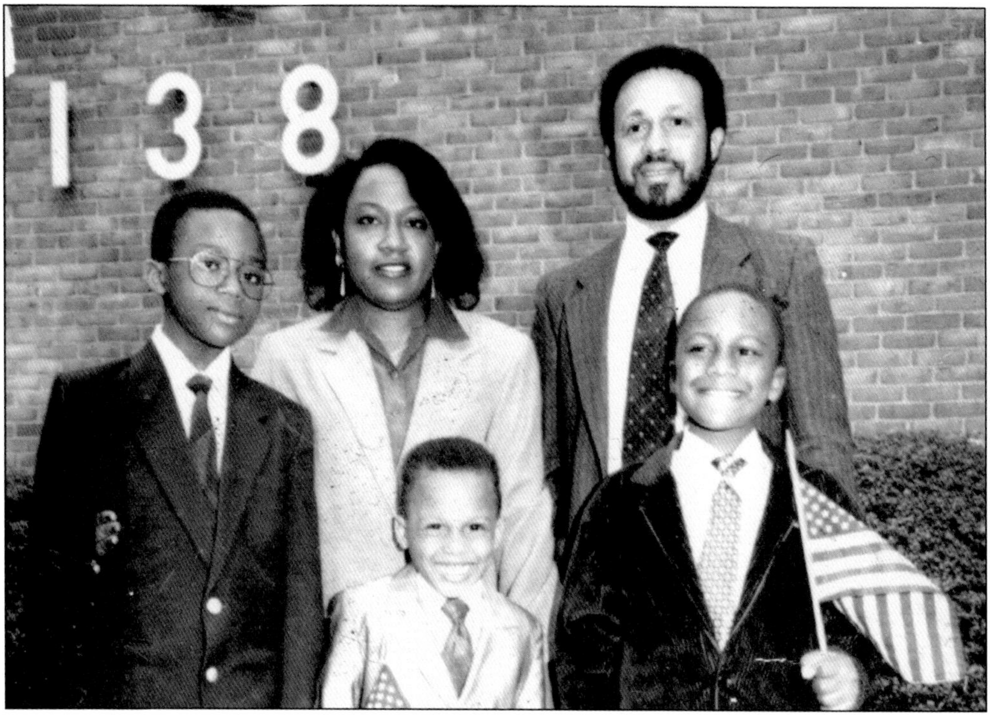

Shown are members of the Robinson family of Coram. From left to right are the following: (front row) Rashawn Robinson and Khalfani Robinson; (back row) Shomari Robinson, Yvonne Robinson, and Clement Robinson. The Robinsons own and manage the Caribbean Delight in Coram, which they have operated for over a decade. (Courtesy of the Robinson family.)

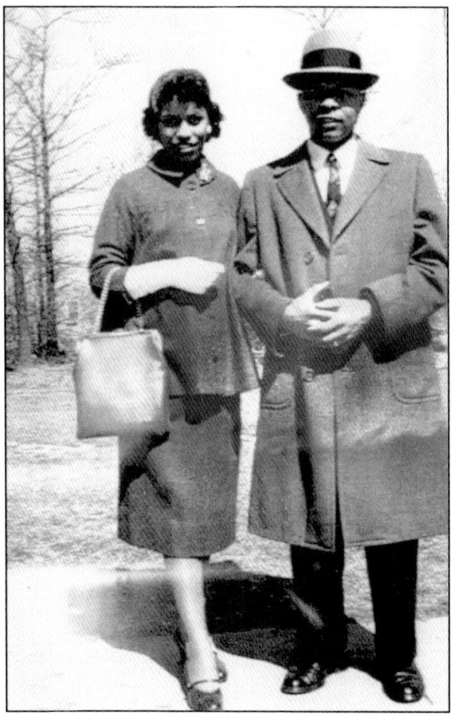

Joan Carpenter and James L. Preston Sr. were married in 1957 and moved to Gordon Heights in 1959. Preston was one of the first African American science teachers in Gordon Heights. He graduated from Lincoln University with a B.S. in chemistry in 1954 and received his master's in education from Temple University in 1956. He served in the U.S. Army from 1956 to 1958. Joan Preston, the fourth daughter of Benjamin Carpenter Sr., graduated from Port Jefferson High School in 1952. She earned her state registered nursing certificate from Central Islip State Hospital School of Nursing in 1955 and worked as a nurse for over 45 years. She received a teacher's certificate from Manhattan College in New York City in 1974. (Courtesy of Joan Preston.)

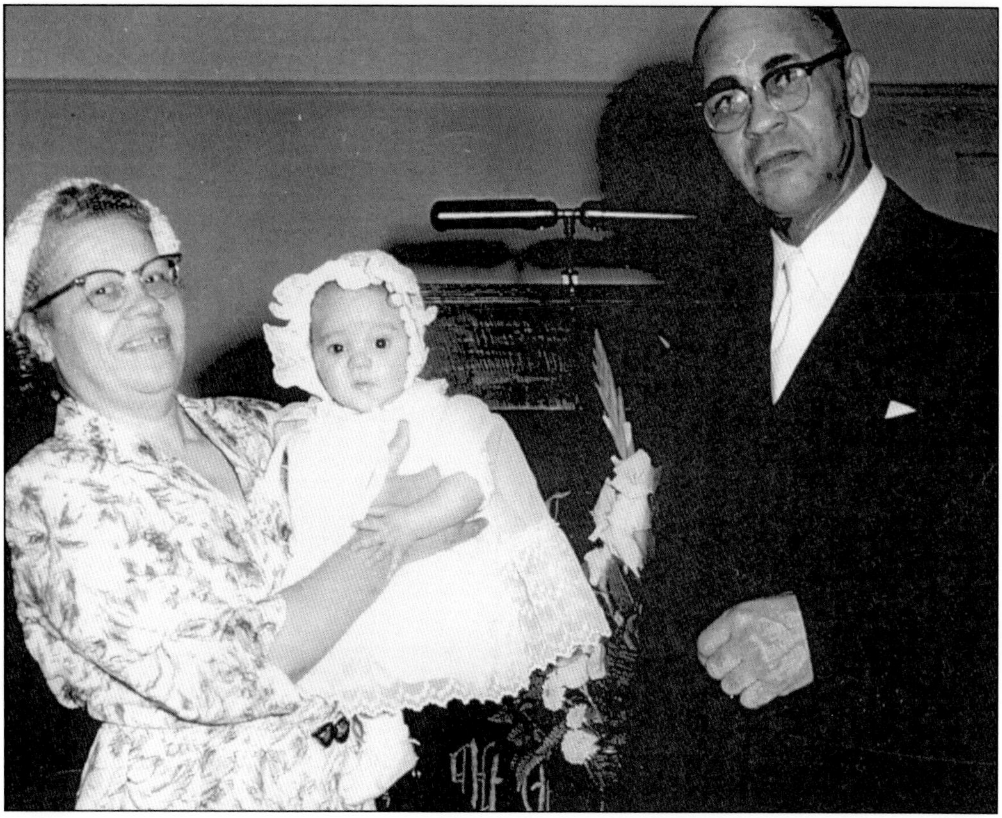

Vivialyn and Hernan A. Johnston were pioneer immigrants to Gordon Heights. Born in Jamaica, they moved to New York in the early 1900s. In the 1930s, they moved to Gordon Heights. Johnston worked with Louis Fife, who sold parcels of land to African Americans. Later, he became an elder in the Seventh-Day Adventist Church. Vivialyn Johnston holds newly christened Lynette Spaulding, who, today, is a lawyer living in White Plains. (Courtesy of Dorothy J. Bishop.)

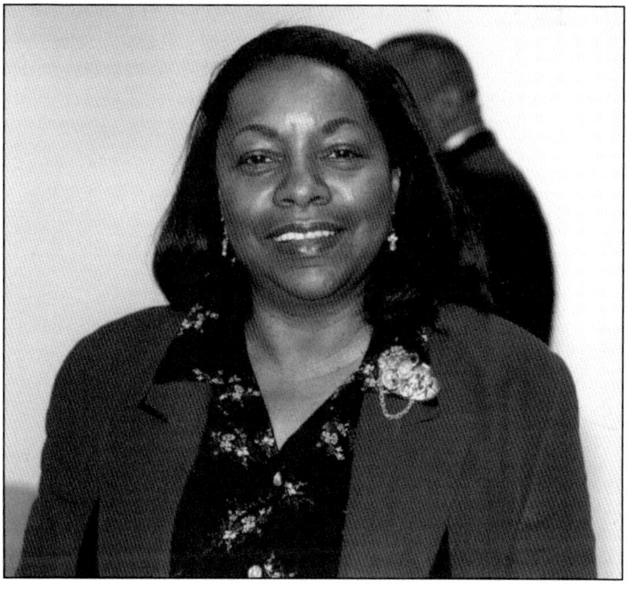

Claire Conquest—community and sorority leader, guidance counselor, and educator—has a ready smile. A respected mentor who teaches and serves with diligence and dedication, she was one of the first guidance counselors on Long Island. (Author's collection.)

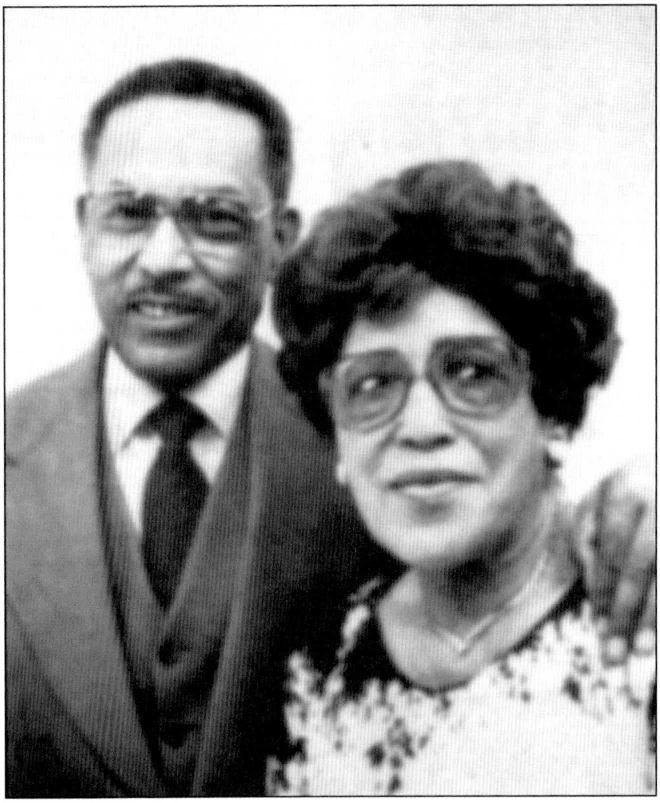

Rev. Herman A Waller was a community leader and organizer of Faith Baptist Church. From 1964 to 1980, the Wallers played prominent roles in the community. (Courtesy of Rev. Adams and Faith Baptist Church.)

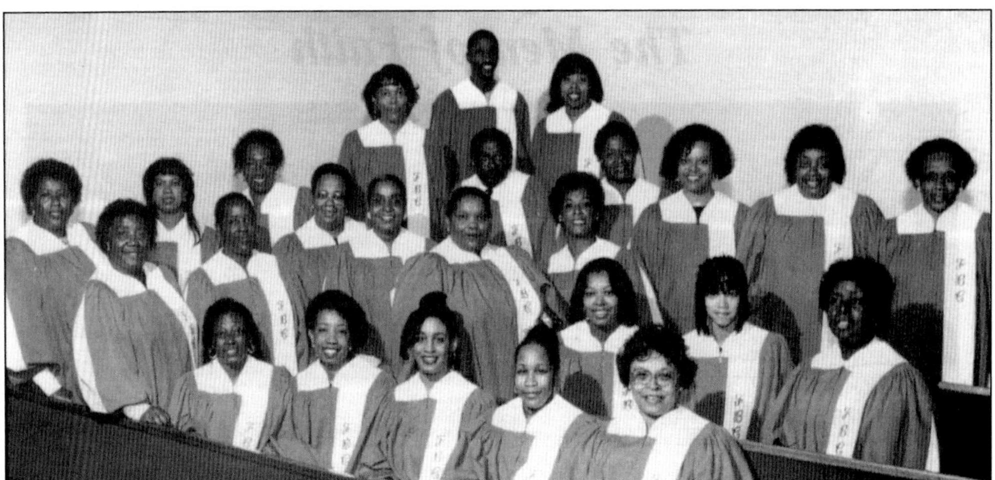

These are the Voices of Faith, the choral group of Faith Baptist Church in Gordon Heights. (Courtesy of Rev. Adams and Faith Baptist Church.)

Harrison Hale, founding bishop of the Cornerstone Ministries Church in Gordon Heights, preaches, teaches, and opens new churches in various parts of the island. Eloquent and dramatic, he attracts a wide group of members to his congregation. (Courtesy of Bishop Harrison Hale.)

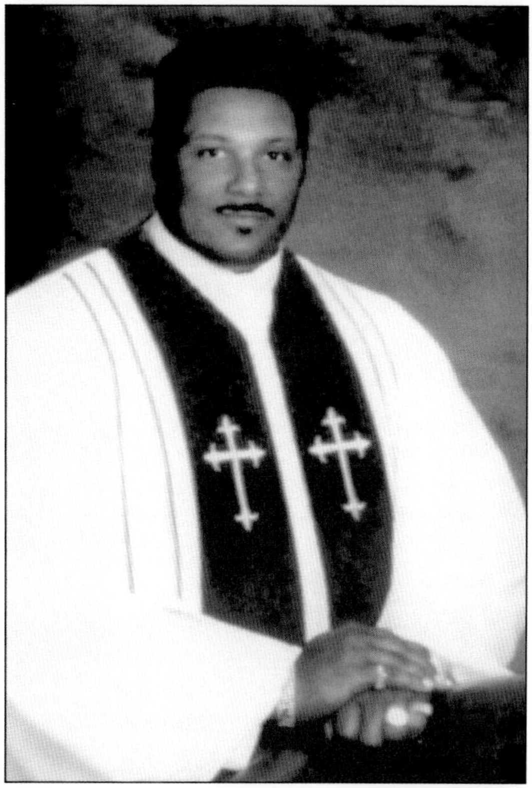

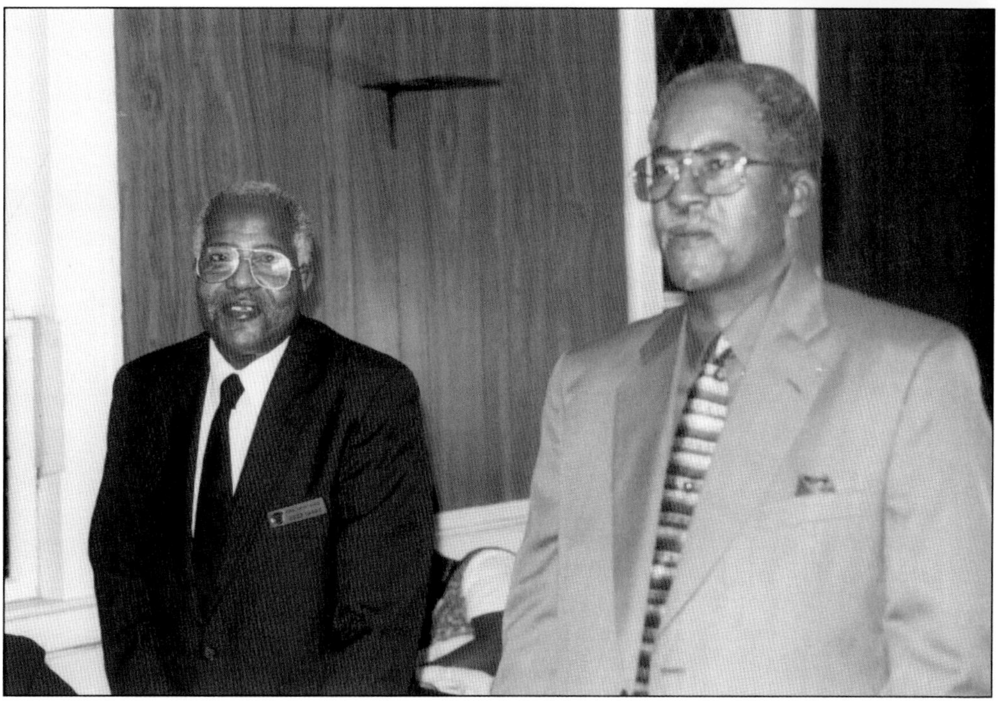

These two men have served as deacons of Christ Baptist Church for more than three decades. (Author's collection.)

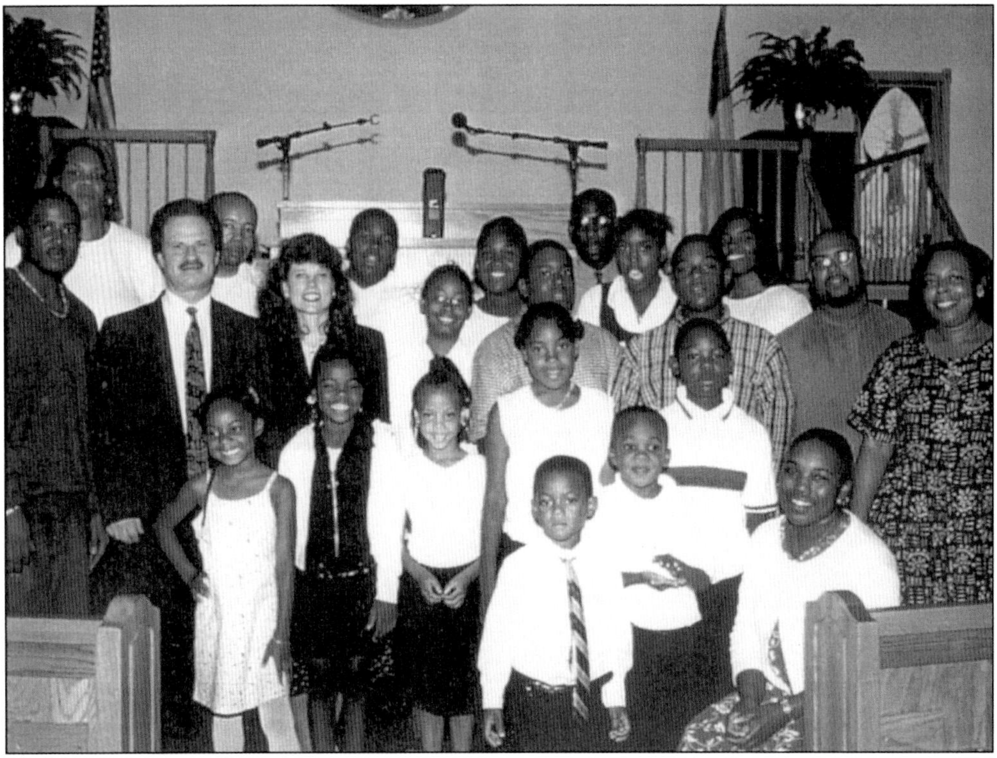

The Mass Choir of Christ Baptist Church attracts families who have roots in the area dating back to the middle of the 20th century. (Courtesy of Pastor Willie R. Jones and Christ Baptist Church.)

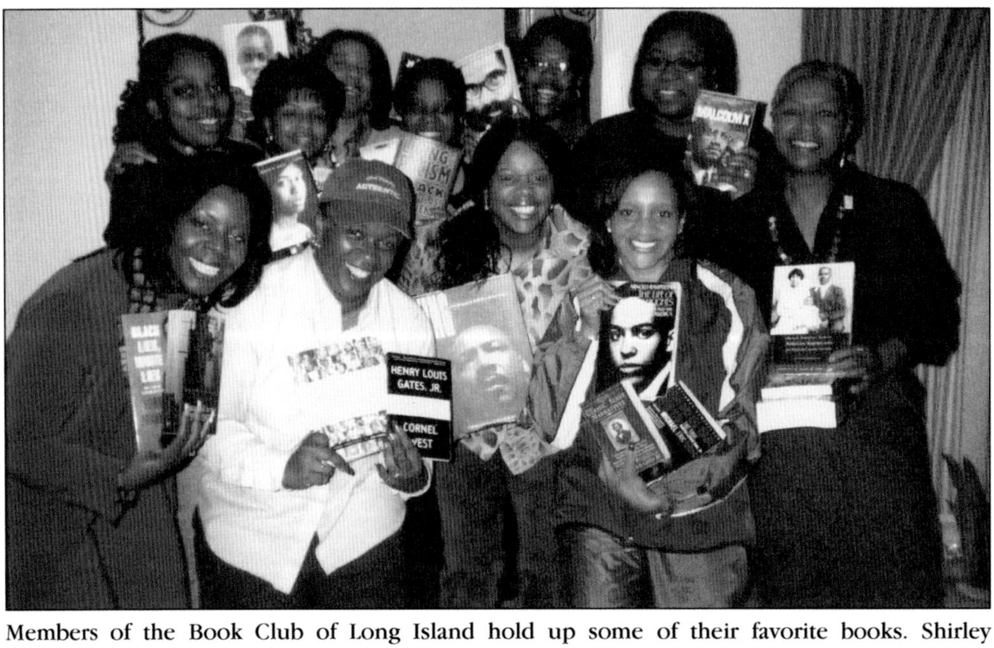

Members of the Book Club of Long Island hold up some of their favorite books. Shirley Bailey (right), former book review editor for Roosevelt's *Community Journal* has the author's companion book, *African Americans of Eastern Long Island.*